ALLENDE:
DEATH OF A MARXIST DREAM

ALLENDE: DEATH OF A MARXIST DREAM

JAMES R. WHELAN

Council for Inter-American Security
Educational Institute

Washington, D.C.

Library of Congress Cataloging in Publication Data

Whelan, James, 1933–
   Allende: death of a Marxist dream.

   Includes index.
    1. Allende Gossens, Salvador, 1908–1973—Death and
burial. 2. Chile—Politics and government—1970–
3. Chile—Presidents—Biography. I. Title.
F3101.A4W46   983.0640924 [B]   81-3490
ISBN 0-87000-503-0   AACR2

Production Services by Cobb-Dunlop, Inc.
Manufactured in the United States of America
9 7 5 3 2 4 6 8

Acknowledgments

First books have deep roots, the deepest of all, I suspect. Those for this book reach back through time and space to the dining room table of a crowded house on the south side of Buffalo, New York, where a teen-age boy struggled with an invincible foe. The foe was English Composition. Though very much overburdened, a patient woman found time to coax and coach the disbelieving young man into the wondrous world of expression. The woman was my mother, and she was overburdened because there were already seven of us—with three more to come. Yet a more caring and competent writing instructor no one could ever have, and it was she who would later encourage me to turn to writing as a career. It has taken me a quarter of a century to find a suitable means for acknowledging this debt.

Later there was a man named Eddie Feinen who was willing to believe that enthusiasm and desire could compensate for still-stunted growth in years and education. He hired me, and thus got me started on a long and exciting career in the United Press International.

A few years later still another UPI warhorse—William H. McCall, then vice-president in charge of the news agency's Latin American operations—also succumbed to the suasions of a (still brash and still too-young) junior reporter anxious for a career overseas. Bill McCall's gamble gave me entrée into the world of international reporting and Latin America, a world I have never really left.

Along the way there were mentors, a few of them great. Two must be singled out. The first was the late Henry Minott in Boston, the vi

finest craftsman it was ever my good fortune to know. Henry taught
me—as he had two or three earlier generations of "Unipressers"—to
respect words and honor accuracy above all else in reporting a news
story. Then there was William Lawrence Frederick Horsey, a grand
old Englishman in Buenos Aires, who took a boy and attempted to
make him a man, as Bill Horsey himself was, both as a foreign
correspondent and as a civilized human being.

Not all of my debt is to people. A large part of it is to a country.
The country is Chile, a land I have loved, increasingly, since nearly
our first meeting back in 1958. There is a word in Spanish, a word I
believe was coined to capture the essence of what Chileans are. The
word is *amable;* it means kind and courteous and sweet and nice and
pleasant and warm and lovable. And that is what Chileans are. Because they are so *amables,* I often find it incomprehensible that they
should have been driven to the depths they were—or that they should
be caricatured so grotesquely as they have been in so much that has
been written about them and their country.

This book I owe, above all, to Helen Tumpson, herself a writer. She
suggested it, encouraged me, stayed with me every step of what
became a much longer and more despairing journey than I had antici-
pated, and she helped me in more ways than I could ever hope to
remember.

In Miami many friends and associates lent me their aid at various
stages of work on the book: Larry Jinks, the executive editor of the
Miami Herald, who bent his own stern rule about letting outsiders
have access to the *Herald*'s immense library riches; Claudio Guer-
rero, an old friend at the Chilean Consulate, and, later, a new friend,
Col. Eduardo Sepúlveda, who opened doors that had been barred to
me in Chile. That I was finally able to see beyond them allowed this
book to grow from the slick journalistic account it might have been
into what I hope it now is: a full and documented narrative of the most
dramatic revolution in Latin America since 1959. Still later the consulate acquired a human encyclopedia named Hector (Chico) Durán,
and he never retreated from my incessant barrage of questions. At
LAN-Chile Jorge Hofer, the general manager for North America, and
his sidekick, my old friend Ciro Correa, were both always ready to
send a badly needed tube or tape or whatever whizzing on its way to
Santiago to rescue a writer and his ailing tape recorder. At the other
end was Harold Beckett, LAN's traffic and sales manager, who
became a good friend as well as a problem-solver.

In Washington Juana Olmos, at the Organization of American States, responded to far more SOS, for research materials and data than it was ever decent to flash, and did so both pleasantly and efficiently.

In Santiago the debts are too numerous to acknowledge—and, in some instances, they must remain so to spare persons with problems enough already further complications. In each and every case I enter a firm disclaimer: the writer and the writer alone is responsible for the opinions—and errors—in this book.

I cannot speak of Chile for more than a minute without remembering Don Manuel Martínez, his wife Morita, and their children, especially my *compinche,* Manolo, and my favorite teen-ager, Isabelita. Because the Martínezes have been for me a true second family, taking me into their home and sharing with me the affection and concern of a loving family, I want to say to them a special "thank you."

Others, too, gave me their warmth and support: Patricia Marín and Daniel Pizarro, two of the finest friends, and doctors, a wayfarer could ever hope to find; the late Mario Carneyro, a newspaper editor strong, very strong, in human qualities to match his superb professional skills; Alvaro Puga, who was never too harried—and he was always harried—to respond to yet another plea for information from the pesky *gringo.*

Sergio Gulisasti Tagle, chief of the Senate Information Office in Santiago, and the admirable Washington González, chief of the library at *El Mercurio,* opened their information treasures, and their memories, to me. Francisco (Gabito) Hernández, at Radio Agricultura, and his staff, took me backstage at what has to be one of the world's spunkiest radio stations.

At the U.S. Embassy, the public affairs officer, Jim Halsema, and press officer, Frank Tonini, shared not only their personal experiences but their own impressive files, including scarce newspapers. Mario Oyarzún and Manuel Bravo—and Manuelita—of the USIS staff were a fertile source of ideas and leads.

At the United Press International in Santiago Carlos Padilla offered not only a base camp to an old UPI alumnus, but also his friendship and constant support. So, too, did other UPI staffers—Ana Villalobos and Roberto Mason in particular.

Miguel (Mike) Gallegos at the Carreera-Sheraton was another valued friend who provided not only hospitality but also insights into experiences few hotelmen anywhere had ever then had.

There was one other in Chile I could never repay. Dr. Patricio Guijón Klein awakened in me a new a awareness of what human integrity and dignity are all about, because he radiates both to a degree and intensity I don't believe I had ever before encountered. Although our political outlooks were completely different, neither he nor his valiant and attractive wife Silvia ever hesitated in opening their home to me. If it were in my power to mend one broken life, the one I would choose, unflinchingly, would be that of Patricio Guijón. But I do not have that power, and so I remain deeply, sentiently, in the debt of Patricio Guijón, a truly great man.

Back home, I could not close without expressing my deep gratitude to two persons whose lot it was to stand and wait: Irma Hernández Whelan, for her patient forbearance, and my son Bobby, deprived by this book, for the better part of two years, of the fatherly care every boy has a right to. If he is one day proud of his father and this book, then it will have all been worthwhile.

Finally, my deepest thanks to my wife, Pamela Ann, for the encouragement she gave me to revive a long-dormant dream, and then the constant help and support she gave me during the long and arduous process of making that dream come true; to Laura and Craig—"the world's greatest 'copycats,' " I called them as they worked so hard and diligently to get me through the last copying and collating stages, and to our infant daughter, Heather Elizabeth, whose smile and mere being lightened even the darkest days.

Contents

one

A
LIGHTNING
BEFORE
DEATH

How oft when men are at the point of death
Have they been merry! Which their keepers call
A lightning before death.

Romeo and Juliet, Act V, Scene III

Man and the elements had made it the bitterest winter in Chile's history, and yet, when the end did come, it came quickly. One day, the stinging winds and infernal mud and the depressing pictures of striking truck drivers staring out from the pages of the newspapers. Then, suddenly, a different kind of dawn, aglow with the warmth of an exuberant sun, a day when Santiago sheds her gray winter pall and seems to rejoice in the luminescence of the snow-mantled mountains in the concave distance. *Clarín* celebrates the event with a low-angle, poster-size picture on its front page—a fetching girl in an excruciatingly minuscule miniskirt. The newspaper explains that the temperature yesterday, August 31, topped out at 31°C (87°F), an all-time record. Since Chile is below the Equator, its seasons are the reverse of ours. September is equivalent to March in the Northern Hemisphere.

The most momentous month in the country's modern history had begun—September 1973.

When day broke on the tenth, Salvador Gossens Allende, President of the Republic of Chile, had less than twenty-four hours to live.

For just a hair over forty years, ending with the cataclysm of 1973, there were two principal power centers in Chile: one, the presidency, ostentatiously visible in recent years; the other, the armed forces, almost sullenly invisible. Since 1841 the presidency had been headquartered in a squat bulldog of a building called La Moneda. If one were to think of downtown Santiago as a tabletop plateau, which it is not, then La Moneda would be very near its southwestern edge. Of much more recent vintage, but no less drab, is the eight-story Ministry of National Defense, on the other side of the city's main stem, Alameda Bernardo O'Higgins, named for Chile's national hero and liberator, who also laid out the expansive boulevard bearing his name. The Alameda was once a branch of the Mapocho River, which now sluices through the city on a safer course east-northeast of the avenue. Since the late 1960s the Alameda had been less a boulevard than a huge trench gashing through the city's heart, which—bulldozers, earthmovers, and money willing—was to become a subway. Meantime, the construction accounted for most of the mud and much of the misery in the daily lives of Santiaguinos. In September 1973 it represented a formidable moat, perhaps 100 feet wide and 50 feet deep.

There are those who find loveliness in La Moneda. But although the streets around it teem with life, it remains stoically unattractive. La Moneda was the neo-classic creation of an Italian architect, Joaquín Toesca, and most of what it was in 1973 had been erected over an eighteen-year period beginning in 1787, the rest (the southern wing) in the late 1920s. The building was originally used as the royal mint, which may explain the four-foot thickness of the walls, a sturdiness of no small consequence come September 1973.

The main entrance faces north, toward the Plaza de la Constitución, which Chileans, a piquant polyphony of romantic and pragmatic, used mainly as a parking lot on top. A *Carabinero* (paramilitary police) post down below was usually cluttered with specimens of what had to be the world's ugliest car, the eminently practical Chilean version of the Citroën. Around the plaza glowered a series of taller buildings, mostly the same height and all the same depressing shade of gray, among them the city's leading hotel. The monotony of this tableau used to be broken every other day at ten in the morning by the ceremony of the changing of the presidential guard, except that the guards wore no-nonsense Socialist brown uniforms.

Inside La Moneda two splashes of nature, both available to the public through the north and south doors, were normally open to pedestrians who short-cut through the grounds. Entering from the Plaza Constitución, you first reached an interior courtyard, its centerpiece a copper water fountain believed to be the first to provide running water for the early settlers. The next and larger courtyard was called the Patio de las Naranjas for the dwarf orange trees blooming there. Emerging into the Plaza de la Libertad on the other side, you came upon a petunia patch of greenery. The greenery survived in almost truculent defiance of the concrete imperium of the ubiquitous parking spaces and the ubiquitous mustachioed men in gray dusters and peaked caps who watched over their patchwork quilt of parked automobiles. La Moneda housed not only the presidency—all of it—but the Ministries of Foreign Affairs and the Interior, a situation whimsically reminiscent of those simpler times in the United States when that gargoyle of a building at Seventeenth Street and Pennsylvania Avenue in downtown Washington, D.C., known as the Old Executive Office Building, hangared both the War and State Departments. (In more recent times it was not spacious enough to handle even the overflow from the White House.) Chile had not yet attained such sophistication, and so La Moneda remained a building of multiple purposes.

The presidential suite of offices was located on the northeastern flank, although Salvador Allende Gossens, Chile's twenty-eighth constitutional president, also expropriated offices along the eastern gallery from the Foreign Ministry. By craning at a corner of a window in that gallery, which became his inner sanctum, Allende could glimpse the northwest edge of the Defense Ministry. But Allende had precious little time for peeking out of windows on September 10. His eye that day was on another military force, some 70 miles away, and his mind was on a quandary of his own creation. The force was Chile's fleet, and the quandary was the presence in Chile, every day more evident, every day more noxious, of a veritable legion of foreign adventurers.

In ways recalling the obtuseness of Louis XVI of France, another ruler who failed to fathom and master the forces coalescing to consume him, Allende relied in those crucial hours on the arithmetic of politics when what he needed was the calculus of strategy. Though trained as a doctor, he had spent practically his entire adult life in politics. On that fateful day in 1973 he was in the forty-first year of his political career and nearing the end of his third year in the presidency. He behaved, on that critical occasion, much as he always had.

"Within him, willpower vibrated stronger than ideas. . . . Allende did not have the political strategy to match this personal sense of decision. He had only scorn for those who possess strategy and not decision, but those who had both at once fascinated him." This posthumous verdict, by Régis Debray, a French Marxist and one of

Allende's most ardent admirers, reinforces the sense of inevitability that he should have fiddle-faddled while his world burned.

Allende arrived at La Moneda late that Monday morning, September 10, as was his custom. At noon he assembled the members of his Cabinet, a curious hodgepodge of humanity, Allende having reshuffled the Cabinet a dizzying twenty-eight times in thirty-six months. The current cadre had been in their jobs less than two weeks.

Four of the ministers were military men, a precedent Allende had set early in his administration when he named a military man on active duty to a cabinet post, the first such appointment in Chile in ten years. Later, following the first of the trucker strikes, he involved the military even more blatantly in the country's civilian affairs, naming all three service chiefs to his Cabinet on November 2, 1972. He turned again to the military following the outbreak of the second "fight-to the-finish" trucker strike earlier that winter. This time he drafted the head of the Carabineros as well as the three service chiefs for his Cabinet. Swearing them in on August 9, Allende said: "This is our last chance." He had similar melodramatic words for the swearing in of this last Cabinet on August 28:

> In this Cabinet the armed forces and the popular parties will defend Chile from the political and economic crisis and will safeguard the security and lives of one and all, and will stop the offensive unleashed by the fascist sectors. There will be neither a coup d'état nor civil war in this country, because the immense majority of Chileans are opposed to such lunacies, conscious as we are of the historic responsibility we all share.

By September 10 the only thing that was clear about "the immense majority" was that it wanted Allende out.

Chile that September day was a country in which public and private services were all but paralyzed by a spreading strike involving a million workers, close to 90 percent of the country's entire urban labor force. Many had vowed they would not return to work until Allende cleared out—or was kicked out. Violence was rife, political tensions intolerable, and there were the ugly rumblings of civil war.

In that cyclonic context Allende's choice of text for his ministerial sermon appears quirky: what to do with the foreigners. Quirky, not because the matter was unimportant, for it was very important, but because obviously there were far more pressing matters crying out for attention. The Minister of the Interior, Carlos Briones, remembers that Allende expressed surprise at the degree of foreign penetration and called for reports and recommendations to remedy the situation. Yet, only a few days before, the General Accounting Office had reported that more than five hundred foreigners were on the public payroll, and an opposition deputy reported a total of ten thousand foreign revolutionaries in the country. Allende had not to look far for an example—his closest political adviser, a shadowy and controversial Catalán named Joan Garcés Ramón.

The cabinet meeting lasted barely an hour, freeing Allende to turn his attention to a time bomb ticking out the last hours of his life and career, one he was confident he could yet disarm. Of all the visible dangers confronting him, none was more obvious than the risk of a full-scale navy rebellion, a risk escalated explosively the previous afternoon by the defiant oratory of Carlos Altamirano Orrego, the firebrand secretary-general of Allende's own Socialist Party. For several days a Chilean squadron had stalled on keeping a rendezvous with a U.S. flotilla steaming south for annual joint naval exercises. If that squadron had actually sailed, Allende knew he could count on a breather of at least a few days, since it represented the backbone of Chile's widely dispersed fleet. And that would allow enough time for his formidable political skills to confabulate new ruses.

Shortly after four that afternoon he received the awaited call: the squadron had sailed from Valparaíso minutes before. Allende had originally been scheduled to speak on nationwide radio and television at ten that morning, then had postponed it to 5:00 P.M. With the new report in hand, he decided to postpone the speech to the following day, when he was scheduled to appear at an "anti-imperialism cultural exhibition" at the State Technical University (UTE), a cauldron of extreme left activists. He wasted little time putting his confabulation in motion.

"Carlos, I want you and Orlando to join me later tonight at Tomás Moro. I'll see if Almeyda can make it too. That idea I mentioned to you Saturday, I'd like to go over it tonight. Around ten."

Carlos Briones had begged off Sunday when Allende asked him to come for a little relaxed conversation at the principal presidential residence, Tomás Moro, on the grounds that he had just been through a withering week of back-to-back crises and negotiations. In his job as Minister of the Interior, Briones was responsible for all internal security, including the 26,300-man national police force, the paramilitary Carabineros. But Allende valued Briones even more in these hallucinatory times for his abilities as a peacemaker, since he was perhaps the only man in the president's inner circle who still commanded the respect of the Christian Democrats, the major opposition party.

There was no question of begging off this time, so Briones made plans to spend a marathon evening at Tomás Moro. The other conferees were to be Orlando Letelier, the improbable Minister of Defense, the "gringo" in Allende's clan, who had returned to Chile only four months earlier after a dozen years in the United States; and Clodomiro Almeyda Medina, a longtime Allende confidant, once again serving the president, this time as foreign minister.

On the surface there was nothing to set September 10 apart from any of the other nerve-racking days of that period in Chile. The editors of *Clarín,* the bawdy, brawling tabloid king of the socialist publishing roost, owned by Allende himself, certainly didn't think so. They greeted their readers that morning with the main headline: "Carlos Is A Dear," and an even bigger front-page picture of soccer hero, Carlos Caszely, kissing the forehead of his fiancée, María de los Angeles. (News of another Carlos—the Socialist Party's secretary-general, Carlos Altamirano—dominated the main news page inside.) *Última Hora,* another Socialist paper owned by Allende's former Defense Minister, José Tohá González, gave over most of its Op–Ed page that day to a commentary on socialism in Korea. In the opposition camp, *La Segunda,* a scrappy tabloid edited by one of the wiliest journalists in Chile, Mario Carneyro, bannered an AP story from Buenos Aires under the headline: "Even Perón Feels Sorry." The story quoted Argentine leader Juan Perón as telling youth leaders: "Allende didn't follow the advice I gave him, and look how it's going for him, poor fellow. It's not a matter of feeling that one would like to do this or do that, it's a matter of doing it and doing it well. . . ."

All eleven newspapers published in Santiago agreed on one theme: still another and dangerous showdown was due the next day. The Court of Appeals in Valparaíso was to hand down its dynamite decision on a suit to strip Altamirano and Oscar Garretón, a radical Marxist deputy, of their parliamentary immunity so that they could be brought to trial. The criminal charge against them: conspiring with thirty-four noncommissioned officers and enlisted men to seize the navy base at Valparaíso.

That port city, situated about seventy miles due west of Santiago, was still tense in the aftermath of the worst riots in the city's history the Friday before. Rumors were rife that the high command of the Movement of the Revolutionary Left (MIR), a Maoist terrorist organization, had moved into Valparaíso with "shock troops." News media in that city of 400,000 received calls from persons purporting to represent the MIR and its labor arm, the Federation of Revolutionary Workers (FTR), threatening to blow the Palace of Justice to smithereens to block the hearing.

Late in the afternoon of the tenth, the Supreme Court in Santiago sent orders to the Appeals Court: rule tomorrow, or place the case at the very top of the Wednesday docket.

Shortly before 4:00 P.M. on the tenth Colonel Julio Canessa Roberts was at his office when he received orders to report for a meeting at four sharp at the Defense Ministry. Canessa, a short man who smiles easily and often and speaks in cackling tones, was then commandant of the Noncommissioned Officers School, situated about a dozen blocks south of the ministry.

At the Defense Ministry he was informed that the next day the army was going to seize control of Santiago, through a meticulously drafted internal security plan. What he did not learn was that the army was also going to oust the Allende government and bring a stunned nation under the iron grip of military rule. "But I suspected," he said, and, suspecting, he went to special lengths to make certain that the 1,200 men under his command would be ready for any eventuality.

The commanders, drawn from a cluster of garrisons and commands ringing the capital, arrived for the meeting in staff cars or jeeps. The meeting was short and to the point.

"We had been over the plan many times, so there was no need to do more than update a few details," Canessa said.

Santiago is walled in on two sides by mountains. The plan called for sealing off the other two sides with a double ring of firepower, one encircling the center of the city, the other on the outskirts, checkmating Allende's private Maginot Line: factories controlled by heavily armed bands of Allende loyalists, known as the "Cordones Industriales."

The plan was to be put into motion at dawn. The commanders were told only that the army was moving to head off street demonstrations certain to erupt in the wake of the court's verdict in the Altamirano-Garretón case—presumably under a long-standing national emergency plan designed mainly to cope with natural disasters.

Nobody bothered to tell Allende. "There was no need to," Canessa said. "It was purely an internal matter, an army matter."

If the comings and goings at the Defense Ministry caught the eye of anyone at La Moneda, across the great gorge of subway construction, there is no record of alarm.

In his private talks with cronies Salvador Allende called him "Pinochito," and exuded confidence that this man he mocked with a belittling nickname could be manipulated as easily as the Pirandellian figure whom "Pinochito" had recently replaced in the post of army commander. But Allende was wrong, dead wrong as it turned out, because Augusto Pinochet Ugarte was as much an unwavering realist as his predecessor, Carlos Prats González, was a testy illusionist. For a variety of tangled reasons, ranging from personal vanity to a sense of soldierly duty, Prats was unswervingly loyal to Allende. As commander in chief of the 32,000-man army, he had been the main reason Allende slept soundly (albeit briefly) night after night. When Prats resigned under pressure on August 23, Allende made the mistake of appointing Pinochet to replace him, firmly convinced he could persuade Pinochet to keep the army, the final arbiter of all political destinies in Chile, neutral. It was a grave miscalculation, and one that should have been obvious from the first. But if Allende ever sensed the danger from that martial quarter, he never let on. Allende had become a man trapped in a hall of mirrors, entranced by a thousand contorted images, mostly of himself.

Augusto Pinochet is a professional soldier, tall, ramrod straight, and powerfully built. His green eyes are warm and friendly, disarmingly so, for they peer out from a no-nonsense face crowned by an abundant shock of black hair, graying at the temples, parted in the middle, and brushed straight back. Thick eyebrows, a leonine nose, and puffed cheeks, streaked lightly by veins, a thin moustache and bulldog chin complete the portrait of his oval face.

Despite his fifty-seven years and the troubled sleep of the previous night, Pinochet arose at 6:00 A.M. on the morning of Monday, September 10, 1973, exercised his customary forty-five minutes, then headed for his office on the fifth floor of the Defense Ministry in downtown Santiago. Pinochet was troubled because he had a problem, a big problem. Under cover of night and immediately after dawn the following day he had to mass, arm, and deploy 4,000 army troops in a city of two million inhabitants. Such stealth was essential because Pinochet was moving that force (whose numbers would swell that day to 10,000 troops) into action for the purpose of overthrowing the government of Salvador Allende Gossens.

That fateful decision—to strike on September 11—had been taken only hours before, at teatime during a birthday party for his youngest daughter, Jacqueline Marie. It was a decision forced by fretful navy commanders, no longer able to restrain the rebellious junior officers and noncoms on the very verge of launching impetuous—and suicidal —pocket revolutions of their own. The navy did not know that two months before, on July 16, Pinochet had ordered—on his own, since he was then only chief of staff, and in sworn secrecy with six other officers—a supersecret plan to depose Allende. H-Hour under that plan had been set, just a few days ago, for Friday, September 14.

"It took me no more than a few moments to realize it would have been suicide for the navy to go it alone," Pinochet stated in an interview in Santiago on October 22, 1974, "even if some army units joined in, as I was sure they would, because it would have taken the refusal of only one garrison to go along to touch off a civil war. So I decided to accept. Only how to justify all of those troop movements?" He discovered the answer shortly after reaching the office. "There it was, in big bold letters—'Altamirano Acknowledges Contacts With Sailors,'—and other stories in the newspapers that morning predicting trouble when the court acted the next day."

"Providence," said Pinochet, a devout Catholic, "was on our side."

With newspaper in hand, Pinochet bounced down one flight of stairs to the office of the new Defense Minister, Orlando Letelier.

In his Estadio Chile (Chile Arena) speech Sunday afternoon Altamirano had defiantly admitted that he had met with navy noncoms accused of plotting a preemptive revolt to oust navy brass. (Of 130 involved, 45 were eventually convicted.) Altamirano, leader of the hard-line extreme left faction in control of his Socialist Party, had added that he would do it again in defense of the constitutional government of Salvador Allende. Though what Altamirano said was technically correct, the truculence of his tone and the perversity of his timing—the country was already at the boiling point—sent shock waves through military commanders and dismay through Allende's ranks. Allende's one remaining hope of survival was in disassociating himself from extremists in his coalition, who for months had been urging troops to mutiny against their superiors and preaching with growing intensity the inevitability of violent seizure of total power.

Pointing to a newspaper story on the speech and warnings of "revolutionary violence" the next day, Pinochet told Letelier: "This gentleman [Altamirano] leaves me no choice but to quarter the troops tomorrow morning—not only over there in Valparaíso, but here in Santiago as well." Letelier mumbled an invective about Altamirano's indiscretion, and Pinochet left. It was 10:15 A.M.

For the rest of the morning Pinochet maintained appearances, even receiving a group of retired generals anxious to air their views on national problems. Late in the morning, he instructed his aide-de-camp to arrange a special luncheon for twelve-thirty in the austere, draperied conference room next to his office that doubled as a private dining room. The guests: Gen. Herman Brady Roche, a close confidant, until recently director of the Army War College, and among the "inner seven" group of plotters; Gen. Sergio Arellano, one of the very earliest senior military officers to cast his lot with the anti-Allende forces, who would command troops in the crucial downtown sector on D-Day; Gen. Raúl César Benavides, another Pinochet confidant, recently named by him to head the army's network of military institutes in the Santiago area; and Col. Augusto Lutz, of army intelligence.

The fifth guest was an even more central figure in the drama: Gen. Gustavo Leigh Guzmán, fifty-three-year-old commander in chief of the air force. Like Pinochet, Leigh had been in his job a scant three weeks. Like Pinochet, Leigh was resolutely anti-Marxist. (Pinochet, for example, had told Allende repeatedly: "I am not a Red general," a stance the president obviously imagined he could soften. Even more adamantly anti-Marxist was the man who was about to seize control of the navy, Adm. José Toribio Merino. In a sharp exchange with the president the previous May, Merino had told Allende: "Chile will never be Communist." The man who would the next day take control of the paramilitary police force, the Carabineros, Gen. César Mendoza Durán, was not only anti-Marxist, but the previous December had become one of the few Carabinero commanders who dared to carry out a court order in defiance of executive wishes, a decision that cost him his job.)

The four army officers arrived first—and found their lives irrevocably changed. Taking the sword presented to him when he was promoted to general, Pinochet asked each, one by one, to swear on it an oath of secrecy, invoking with the sword an old and forgotten army rite. "I told each," Pinochet said, "that the oath was the equivalent of a death warrant, to be executed in case that man should betray the oath. Each of them agreed quickly—and unflinchingly—to swear the oath."

Pinochet then revealed the secret.

"Gentlemen, tomorrow, September 11, we will occupy La Moneda and will expel the government of Señor Allende and his accomplices, giving them the opportunity to leave the country. If there is armed resistance, we will use the means at our command to crush it. The more drastic our action, the fewer lives will be lost. Here are your orders, which you will carry out like good soldiers.

"Units will be deployed in accord with these plans, but make no move whatever until 0730 tomorrow morning. If resistance stiffens in La Moneda, the palace will be bombed by the air force to avoid greater loss of life. In that case, the troops under your command will withdraw and mark their forward positions. Resume the attack immediately after the bombardment. [Someone gave the ludicrous order the following day that the forward line of soldiers should tie white handkerchiefs to the backs of their uniforms so that the jets, swooping in at nearly five hundred miles per hour, could distinguish where the friendly lines ended.]

"If, because of betrayal or suspicion, I should be assassinated tonight, the senior general will take over command of the troops. [Pinochet actually decided to skip over the second and third men in seniority and named Gen. Oscar Bonilla as next in line.] We can neither halt nor falter in our resolve, and much less fail, because at stake is the destiny of Chile; and the fatherland, gentlemen, matters more than all of us.

"Preparations will be made during the night, but I remind you that no one is authorized to move a single unit without specific instructions."

Gen. Herman Brady, maneuvered into the vital job as commander of the Santiago garrison by Pinochet only two days after Pinochet himself took over the top army job, was given overall command of troops in the metropolis. Raúl Benavides was assigned the job of neutralizing the two toughest industrial belts, the fortress-like like factory areas of Vicuña Mackenna and Los Cerrillos, the latter flanking a major military air base in the capital; Col. Felipe Geiger, commander of the Buin Regiment, was assigned control of the northern sector, including major highway accesses to Argentina and the country's north; and an air force general, Mario Viveros Avila, was assigned the southern flank of the city.

The idea, Pinochet explained, was to create a "double ring of fire": the first for the bitter fighting in the center, the other composed of troops moved secretly in from outside garrisons, to converge on the cordones, the industrial guerrilla forces, before they had a chance to surround and decimate the forces in the center of the city. Recent events had given the military ample reason to doubt the danger of massive armed resistance on the part of the vaunted militiamen of the so-called "people's power." Yet estimates of the numbers armed and trained in the factories ringing Santiago ranged all the way up to 100,000. And a few days earlier a retired general loyal to the president reputedly had warned him that a military coup was imminent. Allende's response:

"Don't worry, general. The day the military tries to overthrow me, I'll crush them with the cordones of Santiago. And as for Tomás Moro [the presidential palace in the eastern suburbs], it is an impregnable fortress."

None of the commanders shared Allende's swaggering estimate of the firepower at his command, or of the willingness of his minions to use it. But all of them expected fierce fighting that would last a minimum of three days and cost a minimum of 5,000 lives.

Pinochet explained to the generals that the blueprint for Tuesday's action was an amalgam of two interlocking plans. The first was overt, and he ordered it prepared shortly after he took over as chief of staff of the army in late December, 1971. It was delivered to him on April 13, 1972. Ostensibly, it was a review of the internal security situation, an antisubversive plan. That plan had to be junked and a new one drafted following an abortive uprising June 29, 1973. The new one contemplated "war games" to meet a hypothetical subversive threat. Details of that plan were known to many military commanders, including some loyal to Allende. The second plan was entirely covert. Pinochet had ordered it drafted on July 16, 1973, extracting an oath of secrecy from the two generals and four colonels and lieutenant colonels at the Army War College working on that second—and much deadlier—plan. To protect further against possible leaks, the plan was given the same code name as the open, antisubversive one: "Operación Alborada" (Operation Dawn). The plan was ready on August 3, and turned over to Pinochet in two volumes, the first of 120 pages, the second, 62. It included photographs and biographical sketches of key government people as well as top terrorist leaders. The plan's objective: seize control of the army and then lead a bold assault on La Moneda and overthrow the Allende government.

"I had assurances from a major in the Carabineros that they would not fire at us when we stormed La Moneda," Pinochet said. "We knew that the slightest slip would cost us our careers and perhaps our lives, but we also knew that the chaos and suffering in the country could not go on. So we vowed to act before August 31, unless there was a dramatic change before then... Then came the miracle of the women."

The "miracle" occurred on August 21. At five-thirty that afternoon three hundred women clashed with Carabineros outside the house of the army's commander in chief, General Carlos Prats, who was home at the time nursing a cold. The women were wives of senior officers, including the wives of Generals Pinochet, Bonilla, Arellano, Palacios —all destined to play particularly dramatic roles on September 11— as well as those of Generals Contreras, Muño, and Viveros (brother of the air force general, Mario Viveros Avila, in charge of the southern flank of the city). They were led by a normally mild-mannered brunette named María (Maruja) Medina, whose long years as an army wife (her husband was a retired colonel) had conditioned her to remain quietly in the background. Although opposed to Allende from the outset, one event above all others finally galvanized Mrs. Medina into action: Allende's plan to bring education under total state control —the so-called Unified National Education (ENU) plan bared by the opposition press earlier that year. "We saw our very children, our homes menaced," Mrs. Medina said, "and we saw a general breakdown of morality. I knew I had to do something."

The "something" finally coalesced on that frosty afternoon when she emerged as the symbol of a protest without precedent. Never before had wives of Chile's apolitical military officers gone to such lengths to vent their frustration. Several women were injured in a scuffle with Carabineros, and Mrs. Medina became an instant celebrity—and heroine to her three children and husband—when she boarded a bus and forced a Carabinero lieutenant to free a teen-age boy he was attempting to take prisoner. The gravity of the protest was underscored by the turnout. At that time there were 550 army officers in the Santiago garrison, many of them young bachelors, yet three hundred wives turned out for a protest that snowballed from a few telephone calls. Two days later Prats resigned, and with him the two pro-Allende generals commanding all army troops in the Santiago area. Pinochet once again perceived "divine intercession" in these stunning developments.

"With boundless wisdom," he said, "Providence cleared our path and paved the way for the final action against the government of the Popular Unity."

The two pro-Allende generals collaborated with Pinochet's Providence: they resigned without formally turning over their commands. That breach of discipline enabled Pinochet to parry pressure from Allende to return the two loyalist generals to their troop commands. Seizing the opportunity presented by this "stroke of destiny," Pinochet quickly named Brady and Benavides to replace them.

His outline of the plan completed, Pinochet told his four noontime visitors that absolute secrecy was imperative. They were to instruct Santiago commanders to quarter their troops as of 0630 Tuesday morning, and reveal nothing of the real reason for the move until the following morning. One of the officers, whose forces included the Second Armored Regiment, expressed concern about the armament of the tanks. Pinochet countered that he was confident the general would have the problem solved by the next day.

The men moved into the dining room. There they were joined by an outsider, Gen. Gustavo Leigh Guzmán, commander in chief of the air force.

It had been a momentous day for Gustavo Leigh even before he settled in for lunch with his army colleagues. At 8:30 that morning, he had summoned the twelve air force generals to his third-floor office in the Defense Ministry.

"Gentlemen," he told them, "the dice have been thrown. I move tomorrow, and I am going all the way, whatever the consequences. If any of you don't agree, say so and go home. There will be no reprisals."

None of the generals budged.

"Most," Leigh said, "were frankly jubilant. Then I told them the Chief of Staff would put into effect "Operación Trueno" [Operation Thunder]—the air force's antisubversive plan—and that we would move into action with the least possible commotion. The meeting was over in twenty minutes."

Leigh had one more important meeting before lunch. Late that morning he called Gen. César Mendoza, fourth-ranking general of the Carabineros, and said he needed to see him immediately on an urgent matter, could he come to his office?

Mendoza arrived at 11:50. (He had actually arrived at the Building from his office in the Norambuena Building, two and a half blocks up the Alameda, at 11:40 A.M., but had to double around to a back door; several hundred women, including many officers' wives, were again demonstrating, now outside the Defense Ministry itself, demanding nothing less than the ouster of Allende.)

Once inside, Mendoza learned for the first time, formally, that he had been selected by the other service commanders to lead the Carabineros in the revolution, and that D-Day was dawn the next day. September 11 had another significance for Mendoza: it was his birthday. At fifty-five, Mendoza retained the svelte physique and agility of movement he had in 1951 and 1952 when he won the gold medal in the equestrian event in the Pan American games and bronze medal at the Olympic games in Helsinki.

The navy, at Admiral Merino's direction, had taken the initiative in contacting the Carabineros, working principally through Gen. Arturo Yovane Zuñiga, based with Merino in Valparaíso. Over a period of months the two had cautiously felt each other out until they were finally both convinced they shared the same anti-Marxist ideas and could trust one another.

The delicacy of these contacts illustrates a reality of the precoup period: no one trusted anyone else, a problem heightened by traditional aloofness among members of one branch of the armed forces from those of the others.

The result was that each of the services, except the Carabineros, developed their own plans independently and without knowledge of those of the others. Civilians tended to provide the putty among the services, breaking down traditional resistance to civilian interference in military affairs, then locating and identifying rebellious-minded officers and noncoms, and finally, if cautiously, bringing them together. But these contacts were at the informal level, and as Pinochet has remarked, none of the army officers involved, however bold and daring, had decisive troop commands.

Again, it was the navy that took the lead at the official level, lining up allies in the other services, then sharing its secret planning, first with the air force, then with the army. Pinochet's situation in the army was more difficult, inasmuch as his commander in chief was the man most committed to Allende. So, until the very end, he not only limited his contacts with the other services to a few personal pipelines (such as the major in the Carabineros), but even within the army worked with the compact group of six sworn-to-secrecy plotters.

There was another reason the air force and navy could reveal their plans: both were ostensibly defensive in nature, designed to thwart subversion, although both services were prepared, in case of extreme desperation, to convert those plans from antisubversive to frankly subversive. In that case, each looked to the other services to do little more than refrain from opposing them.

Pinochet, on the other hand, was constructing an explicitly aggressive plan to overthrow Allende and seize power.

"We held the key," he said, "and that's why Allende's intelligence people kept a much tighter watch on us. That made planning all the more difficult, and that was another reason for assigning the job to trusted associates at the War College—we didn't need a pretext to meet there regularly."

Yovane and Mendoza renewed an old friendship in late May 1973, after Yovane also lost his job as prefect of Valparaíso (but not as chief of the Second Carabineros Zone there) because of his brusque handling of far-left extremists. Over lunch at the Norambuena Building the two reached a tacit agreement to take Carabineros into the anti-Allende camp if and when the need and opportunity should arise.

Now, only a few days before the Leigh-Mendoza meeting, on September 6, Yovane had been summoned to the army's Military Academy in Santiago and given the word: the time had come. Col. Nilo Floody Butón, commander of the school, told him the blow would be struck the following week. He would be advised of the exact details in a telephone call informing him of the date and time of a meeting of the Cooperative Los Ositos.

Mendoza, meantime, was meeting in those same fateful, final days with General Arellano, as well as lower-ranking emissaries from the navy and air force. Once they met in a Santiago hotel room, another time at the country home of a friend. Telephone conversations were staccato exchanges, tense, vague, but revealing.

Leigh wasted no time when Mendoza arrived at his office. He showed him the proclamation that would be read to the nation by radio the following morning, calling on Allende to resign and turn over power immediately to the four members of the Junta. Mendoza's name appeared on the proclamation, representing the Carabineros. Leigh had already signed, followed by a remarkable man named Patricio Carvajal Prado, a vice-admiral and chief of staff of the Defense Ministry, who signed for Merino, anchored in his Valparaíso headquarters. Mendoza declined to sign, on the grounds he believed Pinochet should sign first. Leigh assented. (Pinochet signed at lunch. Mendoza returned to Leigh's office at five that afternoon and signed. He was accompanied by General Yovane. He remembers Leigh removing the proclamation—typewritten on plain paper—from a strong box in his office.)

Next Leigh asked Mendoza what preparations he had made. The answer caught Leigh off balance.

"None," Mendoza said.

He went on to remind Leigh that the top two generals in the Carabineros were loyal to Allende. (He might have added that, besides himself, there were only six other generals among the sixteen then of flag rank in the Carabineros who could be counted on to oppose Allende. Two others were in the doubtful category.) To complicate even further their plight, the Carabineros were administratively attached to the Interior Ministry, and that, of course, was infested from top to bottom with Allende people.

But Mendoza was quick to add he was confident the Carabineros would respond to the new leadership. Although the ranks of senior officers—lieutenant colonels and up, and a few majors—were rife with Allende sympathizers, the levels below seethed with resentment about having been used repeatedly as government bullyboys to quell popular protests.

"I had thirty-five years' experience to back up my confidence," Mendoza said. "As it turned out, even the most remote outposts, which we couldn't reach fast enough with our instructions, even they responded on their own when they learned of the coup."

After leaving Leigh, Mendoza went back to his office and arranged to send a messenger to one vital field commander: Col. Mario Mackay

Jaraquemeda, in charge of the Carabinero garrison in the country's third city, Concepción, 325 miles southwest of Santiago. Concepción was the birthplace of the Movement of the Revolutionary Left, the Maoist organization committed to violent change. Mendoza's was not the only messenger afield that day. Pinochet had also dispatched couriers in army planes to reach the commanders of key garrisons.

Gustavo Leigh hated cold water almost as much as he loved the beach, especially the beach at Llolleo where he vacationed as a boy. So it was no surprise to those who knew him that, as a cadet at the Military Academy, he balked when ordered to follow the other cadets off the high board at the military swimming pool in Santiago's Cousiño Park.

"I don't know how to swim, my lieutenant," Cadet Leigh told Lt. Donald MacLean, the officer in charge of the exercise.

"Dive in," MacLean ordered.

Leigh repeated his plea three times. MacLean persisted in his order three times. Leigh's comrades in the Military Academy looked on silently as he slowly scaled the ladder. Suddenly there was a loud splash: the entire water polo team had plunged into the pool and formed a circle beneath the diving board.

"I think we grabbed him before he even hit the water," Oscar García Gajardo remembered. Leigh climbed out of the pool and presented himself before MacLean.

"Your order carried out, my lieutenant," the shivering cadet said.

There were other instances of hesitation in his career, but they were few and far between. He had hesitated long and hard through one of the most nerve-racking weekends of Chile's modern history—a crisis-packed weekend, which began Friday, August 17, and ended early Monday evening, August 20—before finally accepting the job as commander in chief of the forty-three-year-old Chilean Air Force, one of the oldest air forces in the world.

But on one historic issue Leigh was unflinching: his resolve, once convinced that the Allende government was beyond salvation, to rid Chile of what he regarded as the scourge of anarchy and certainty of civil war. A flag officer recalled Leigh's response to navy prodding at the end of the first turbulent week of September: the air force, he said, would be ready to move on an hour's notice.

On September 10, 1973, Leigh was nine days away from his fifty-third birthday, and, after thirty-five years in the service, only three and a half months away from hoped-for retirement. At lunch with Pinochet on the tenth, Leigh was emphatic in agreeing with the army chief. Should their revolution succeed the next day, the best course to follow would be to give Allende and his family safe conduct to fly to whatever country he chose.

Leigh drew a geographical line, however.

"If he chooses Mexico, for instance, nothing doing," Leigh told the others. "No farther than Venezuela."

The reason: Leigh was worried for the safety of his crews, "orbiting the world with that man." Leigh wanted his crews to be able to fly to the exile destination in a single hop and return immediately. (Santiago-Caracas is 3,045 miles one way; Santiago-México, 4,197 miles by the most direct route, practically all over water, which almost certainly would force a detour, via Panamá, and a stopover, making the one-way distance 4,482 miles.)

After lunch Leigh went back to his office to make ready for the next day. His afternoon ended on a rancid note. Shortly after Mendoza had sworn his oath and signed the proclamation, Leigh was visited, at five, by a commission headed by one of the most hated men in the Allende regime, a scofflaw turned policeman named Alfredo Joignant. The previous November, the Senate, by a 32-14 vote, ordered Joignant removed as mayor of Santiago for his "repeated violations of the Constitution," including systematic defiance of court orders. Allende then appointed the tough-talking Joignant head of Investigaciónes, a nationwide detective force, performing, during the Allende years, as a veritable Gestapo. It was the sort of appointment Allende frequently made to mock the Congress after it had impeached one of his men, a frequent occurrence.

The previous Friday, September 7, an air force detachment on a routine raid for clandestine arms suddenly came under heavy fire from the SUMAR textile factory on heavily traveled and congested Vicuña Mackenna Avenue. Rather than risk countless casualties, the air force unit withdrew, but not before wounding three of the attackers and rounding up twenty-three prisoners. The following day Allende harangued the three service commanders, including Leigh, for "repression" of worker groups, and ordered that a commission be named to investigate the shooting incident.

Joignant arrived at Leigh's office accompanied by two of his inspectors and three air force technical officers also on the commission. He started to tell Leigh that he planned to order ballistics tests to determine who had fired first.

"What ballistics tests!" Leigh exploded. "Just follow the trail of bullet holes from the factory to the house where my men were, and you'll see who fired at whom. In fact, we have counted more than three thousand rounds fired at my men."

Joignant cut him off to say that Leigh had lost control of himself.

"Say what you like, carr——," Leigh said, unleashing a vivid curse word. "My men say they were fired upon, and air force men don't lie. Now get out of here—right now!"

Joignant left, pale and enraged.

Joignant must have winced, remembering the incident a few hours later as he embarked on the biggest—and last—investigation of his career.

At first glance he might strike the observer as a popinjay, strutting and posturing and puffed up with self-importance, because he does tend to prance, and there is something of the dandy about him. But upon closer inspection the image of vaingloriousness gives way to a more beguiling one, that of a pixyish person full of devilry. Neither image captures the reality of José Toribio Merino Castro, but it is true that there is an impishness about the second-ranking admiral with the Groucho Marx moustache that rules out putting him down as a pompous man. While the casual observer might be forgiven momentary confusion between those two images, few familiar with him would fail to remark other qualities: spontaneous warmth, an affectionate, generous personality, deep love of the sea—and the inner strength and resolve of a man of profound convictions.

José Toribio Merino was born on December 14, 1915, in the hometown of his mother, the charming, four-century-old city of La Serena, without peer in all of Chile for its colonial character, and famed for its sweets, which may account for Merino's lifelong weakness for them. His father, grandfather, and great-grandfather before all bore the name of José Toribio, and he was set to follow in his father's footsteps as commander in chief of the Chilean Navy. And, like his father, who had been a thorn in the side of Chile's dictatorial president, Carlos Ibañez del Campo, back in the late twenties, he was at irreconcilable odds with his president. He became the senior service chief who most defiantly confronted Allende. In a heated exchange during the first week of September, Allende shouted: "Then I am at war with you; I am at war with the navy!" To name or not to name Merino to the top navy job had become the Scylla and Charybdis of Allende's career. As in the case of the army, Allende had protected himself by maneuvering into the top navy job a man who was, while not so vain as the army's Prats, at least pliable and amenable to the president's purposes, Adm. Raúl Montero Cornejo. Montero was too passive, as it turned out, to the point that the clamor for his removal by senior navy officers compelled Allende to replace him. Merino was, from the start, plainly and implacably antagonistic to Allende.

Not that Allende or his cohorts suffered Merino in impassive silence. Merino had been fired upon twice: once on August 2 or 3, with a bullet fired from a gun with a silencer, another time by a machine gun as he emerged from the long Prado tunnel on the highway between Santiago and Valparaíso. Two of those bullets pinged off the back bumper of his car.

Finally, there was the ominous report that reached Merino late on the afternoon of September 10. At lunch that day in La Moneda, Allende told the servants to withdraw and, over dessert, was heard to tell Alfredo Joignant, head of Investigaciónes: "I'm going to have to name Merino Wednesday. You take care of him before then." The conversation was overheard by a navy steward, who reported it immediately to his superiors. But Merino could afford to relax, because he knew that Wednesday would never come—at least not as Allende envisioned it.

It was Merino, in fact, who had set the hands on destiny's clock. Late Friday night, September 7, he realized there was no longer any hope of deflecting Allende from his nation-wrecking path. On the morning of Saturday, September 8, he selected the time and date. On Sunday afternoon, September 9, he scribbled the sixty-word note that sealed Allende's fate—and with it an entire epoch of Chilean history:

Gustavo & Augusto: Bajo mi palabra de honor el Día D será el Día 11 y la hora H 0600.

Si Uds. no pueden cumplir esta fase con el total de las fuerzas que mandan en Santiago, explíquemelo al reverso.

El Almirante Huídobro está autorizado para traer y discutir culquier tema con Uds. Los saludo con esperanzas de comprensión. Merino.

On the back, he added a stunningly dramatic postscript:

> Gustavo: es la última oportunidad. J.T.
> Augusto: si no puede toda la fuerza del primer momento, no
> viveremos para el futuro. Pepe.*

That afternoon, in the studio of Pinochet's house, Leigh and Pinochet read the note. Without hesitating, each took pen in hand, and, across the back, scribbled the word *Conforme,* each adding only his signature ("Gustavo Leigh" and the one word, "Pinochet.") The countdown for the most momentous revolution in Chile's history had begun.

Though scribbled as an afterthought, at the suggestion of an aide, the note was a masterpiece of ultimatum, of appeal—and the possibility of negotiation. What Merino did not know, but would soon discover, was that the army under Pinochet was as ready to act as he expected the air force would be.

On the afternoon of Monday, September 10, 1973, Merino shared with Allende a major preoccupation: the squadron at Valparaíso, slated to rendezvous with a U.S. squadron for the annual Operation Unitas exercises. The ships: the cruiser *Prat,* the destroyers *Cochrane, Blanco Encalada,* and *Orella,* the oiler *Araucano,* the submarine *Simpson.* The fleet was under the nominal command of Adm. Pablo Weber Munich, but actually under Merino's tight, personal control. Weber's vacillating attitude on the Montero resignation had cost him the confidence of Merino and other top navy commanders.

The squadron began to weigh anchor at noon, and set sail starting at two that afternoon. The last ship sailed at 4:00 P.M. Their orders: sail north, at 10 knots, until rendezvousing with the American flotilla

---

*"Gustavo [Leigh] and Augusto [Pinochet]: On my word of honor, D-Day is the 11th and H-Hour 6:00 A.M.

If you cannot take part in this phase with all of the forces you command in Santiago, explain on the other side.

Admiral Huídobro is authorized to bring and discuss any topic with you.

I greet you in the hope of understanding."

The postscript:

"Gustavo: This is the last chance. [The initials J.T. were those of Merino's first names, José Toribio.]

Augusto: If you can't [commit] your full force from the outset, we will not live [to see] the future. Pepe."

west of Caldera, a two-day voyage, just under 500 miles to the north. The American ships were, at that time, just entering Chilean waters west of Arica, about 600 miles north of the rendezvous point. Weber was given orders to be opened at sea. The ship captains received sealed orders not to be opened until midnight.

Shortly after the fleet had sailed, Merino moved from the traditional headquarters on the principal plaza of downtown Valparaíso to the Naval War College. Communications had already been installed there linking him with navy bases around the country and, through the navy's private "green telephone" system, with Santiago. The move was made on the pretext of security, since the War College, on the second floor of a building in Valparaíso, a few blocks from the port, was far more defensible than the downtown site, and trouble was expected the next day over the Altamirano affair.

At that point, only Merino, the five members of his general staff, and two or three other top commanders among the 18,000 men in the Chilean Navy knew the real dimensions of the "trouble" that awaited Chile the next day.

It is unlikely that Iván Sáez Ayala thinks of himself as a pawn of any kind, but he fits at least one definition of the role. Iván, on that day in September, was a twenty-three-year-old bachelor and also a professional soldier, a career he began at eighteen. On September 10 Sáez was finishing up a three-day pass in his hometown of Talca, 155 miles south of Santiago, a city famed in history as the place where Chile's Declaration of Independence was signed, and important now as the capital of the country's leading wine-growing province.

Sáez had ample reason to feel satisfied with life. He was moving along well in his career—he was then a corporal, second class, and a member of the cadre of the prestigious Command of Military Institutes in Santiago, the umbrella organization for the clutch of army schools in the capital. At that particular time he had his soldier's life "by the tail"; he was on detached duty, training for the pentathlon event in the armed forces' annual track and field games scheduled for midweek.

If that weren't enough, Sáez would soon be with his girl. She lived in San Bernardo, just a few miles south of Santiago. That afternoon he would catch a train and spend the night at her house before reporting for duty in the morning.

Not even the nagging of his family could mottle Corporal Sáez's spirits. Of course, they weren't exactly nagging him, either, when they asked, with growing exasperation these past few days, "When are you bums going to do something?" Everywhere he went, people put the same question to him, and Sáez didn't have to ask what they meant. There wasn't a man, woman, or child in all of Chile who did not know what it meant: How long before the military finally gets rid of Allende?

Another corporal had a date that day—of a very different kind. Iván Figueroa Araneda, twenty-four, one of the early ringleaders of the plot to subvert the air force, was due that day at the office of Capt. Raúl Vergara Meneses, a key man in a plan to seize the Air Academy and convert it into a bristling armed bastion of a general counterrevolution. The plotters had arrived at the conclusion that by no later than October 12 an attempt would be made to oust Salvador Allende, either by legal means, in Congress, or by violence. Of four options, they finally decided that those known to be loyal leftists would flee their units to join prearranged commando bands. On September 10 Figueroa was to receive from Vergara his "combat" instructions, including hideouts and passwords.

"I told him I couldn't make it that day," Figueroa said, "but I would see him the following day." That was a tomorrow that would never come.

Orlando Letelier had spent practically his entire adult life outside of Chile. After college he moved directly into a government job, which kept him much of the time abroad, attending international conferences. Next came two years in Venezuela, in a job Salvador Allende helped him get. From there he moved to Washington, with the Inter-American Development Bank (IADB), recruited by a fellow Chilean and Allende crony, Felipe Herrera, longtime president of the Bank. In ten years in that bureaucratic behemoth Letelier climbed steadily upward, finally reaching a key, third-echelon job. A month after Allende took office, he tapped Letelier for the tough post of Chile's ambassador to the United States. Then, in May 1973, Allende summoned him to Santiago to take over as Foreign Minister, a move widely interpreted as a sop to soft-liners within the Allende coalition and the increasingly wary opposition outside. In the whirlwind of the ensuing months Letelier also served briefly as Minister of the Interior, winding up finally as Minister of Defense in Allende's last fling at Cabinet roulette, a dozen days earlier.

Letelier was on his way to an appointment with the dentist when he learned he was to have dinner that night with Allende. He decided to keep the dental appointment, and the dentist started root canal work, a painful process even in normal times.

Letelier did not know it, of course, but normality was rapidly vanishing from Chilean life.

But another man did know it. For very important personal reasons, that man chooses to remain anoymous. We shall call him Mario. Mario is an engineer who makes his money in real estate, but finds his satisfactions in amateur radio. Like countless "hams" around the world, Mario is so dedicated to his hobby that he finally knows more about the workings of the radio rigs he uses than do the manufacturers who make them. He enjoyed a peerless reputation among Chile's three thousand radio hams. It was that reputation that would catapult him, together with three other civilian amateur radio operators in Santiago, into a pivotal place in the impending drama.

Mario is a devoted family man and an ardent patriot. One might question his views, but never their intensity or sincerity. He felt a growing heartsickness about the fate of his country under the Allende regime and had been making arrangements to move his family to Ecuador, 2,400 miles to the north. The turbulent events at the end of 1972 persuaded him, however, that Chileans would not allow their country to go down a socialist drain.

"In January of 1973 I liquidated everything I had in Ecuador," Mario said, "and decided to fight to the finish in Chile."

Another man had made a similar decision, and found himself also in a central if shadowy role. We shall call this man César, because he has something of the handsome good looks of oldtime movie star César Romero: gray hair, curly in the center, tall and erect as befits a retired army officer (which he was). An electrical engineer with experience in broadcasting, César was approached informally early in 1973 by a number of organizations: the armed forces, Patria y Libertad (Fatherland and Freedom, the small but increasingly aggressive right-wing terrorist organization), and others, all chafing restlessly in the embittered atmosphere of a disintegrating country. But it was early July before he received the first official nibble.

The "nibbler" was Col. Julio Polloni Pérez, a man admired by his professional peers as an inventive genius of communications. César had served with Polloni years before on a military mission to the

Chilean Antarctic. Early in July, a few days after the abortive tank regiment uprising, Polloni, then chief of telecommunications for the army, called César and asked him to come to his office in the Defense Ministry.

"When I got here, he came straight to the point," César said. "He asked me how would we go about silencing commercial radio stations, swiftly and surely."

Bluntness was not Polloni's usual style. Then forty-nine years old and rounding out his thirty-first year as an officer, Polloni was usually the soul of discretion (a characteristic that would later get him named chief of army intelligence.) Mustachioed, his black hair combed straight back, accenting the ruddiness of his face, Polloni normally peers at visitors through light gray-blue eyes that seem to be issuing an appeal for help in forming the next phrase.

That quality of deflecting detachment quickened Pinochet's confidence in Polloni and encouraged him to ask Polloni, in April 1973, to design a twin-pronged communications plan with the overall name "Operation Silence."

Phase One: On signal, silence all commercial broadcasting—radio, television, international cable and telex services, new agencies, long distance and international telephone, and special cases, such as transmitters operated by private firms—and the powerful equipment installed in the warehouse of the state-run Development Corporation, providing a twenty-four-hour radio link with Allende's most vocal international ally, Fidel Castro.

Phase Two: Design and set up a secret, backup communications network for the army, connecting points stretching 2,700 miles from Arica near the Peruvian frontier in the north to Punta Arenas, hard by the Straits of Magellan to the south.

César was the key outsider working with Polloni on Phase One. Mario and two close friends—officers of the Radio Club de Chile— were the key men on Phase Two, later given invaluable help by a civilian colleague in Talca. For all of these men the commitment meant months of hard work, sacrificing family and personal fortune, for they had not only to leave their businesses to run themselves but also to finance their own, often considerable expenses and provide their own equipment. Nor was there glory in what they did. If the revolt finally came and succeeded—as it did—they would have to remain anonymous, since, as civilians, they would be easy prey for terrorist reprisals. Finally, there was danger, real danger. In those uncertain times there could be no guarantee that if caught, or if the plot should fail, the military would—or could—stand behind them.

"At first, I was a little nervous," Mario said with deliberate understatement. "For one thing, I couldn't be sure that Polloni wasn't some kind of a nut, acting on his own, especially after the *tancazo* [an abortive uprising in June 1973 by elements of the Second Armored Regiment]. But gradually, as others got involved, I realized it was on the up-and-up, and we got busy."

Months of tension and frustration culminated in a frenzied rush through that climactic weekend in September, and finally coalesced into the decisive action of Monday, September 10, all had been awaiting.

"Julio called me Monday morning and told me to get right over, it was an emergency," César said. "When I got over there, he said we had to duplicate the links from the Defense Ministry to the two radio stations we had long since decided would be the official stations left on the air in an emergency: Radio Agricultura and Radio Minería. We had set them up to operate on 150 MH. frequency; he wanted to add 320 MH., to give better international coverage."

César set to work immediately, without asking questions. Nor did Polloni tell him what he had known for the past forty-eight hours, that H-Hour was set for dawn on Tuesday. Polloni had known ever since Merino had made up his mind and communicated his decision to the Defense Department's General Staff on Saturday. (Even before, it turned out, the navy chief had addressed his urgent appeal to the other service chiefs.)

Once he had finished with César, Polloni focused on a new and crucial problem: installing, practically from scratch, a radio network to connect the three critical posts in Santiago: the Defense Ministry, the army, and the air force. Shortly before noon he put in a call to Mario, who was then back at his office on the top floor of an office building just three blocks from La Moneda.

Polloni, Col. Julio Sánchez of the Military Intelligence Service (SIM), and another man who had won the abiding respect of the radio amateurs, Major Valdivieso, Defense Department communications officer, were waiting for him. The four men had met often, together or separately. By now they were friends. But even among themselves the game of semantic charades had to be played out to the end.

"Right up until the early part of September," Mario recalled, "there was nothing definite about what we were doing, or why. But by that last week, we knew, we knew."

Still, Polloni kept up appearances.

"Mario, there could be a problem tomorrow," Polloni told him. "You know about Altamirano, I'm sure. We've got to be ready. Are we?"

Mario thought they were "98 percent ready," but then he didn't know yet what his military "clients" had in mind.

The men went immediately to Valdivieso's office on the top floor of the Defense Ministry. There Valdivieso sketched for them the entire communications plan, including the amateur backup net for military communications patched together in ten to fifteen meetings over those recent months. The hub of the network was an installation in the heavily guarded Military Academy in the posh Las Condes suburb of Santiago. The academy had already been linked to the Defense Ministry, five miles due west in downtown Santiago.

Fifty-seven stations around Chile were hooked into the emergency network, for use in case saboteurs knocked out the army's regular communications, mostly carried over vulnerable microwave links. Transmission would be on a seldom-used (144.48Mc.) frequency. In Chile at that time the relatively few hams on the air operated on 144.60 Mc.

The lower frequency also had the added advantage of being viewed as highly improbable for army use, since regular army equipment was not suited for that frequency—a problem Mario had solved by borrowing two used Motorola sets, installing one in the offices of COFA (Armed Forces Command Center) on the fifth floor at the back of the Defense Ministry, the other at the Military Academy. These three-watt, $170 sets would soon crackle with the commands of the most profound revolution since the birth of the republic.

Polloni had about a hundred soldiers and an equal number of airmen and sailors assigned to him in Santiago for the twin purposes of silencing unwanted communications and supervising the emergency network. In all of Chile more than a hundred civilians were plugged into the network, assigned to the primary mission of tuning in on, and recording, "enemy" radio conversations, up to and including the day of battle. In Santiago twenty civilians worked with Polloni and his men through August, but during the hectic weekend just concluded their number had been narrowed to five or six, and now, in the final crunch, there were just these four: Mario, César, and the two Radio Club officers.

Valdivieso quickly explained the problem: the COFA installation had to be moved immediately to the front of the building and the fifth-floor office of Vice Admiral Carvajal, chief of staff of the Joint Chiefs of Staff. Even more important, new installations were needed at the Signal Corps garrison at Peñalolén, 7.5 miles east-southeast of the ministry, and another at the Air Academy, about seven miles north of Peñalolén. The first was to be the combat headquarters of General Pinochet, the second that of General Leigh. Pinochet had originally planned to install his headquarters at Peldehue, twenty-one miles north of Santiago, part of a constellation of army, Carabinero, and air force garrisons in that area. Leigh had persuaded him during their decisive Sunday night meeting to move closer in. Up to that point none of the service chiefs had informed any of the others where they planned to locate, revealing the degree of cautiousness and independence surrounding the separate service conspiracies. The following morning Polloni, as chief of communications, was given the word, and instructed to connect each headquarters to the others—a new dimension in his planning.

Once Mario had been cued in on these arrangements, he went from the ministry straight back to his office. There he was joined at 2:00 P.M. by his two Radio Club companions. Mario took on the job of moving the set from COFA to Carvajal's office. When he finished, he drove out to the Signal Corps garrison at Peñalolén.

One of the Radio Club men borrowed another set and installed it at the Air Academy. The third headed out to the Military Academy, where a transformer had to be changed. A hefty man, he peeled off a few pounds that day bounding up and down four flights of stairs more times then he would care to remember. The equipment had been squirreled away there for security's sake, away from prying eyes, in a room on the top floor of the cadets' dormitory, then vacant because of a recess in classes.

At Peñalolén and the Air Academy problems plagued the men far into the night. Since the installation had been made previously at the Military Academy and it was only a matter of repairs, the man assigned there finished his job around 6:00 P.M. He was told to report "first thing" the following morning.

"Should I bring a toothbrush?" he asked the commandant, Colonel Floody. "It might be a good idea" was the wry answer.

Radio Agricultura was an inevitable first choice to carry the revolutionary voice of the armed forces to Chile—and, during the first hours of the revolt, to the rest of the world. As an added safety measure, Radio Minería was later added, and, at the last minute, Radio Balmaceda, the Christian Democrat station, was also allowed to continue broadcasting. But the pilot station in all of the planning, from the very first, was Radio Agricultura. In light of the sacrifices and risks of so many others in the media during the Allende years, there is an element of perversity in singling out any one person or entity for special mention. Yet it is certainly true that of all of the radio stations in Chile, none was more combative than Agricultura.

Radio Agricultura became what it did thanks largely to the fighting spirit of two men at the station—its general manager, Carlos Ashton, and an extraordinarily dedicated and able man named Alvaro Puga, who, in the phrase of his friend, the distinguished writer Enrique Campos Menéndez, has always had as the thrust of his mission "to sow rather than to harvest," to fight for a cause rather than profit by it. But they were not alone. Of Agricultura's eight gifted and pugnacious commentators, no fewer than five won seats in the Chamber of Deputies in the bitterly contested parliamentary elections of March 1973, a vote of confidence in independent campaigners without equal in Chilean politics or journalism.

As a measure of the station's gadfly effectiveness, it was closed seven times by the government during the last ten months of Allende's administration, its key personnel frequently threatened and occasionally jailed (Puga was, for instance), and the station made the target of sporadic gunfire from Communist Party headquarters diagonally across Teatinos Street in downtown Santiago. Through its two satellite stations—one in Los Angeles (closed by the government for ten weeks in late 1972) and another in Valparaíso, plus an occasional nationwide network of eighteen to twenty stations, the station's scrappy voice was heard by as many as 80 percent of Chile's six million radio listeners.

Any one of these considerations might have been enough to earn the station the confidence of the military. But it was the fickle circumstance of chance encounter that finally mattered more than cold calculation.

On October 15, 1972, at the peak of a debilitating national strike, the Allende government ordered radio stations to join, on presidential command, in national networks—an order the presidency would persist in issuing despite repeated court rulings that such enforced *cadenas* (chains) were unconstitutional. Army troops frequently were sent to aid Carabineros in enforcing the orders. On October 23, 1972, three stations among the hundred-odd then on the air in Chile defied the decree and withdrew from the network. One of them was Radio Agricultura. One of the "enforcers" sent to the station that day was Julio Polloni. He was to return often.

In the process, Polloni, Ashton, and Puga began to discover, gradually, cautiously, that they shared the same distaste for the Allende government. Eventually, Polloni began consulting them on communications matters, and, finally, involving them in the actual plotting. (Puga remembers one time, in late August or early September, when he and Polloni had spread out Operation Silence maps on the floor of his office when Carabineros arrived on a raid. He stuffed the map under a file cabinet just before they burst in.)

The breakthrough came in early July 1973. The first phase of Operation Silence was concerned mainly with zeroing in on the dozen or so radio stations rabidly loyal to the Allende government, since it was assumed that the others would knuckle under to a military command if and when the revolt should come (and they did). But parallel with that was the concern of assuring that at least one station would remain on the air to relay official messages to the public.

It wasn't enough to single out Radio Agricultura. Polloni and his cohorts—principally César and an army captain, a former student of César's whom Polloni had assigned to work with César—had to provide for the possibility that the station might be forcibly seized during the first fighting: armed protection could not be provided in advance because that would have attracted attention, and once the revolt was officially announced, Communist street commandos permanently bivouacked in the party's headquarters across the street might easily have reached the station before "friendlies."

So, at César's instigation, three VHF links were installed: one from the Defense Ministry to a special studio in Radio Agricultura, connected then by the usual means to the station's transmitter on the southeastern outskirts of the city; another from the ministry direct to the transmitter hut; and the third to an inconspicuous house at 2199 Julieta Avenue in the eastern suburbs, about four miles from the station. That house belonged to Francisco (Gabito) Hernández, a house he shared with his seventy-two-year-old mother, Francisca, and seventy-four-year-old aunt, Teresa. Hernández, a man in his mid-forties, was then a second-echelon executive of Radio Agricultura. Weeks before, a transmitter had been installed in the one-story house, small but capable of becoming the voice of revolution should first-line communications fail or be knocked out.

Inasmuch as Ashton had been sidelined with a bad case of hepatitis since August 3, Puga was in charge at the station and was the first to learn about the impending coup. The previous Friday, September 7, Puga was alerted by Admiral Carvajal to have the station ready; there was a chance of action as soon as Saturday or Sunday. It was then he learned that the general staff of the Defense Ministry had completed its planning and was ready to respond to escalating navy pressure to move. Early Friday evening Lt. Col. Gonzalo Albiña, the air force liaison on Operation Silence, told him that it looked as though Monday would be the day, and that he would be picked up at the station. Puga put in a restless weekend, awaiting final instructions. He got them Monday morning, but shared the secret with only two persons that day: Ashton and Jorge Fontaine, president of Radio Agricultura (and president of the Confederation of Production and Commerce, an amalgam, roughly, of the membership of the U.S. Chamber of Commerce and the National Association of Manufacturers, were they to be combined). To two other friends, Enrique Campos and Gen. Alfredo Canales, who stopped by the station that afternoon, he remarked only that he understood trouble was expected Tuesday over the Altamirano affair. General Canales would have been particularly pleased had he learned the real news: only a few months previously he had been fired as army training chief for his firm resistance to Marxist penetration of the army.

There was another man with a secret on September 10—and a pledge to share it. That man was Rear Adm. Sergio Huidobro. He was one of the first men to know the virtual ultimatum on D-Day, H-Hour, and one of the first five to know when it had finally been ratified. It was a secret he had promised to share with his close friend, Rear Adm. Horacio Justiniano, commandant of the Third Naval Zone in Punta Arenas, 1,500 miles to the south. Monday morning he put in a telephone call to Justiniano over lines both were sure were monitored. "Horacio," Huidobro said, "Helena, Amanda, Fabiola, and Carolina will be at your house tomorrow." The names were fictitious; the first letters of each spelled out a prearranged code, which told Justiniano that tomorrow was D-Day, and that all three services and Carabineros would join in the revolt. Justiniano understood immediately, but doubted all the same.

"Are you sure all four are coming?" he asked, "Because there aren't enough beds."

"You'd better get the beds ready then," Huidobro shot back, "because these girls are very rebellious."

Huidobro chuckled.

"They were probably still trying to figure that one out," he remarked months later, "when it was too late to worry about it any more."

Though he didn't yet realize it, chance was, for our last protagonist, a sadistic Tantalus teasing him out of the comfortable obscurity he preferred, pushing him instead into a situation that will torment him to the end of his days.

His name is Patricio Guijón Klein. He is a surgeon, forty-one years of age at the moment he stumbled onto history's stage, father of four children and husband of a blonde-haired woman named Silvia. He is a slight man, standing perhaps 5'6" and weighing no more than 140 pounds. His brown eyes have an appealing quizzical quality.

In October 1972 Dr. Arturo Jirón, who had been Allende's surgeon, was appointed Minister of Health. Dr. Patricio Arroyo, an Allende intimate and former classmate and close friend of Patricio Guijón, succeeded Jirón at La Moneda, and asked Guijón whether he would like to join the presidential medical staff. Although his affection for Marxist ideas dated from his youth, Guijón was not a political activist and described himself, in fact, as a "Platonic leftist." He decided to accept.

"Look, what doctor wouldn't? Not only for what it represents in terms of prestige, an opportunity to become known, but for the public recognition of what a man is, what he's accomplished, as a professional. Of course I accepted."

The job was ad honorem. It turned out to be all ad honorem, in fact, because Guijón not only never got to examine his famous patient; he never even got to meet Allende personally. Nor, for that matter, did he suddenly appear on everybody's invitation list or in the society or news columns. None of these things happened. As a result, he moved no nearer the ideal of most Chilean doctors of developing a private practice above and beyond the drudgery of a mandatory, time-clock workload than he had before the appointment. In Chile medicine had long been socialized. To have a lucrative private practice, a doctor had to be extremely distinguished or extremely famous—or both. Otherwise, he punched a clock, literally, and took home a very anemic paycheck. Like most doctors, Patricio Guijón punched two: at Hospital del Salvador and the Clínica Alemána.

All that did happen to Dr. Guijón in his new role was that he got to attend weekly meetings with the other five "presidential" doctors (only one of them actually ministered to the president's needs). The meetings were held in a nondescript office just off the north entrance of La Moneda, which was about as close as Guijón got to Allende.

But politics cast an enticing spell, and in the process of living even on the periphery of power, platonic Patricio became, inevitably, partisan Patricio, a man of hardening commitments. That entitled him to worry, along with the rest of Allende's loyalists, about the sanity of the opposition and, by the time September 10 rolled around, whether that opposition would even go so far as to bring the country's democratic institutions down upon their hectoring heads.

"Chile Will Be Transformed Into Another Heroic Vietnam."

So proclaimed the headline over the page 3 story in the September 10 issue of *Clarín* on the explosive speech made the day before by Carlos Altamirano Orrego.

"The Socialist Party," Altamirano told his cheering Estadio Chile audience, "is willing, is decided, to fight, to triumph over the right-wing conspiracy. The betrayal of the Right will be crushed only by the force of a people united. Chile will be transformed into another heroic Vietnam if sedition tries to lord over our country."

As for the enemy, combat-ready Altamirano had them sized up.

"They are cowards!" he said. "They hide in embassies, and seek asylum, and flee from Chile, so as not to face up in a manly way to the consequences of their deeds."

Fighting words they were. And they fell into the wide chasm that separated words and deeds in the Chile of September, 1973.

two

UNDER COVER OF NIGHT

I. The Sleepwalkers

On the statistical surface, September 10, 1973, was a day heralding the coming of spring: the temperature that day had peaked at 72 degrees (22°C) before sliding down to an overnight low of 41 degrees (5°C). But September 10 was not a time like any other in Chile. It was the one thousand forty-third day of a journey on a fool's errand, *la vía chilena al socialismo*—Salvador Allende's much-celebrated "Chilean road to socialism." As night fell on Santiago, portents were everywhere that the road had led to the edge of an abyss.

Darkness had just settled over the sylvan tranquillity of Langley, Virginia—5,015 miles almost due north—when word of those portents reached official Washington.

A clerk in the communications center of the Central Intelligence Agency tore the coded message off a teletype machine as it came in and rushed a copy to David Atlee Phillips in his third-floor office. A strapping man with a resonant voice, intense blue eyes—and long experience as a spy—Phillips then headed the Latin American area of CIA's Clandestine Services Division.

"It was a message like so many others we had received from Santiago during those days when revolution was the number one topic of talk in Chile," a former CIA man close to the case said. "Except that this one said the army was ready to join in, and that gave Dave a feeling at the back of his neck that this time it was for real."

Phillips was a man especially suited for "feelings at the back of his neck" on this subject. He had served in Chile early in his twenty-four-year spying career. He was posted to Chile in the 1950s as an undercover agent (he would remain so for most of his career). His cover: editor of the English-language weekly, *The South Pacific Mail*.

Next he went to Havana, where he remained during the last two years of Fulgencio Batista and the early days of Fidel Castro. Still working under cover, he wrote a weekly column for the English-language *Times of Havana*. Next he surfaced in Miami, as a conduit of funds for exile newspapers kept alive not only to fan patriotic zeal among Cuban exiles but also in the expectation that they would resume publication on their home territory following the triumph of the CIA-orchestrated invasion. This operation collapsed suddenly in the Bay of Pigs debacle. Following a stint in Washington, Phillips was dispatched to the Dominican Republic shortly after the 1965 civil war broke out there and remained to become CIA station chief. Next he went to Brazil, where he was when Salvador Allende was elected in 1970. In September and October of 1970 he was detailed to special duty: head of a special CIA task force created in mid-September in response to Richard Nixon's decision to prevent Salvador Allende— by whatever means—from assuming the presidency in Chile. Over a period of a month the CIA attempted moves, some bordering on the desperate, to carry out Nixon's edict. By mid-October, before the fateful negotiations had been concluded that would give minority-candidate Allende the votes he needed in Congress, the CIA had ended its own bumbling operations. Although there were some CIA links to the plotters, who would eventually kill the Army's commander-in-chief, René Schneider Chereau, the CIA operatives for the most part shunned them and were certainly excluded from the operative inner circle that actually carried out the bungled kidnaping and assassination.

In 1973 Phillips took over as head of the "company's" clandestine services for all of Latin America. The author of the message handed him that night in September was a man of experience comparable to Phillips's own: Raymond A. Warren, fifty-one, then rounding out the third year of his second tour in Santiago. His "cover" was a standard one used by espionage operatives of all countries. He was, theoretically, a member of the political section of the U.S. Embassy.

The two-hundred-word message handed to Phillips on plain tele-type paper said the revolution to oust Allende would begin around 7:30 A.M. the following day.

"Although copies had gone simultaneously to other agencies in Washington," the former CIA man continued, "Dave decided this one was important enough to flag for the attention of a couple of key people, because he knew official Washington was closing down for the night. Important enough to do that—but not conclusive enough to recommend any immediate action. After all, you can't call a meeting of the National Security Council on the basis of a feeling at the back of your neck, and certainly not after literally scores of messages saying just about the identical same thing—now it's on, now it's off, and so forth."

So, the agent added, Phillips "covered" official Washington, as CIA's director, William Colby, would later express it in congressional testimony: he telephoned counterparts to both the State Department and the National Security Council.

"I have a feeling," Phillips told them, "that this is it. This time it looks as though the army is in."

Phillips then went home and to bed, and so did official Washington. They would awake the next day to the news that their spy in Santiago knew what he was talking about—this time.

Official Washington could be forgiven for failing to react to the portents. For they remained, after all, invisible even to Salvador Allende.

"He [Allende] was worried because he understood the gravity of the situation, what with the reaction to the Altamirano speech and all," the Interior Minister, Carlos Briones, recounted later. "But he was certainly not beside himself—that just wasn't his style."

Not only was he not beside himself, he exuded confidence as he left La Moneda that evening and headed for his rendezvous with Briones and two other advisers, Defense Minister Orlando Letelier and the shadowy Spaniard, Joan Garcés Ramón.

"I am absolutely confident and optimistic we will overcome the difficult hours we face," Allende told newsmen as he left the Palace. "Even more so: I am fully confident we will."

With that, Allende sank into the back seat of the blue Fiat 125 for the ride to Tomás Moro, the impregnably fortified manor in an eastern suburb that he liked to use on week nights.

As chance would have it, Hortensia Bussi de Allende, his wife of thirty-three years, was present at that last dinner they would have together. Tencha, as she was called by her family and friends, had returned only the night before from a five-day visit to Mexico, heading a Chilean delegation taking relief supplies to that nation in the aftermath of an earthquake. Although their relations had been strained the past three years, tonight Allende was amiable and solicitous in his attitude to her. (The reason for their strained relations everyone knew: La Payita—Miria Contreras Bell de Ropert—his private secretary.)

Others at dinner that evening were Allende's youngest daughter Isabel, a twenty-eight-year-old sociologist, and, like her older sister, Beatriz, a political firebrand; Briones, who drove straight to Tomás Moro from his downtown office; Letelier, who also could not find time to stop home first, and arrived late for the dinner gathering; and Garcés.

Of all the men and women around Salvador Allende, none managed to be more invisible than Joan Garcés Ramón. Nor is it likely that any of them wielded greater power, if one defines power as the ability to influence events, because Garcés exercised enormous influence over Salvador Allende.

His past was as mysterious as his present for Chileans. One version has it that he held a doctorate in political science from the University of Madrid, another that he took his doctorate at the Sorbonne. Most seem to agree that he insinuated himself into Salvador Allende's life from the anonymity of a small village in Spain's Catalonia region by sending him a twenty-page letter in late 1969 or early 1970, just prior to Allende's nomination as the Popular Unity presidential candidate.

In the letter Garcés charted a Marxist strategy for winning and consolidating power in a revolution without violence—ideas with an immense emotional appeal at that time to Salvador Allende. As the story is told, Allende cabled Garcés the day of his nomination inviting him to fly to Santiago, all expenses paid, for "conversations."

If there had been no Joan Garcés, one would have had to be invented to comply with the natural law of equilibrium. None of Allende's advisers were pensive, meditative men. Briones came closest to being so, but he was brought in only at the very end and was promptly sucked into a whirlpool of overwhelming events. Garcés fulfilled the need for a resident philosopher, a strategist of ideas. None of those around Allende were noted for moderation. Garcés was a man of retiring, Trappist-like austerity.

The contrast was even sharper between the man and his master. Of Salvador Allende, it has been said and written many times that he "never read a book through, not even one by Marx." It has also been noted many times that he possessed a retentive, vacuum-cleaner mind, capable of suctioning complicated data in quick gulps and later parceling it out with great precision.

Garcés, on the other hand, was a man of ponderous, methodical phrases, who quoted and disputed a wide range of political thinkers in his own writing, writing that was a latticework of carefully, cautiously, elaborately constructed political blueprints.

Garcés became a key behind-the-scenes man in the campaign that carried Allende to the presidency in 1970. He went on to become Allende's principal speechwriter. It is interesting to speculate which of the partners in this marriage of convenience—the bon vivant man of action and the ascetic man of convoluted ideas—was responsible for the intellectual barrenness of the union, or whether it was, perhaps, less a mating of complementary talents than an immolation of mutually destructive styles. The fact, noted by a number of critics of the Allende years, is that in all the "flood tide of his speeches, it is not possible to extract a single theoretical concept, a single philosophical orientation . . . a single original idea . . . or thought endowed with depth or sharpness. . . ."

The Spaniard was in his thirties when he teamed with Allende. Little is known of his personal life in Santiago, except that Allende finally managed, apparently, to ease him onto the payroll of the United Nations.

Newspaper accounts portrayed Garcés as the voice of quiet reason within the president's inner councils, the man who learned to abhor violence in his native Spain, where several members of his family died in the annihilating civil war. A closer reading of his work would have revealed that there lurked in the soul of this pacifist the same duality that ruled Allende: total power by peaceful, "legal" means so long as it was possible, by deceit and violence when it was not.

Apart from this group, there was one man who did not come to dinner that night: Clodomiro Almeyda Medina, once again Allende's Foreign Minister (the job he had in the first Allende cabinet), a self-styled Maoist and one of the president's closest and most trusted advisers. Almeyda had returned only at seven that evening from a conference Allende himself had planned to attend, the meeting of so-called nonaligned nations in Algeria. Almeyda returned too late to make dinner—but too early to escape the effects of that night's events on his future.

Doña Tencha dominated the talk at the dinner table, recounting her experiences in Mexico.

Around eleven o'clock the four men—Allende, Briones, Letelier, Garcés—excused themselves and went to Allende's first-floor study, adjoining the bedroom he used at Tomás Moro. (Mrs. Allende slept in a bedroom on the second floor.)

A waiter served them coffee and Cognac. A fire crackled in the fireplace, causing the glass on the French doors facing the swimming pool to steam up.

Allende came straight to the point. The following day he was to make a speech at 11:00 A.M. at the State Technical University's "antifascist rally." He planned to throw a bombshell: announce his intention to call for a plebiscite to confirm or reject him and his policies.

"The day had been just too busy for us to talk about it," Carlos Briones said, "and that's why he kept postponing the speech Monday. The idea was, of course, unconstitutional, but he wanted to see what kind of a formula we could come up with. He wanted Letelier there because he had such an excellent pipeline into the Socialist Party and was particularly close to Altamirano. Almeyda had the broadest political base of anyone in the Cabinet."

Briones brought to the conversation two valuable qualities: one, he was an expert on constitutional law, having taught it for years at the University of Chile; and two, he still had the respect of some members of the opposition, and probably offered the most realistic thinking on their moods.

"Whatever the formula, Salvador made one thing plain," Briones said later, "and that is that he would accept the verdict of the plebiscite no matter what the outcome. If adverse, then he would pack up and leave the presidency. Contrary to what many have said about him he was profoundly democratic."

"Anyway, we didn't have a chance to get very far before the telephones started ringing."

The lights burned late that night in La Moneda. In his first-floor office on the south side of the building, René Largo Farías fought drowsiness at the end of a fourteen-hour day. Farías, the chubby, snub-nosed chief of radio of the presidential Office of Information and

Broadcasting (known by the acronym OIR from the Spanish initials), had been tipped off about troop movements at different points around the country. The OIR logbook reveals the beginning of a tense vigil at five minutes past midnight: a call to the governor of the Province of Aconcagua to check on reports of troop movements there. The governor confirmed that "something" was afoot, and promised to call Farías back as soon as he smoked out the details.

But Farías was not alone in his anxiety. The telephone in the study at Tomás Moro had rung earlier with a call for Briones. The caller was Alfredo Joignant, head of the plainclothes police force, Investigaciónes, a nationwide agency attached to the Interior Ministry. Briones put the phone down.

"That was Joignant," he told the others. "He's picked up some alarming reports about troop movements, the confining to quarters of the Santiago garrison. He said it was ordered by Brady [the disarmingly mild-mannered general named by Pinochet to command the Santiago garrison only three weeks before]. Do you know anything about it, Orlando?"

Letelier, less than two weeks on the job as Minister of Defense, said he did not. The two men began immediately to make calls.

"General Brady, I'm here at Tomás Moro with President Allende. We have heard reports of troop movements in San Felipe, in Los Andes, here in Santiago. What's going on, General?" The caller was Orlando Letelier.

"Troop movements? There are no troop movements, Mr. Minister. Everything's quiet. Nothing to be alarmed about." Brady told the minister he'd advise him should anything of importance happen. Brady's report did not, however square with other information trickling in—from Joignant, now hard at work on the most crucial "investigation" of his career, from the increasingly troubled Farías, and from the field.

The mayor of San Felipe—capital of Aconcagua Province, situated just over 50 miles due north of Santiago—called to report "intense activity" at the Yungay and Aconcagua Regiments. The most disturbing news came in a call from Los Andes, a city of just under 30,000 inhabitants astride the main highway to Argentina, some 40 miles north of Santiago.

"The military have started to requisition trucks and buses," the major reported. "They say they're needed to transport the Guardia

Vieja Regiment to Santiago. I hear they're moving troops from other points to Santiago, too. What's going on?"

Carlos Briones could not answer that question, but he intended to find out. The man who would have the best chance of finding out, he decided, was Daniel Vergara, the number two man in the Interior Ministry since the outset of the Allende administration. Vergara had direct control over the Carabineros, Investigaciónes, the provincial governments, and direct access to the nationwide communications network of the Carabineros. But Briones was unable to reach Vergara, a frustration that would be repeated again and again during the long night for both Briones and Letelier. They did not know it then, but an invisible wall of silence was already being built up around them.

Briones did manage to get through to a few subordinates: Joignant, in his second-floor office in the gloomy Investigaciónes building at the edge of the downtown area; the mayor of Valparaíso, who said there was no sign of the fleet, but there *was* "unusual" activity at the navy installations around the city; and the mayor of Rancagua, 55 miles to the south, who reported all quiet in that area.

The signs were disturbing, yet there remained the reassuring departure of the fleet. Besides, Allende's attention was riveted on the bombshell speech he still planned to deliver that morning, a speech that would, at the very least, neutralize the opposition long enough for him to devise new stratagems.

Shortly after 1:30 A.M. Allende sent the two ministers home so that they could rejoin him first thing in the morning. Allende continued work on the speech with Garcés. It was four in the morning before he would finally go to bed, still unsuspecting.

Unsuspecting, but not entirely unprepared. Before retiring, Allende ordered Alert One for his Praetorian guard of private gunslingers.

He called them, with withering irony, the Grupo de Amigos Personales (Group of Personal Friends), the GAP. Their trademarks were Fiat 125 automobiles (blue), submachineguns, and bullyboy manners. They had no precedent in Chilean history, and no place in Chilean law. The Law of Internal Security prohibited the existence of armed forces in Chile other than the army, navy, air force, Corps of Carabineros, and Gendarmerie of Prisons. So, too, did Article 22 of the Constitution.

Nevertheless, shortly after the election on September 4, 1970, when a mob demonstrated outside the Allende house on Guardia Vieja

Street, Allende felt "obliged to resort to a personal political guard." Allende gave them their name. Asked at a news conference to explain this unprecedented cluster of bodyguards, he replied: "It's a group of personal friends of mine, in whose loyalty and valor I have absolute confidence." The name stuck, and so did they, despite repeated demands to have them disbanded, and despite the fact that, once in the presidency, Allende could, and did, install his own people in control of the regular security forces.

Isabel Margarita Morel Gumucio Letelier is a woman who radiates warmth. At a distance, she is an attractive woman; close up, she is a beautiful woman, not so much for her rusty hair and peaches-and-cream complexion and soft features as for the sweetness of her voice, her gracious style, and her gentle affection for people in general.

The night of September 10 the telephone rang incessantly. She referred the callers to Tomás Moro, where her husband was conferring with his president.

"I woke up when Orlando came in," she said. "I have no idea what time it was. When he came in, I asked him about his teeth—he was really in terrible pain. He took something the dentist gave him and two aspirins.

"Tired as he was, we chatted a bit: I asked him about the press conference he had given that afternoon, and he said it went fine. Then he gave me the big news:

" 'Tomorrow we go to a plebiscite,' he told me. 'The president is decided to do it, and he's going to announce it tomorrow. It's going to be all or nothing.' "

Minutes later, Orlando Letelier was sound asleep.

II. The Sleepless

It was a night of improvisations for César, a night of little sleep, a night of hearing the news he had long doubted would ever come. This latest, and last, assignment was proving a tough one: install in the COFA (Armed Forces Operations Center) offices on the fifth floor of the Defense Ministry the equipment needed to convert it into the radio voice of revolution. From that office, over nationwide radio, would issue the proclamations and communiqués and special instructions to a nation at war.

He called in three of his own technicians to help him, but despite their best efforts, they were finally defeated by the lack of a length of coaxial cable two to three yards long. Finally, he sent the others home and instructed another technician to report with the cable at dawn. He also alerted the key engineer at Radio Agricultura to be ready to hook into the patch from the Defense Ministry as of 6:00 A.M.

There was a reason for his urgency. Earlier that night, as he collided with one problem after another, he turned to the communications chief, Colonel Polloni, and said:

"Look, this is more than I can handle in one day. I'll finish up tomorrow."

"I think you'd better finish tonight," the colonel replied.

"Why? Is tomorrow the day?"

Polloni winked.

"If this fails, then all of Chile fails."

Augusto Pinochet left his afternoon visitors with that ominous thought. He would repeat it early that evening for three other generals.

"I called them into my office at 7:00 P.M. and made them swear the same oath the others had. Then I told them the plan, and gave them their assignments: they would work out of my office—the Commander in Chief's office in the [Defense] Ministry—controlling action around the entire country." One was to function as Chief of Staff of the General Staff, one as head of G-2 (intelligence), and the third was put in charge of operations.

Two of the three were third and fourth in army seniority: Generals Oscar Bonilla Bradanovic and Gustavo Alvarez. (The general, second in rank to Pinochet was Orlando Urbina; he was excluded from the planning and the coup itself because it was felt that his sympathies were with Allende.)

That night Pinochet also dispatched special couriers with orders for garrisons in Valdivia and Concepción in the south, Iquique and Antofagasta in the north.

Each was told that his combat command post would be set up at 0730 Tuesday morning and that if, for any reason, he should not arrive at his command post by that time, the Chief of the General Staff should take command immediately and put into operation the revolutionary plan.

Pinochet was emphatic about the need to maintain normal appearances.

"Until 0730 tomorrow morning, everything must be done in as normal a fashion as possible," he told his generals. "No unusual troop movements, nothing out of the ordinary, because if the government stumbles onto what we are doing, it will be war without quarter."

Before leaving his office, Pinochet went over with members of his General Staff the proclamations that would be read the next day; the first, heralding the start of the revolution, had already been signed by all four service commanders and would shortly be recorded.

His own touch of "normality" included going through with the charades of attending to a husbandly chore: sending out to buy pastry for a late morning party his wife was giving the next day. At 8:00 P.M. he left his office and headed home.

Inevitably, it was a restless night. He played with his dog, made an attempt at desultory conversation, but most of all reviewed the plans for the most momentous day of his life.

Even if he had found much to change, it is unlikely he could have done so without risking the secrecy he had striven so hard to preserve, secrecy essential to the success of the operation.

Using the closely monitored telephones was, of course, out of the question. But control of General Pinochet went further. Every night a patrol car lazed around the block past his house, at midnight, and again at 3:00 A.M.

"When I got home, I left the light on in my study so they would be sure to see me. Just before retiring, I went for a stroll outside so they would be sure to see me even better. Then I went inside, turned out the light, and went to bed. Of course, I did not sleep."

Another emergency. Around 9:00 P.M. it was discovered that the radio link between the command posts of General Pinochet and General Leigh did not work. The two top amateur radio men joined Mario at Peñalolén to repair the equipment. They worked on into the night, but to no avail. Finally, Mario was told to return at eight Tuesday morning to raise a higher antenna to see if that would do the trick. He still did not know that the final countdown had started.

Gabriela Leigh was also planning a party the next day, a farewell tea for Mrs. César Ruíz Danyau, wife of the man Gustavo Leigh had replaced as commander in chief of the air force. Her suspicions had already been aroused Sunday afternoon by the unusual traffic in and out of the house. The callers were generals and other high-ranking air force officers, alarmed by the Altamirano speech. One after another, they asked: How much longer are we going to stand idly by and watch the flames of class warfare be fanned? If we wait much longer, they argued, they will consume not only ourselves, but all of Chile. Leigh listened mostly, but a silent decision was already forming. Late that afternoon he called Pinochet and said he needed urgently to talk to the army commander. Gabriela Leigh overheard the call, and understood how unusual it was. Still, she went ahead with plans for the Tuesday tea party. She had long since learned that with Gustavo Leigh things would make sense and fit snugly into place—in due time.

The couple had met in the late 1950s at the ranch of a mutual friend, a colonel in the air force, Sergio Crespo Montero. In 1960 Leigh was transferred to Washington as air attaché. The couple toyed with the idea of a hastily arranged wedding, but decided to wait. A long wait it was, until his return to Chile in 1966. Leigh was at the time a widower, father of two children. Two more were born to the second marriage.

At three o'clock Monday afternoon Gabriela Leigh's suspicions were fired even more. Her husband told her to pack a couple of suitcases, take the children, and go to the home of a close air force friend, Col. Eduardo Sepúlveda Medel and wait for him there. It was a date he almost did not keep.

After tangling with the head of Investigaciónes, Alfredo Joignant, Leigh still had two urgent matters demanding his attention.

The first was with a group of carefully selected pilots, copilots, and flight engineers of LAN-Chile, the national airline. The previous Friday, 96 percent of LAN's pilots had voted an indefinite strike in solidarity with truck drivers, professionals, small shopkeepers, clerical workers—around a million Chilean working men and women, all protesting Allende's policies, many demanding he resign. As a precaution, the pilots immediately flew the airline's fleet of planes to air force bases to safeguard against sabotage, an act that enraged Allende. In an interview a month later Leigh said:

"I told the pilots the government was pressuring me to return the planes, and that I had agreed to do so the next day, at 11:00 A.M. They asked me not to do it—and that's when I broke the news to them. That we were going to strike the next day, and that I needed their help. I had already decided that the LAN planes would be invaluable for transporting troops [they were], and so I would need crews for the 707s and 727s. They agreed immediately to help.

So as not to attract any attention, I asked them whether they would spend the night at the Air Force Hospital, which they also agreed to do. So the twenty of them—four crews of five men each—became the first 'recruits' for the revolution."

Leigh had one more fateful meeting Monday, September 10, before closing out one chapter of his career and embarking on a new and frightening one. He had earlier sent for the commander of Group 7, based at Concepción, an hour and twenty-minute hop south of Santiago by subsonic jet.

"He came in around 9:00 P.M. I went straight to the point," Leigh said. " 'Your unit is going to be in the thick of things tomorrow,' I told him. 'Crews under your command are going to be called upon to perform special missions. They will receive their orders in the air. They are to use only rockets and machine gun ammunition—no bombs. You've got to be ready to carry out whatever orders you receive, even if it means bombing La Moneda or Tomás Moro should that be necessary.' "

With that, Leigh dismissed the group commander and turned his attention to the day ahead. For the subordinate, the flight back to Concepción that night was a time of exhilaration and grave concern: selecting the pilots for the most dramatic mission in the history of Chilean aviation.

Leigh went from the Defense Ministry directly to his house near the Air Force Hospital in Las Condes. There he picked up a "ditty bag" with his toilet articles and headed for the Sepúlveda house.

Gustavo Leigh and Eduardo Sepúlveda had been friends since the early days of their service careers, when Leigh was a captain and Sepúlveda a shavetail lieutenant. The friendship was consolidated a number of years later when the two were aboard a U.S. Air Force plane that was damaged on landing at Easter Island. The two of them were stranded together on the island for a month and a half until replacement parts arrived and repairs were made.

In May 1973 Sepúlveda was shifted from his command of the air force base at Quintero, on the coast just north of Valparaíso, to Santiago, to become public relations chief for the Air Force. When Leigh took over as commander in chief on August 20, Sepúlveda was the very first subordinate Leigh confirmed in his job.

But it was likely that more than friendship influenced Leigh's decision to send his wife and two smallest children to that particular house. The Sepúlvedas lived on a rustic four-acre lot in the Los

Dominicos section on the eastern outskirts of the city. The house at 9600 Camino del Alba surely would have been one of the last places the general's enemies would have looked to find him—or his family. Gabriela Leigh, a strikingly pretty, soft-spoken woman, arrived about 6:00 P.M.—with two suitcases, two toddlers (then aged three and four), their bottles and milk in pans ready for heating, and the chicken she had planned to have for dinner that night. Marisa Sepúlveda had already evacuated her daughter's bedroom (one of four in the house—none too many, since the Sepúlveda's four children were all still living at home at the time). Neither woman knew it then, but the "overnight" visit would stretch out through the week, and Gabriela Leigh would begin her still unimagined career as one of Chile's four first ladies sharing a rollaway bed and small bedroom with her two children (and, one of those nights, with her warrior husband).

Leigh arrived at about 9:30 P.M.. He told the women the reason for the sudden upheaval was the trouble expected in the city the next day; both women suspected otherwise, but did not press him. Over dinner the Sepúlveda's eldest son, Reynaldo, made a remark about his work as a technician at the state television station and a job that needed to be done the next day.

"Tomorrow you stay home," his father told him. "There's going to be trouble."

"But, dad," the boy said, "there's supposed to be trouble every day."

"Tomorrow is different; you stay home."

After dinner, the Sepúlvedas tactfully slipped out so that the Leighs could be alone for a final farewell.

"There were no tears," Marisa said. "Gabriela is a very serene woman—affectionate, but serene. Before going, Gustavo looked in on the sleeping children, kissed his wife, and shook hands with Eduardo. They wished each other luck—and then he left."

While still at Sepúlveda's house, Leigh had received a call from the secretary-general of the air force, the only subordinate who knew his whereabouts. He told Leigh the president had been calling all over town trying to reach him.

"I decided not to call [Allende] right away," Leigh said, "but wait until I got to my headquarters."

Leigh drove alone to the Air Academy, a mile or two away, in bucolic Lo Barnechea. He arrived there shortly after 11:00 P.M. There he put in the call to Allende at Tomás Moro.

"I had imagined just about everything—that Joignant had protested, that he [Allende] was on to something, anything—except what it turned out to be. He wanted to talk about the LAN planes.

"That morning he had called me and very heatedly told me I should get the planes back, that I was protecting seditious outlaws. I had told him I wasn't protecting outlaws, simply protecting state property. He ordered me to return the planes. I said, all right, you'll have your planes tomorrow. Now he wanted to tell me he had since talked to the president of LAN, who told him I was right; better leave the planes at the air force bases.

" 'Ah, so you trust the president of LAN, but you don't trust me,' I said to him. With that, I thanked him and said goodnight. It was the last time I would ever speak to him."

The telephone rang at midnight in Alvaro Puga's house. The conversation was brief, because it was the call he had been waiting for—a wait that began for him three years earlier.

Even before the Chilean Congress met on October 24, 1970, to choose a president from the candidates who polled the highest vote totals in the September 4 balloting, Alvaro Puga was battling Salvador Allende. His weapons: the microphones of Radio Agricultura (where he had a morning program) and his sassy column in the pages of the Santiago tabloid, *La Segunda* written under the pseudonym "Alexis."

A few days before the Congress met, when the Christian Democrats, who held the decisive votes, were clearly tilting for Allende and offering him their votes in return for a passel of constitutional "guarantees," Puga wrote:

"If the Christian Democrats agree to be the guarantor [of legality under Allende], they may find that the bank of history will collect their guarantee with considerable interest."

A few days later, when the Christian Democrats gave Allende their votes, he wrote:

"Yesterday is all the time elapsed before September 4; today is the moment we live until November 4 [date of Allende's inauguration]; tomorrow is what will happen after that date. . . .

"Yesterday, we lived in a world of deception; today, we face an unexpected reality; and tomorrow we will find ourselves facing a future we had each of us envisioned in one of two ways: as an illusion or a nightmare."

Puga left no doubt that he viewed the impending drama as a nightmare. Over the next three years, in broadcast after broadcast, column after column, he chronicled the unfolding bad dream. But Alvaro Puga was no mere passive spectator. He had already been through several careers, and was still but forty-one years old, his hair a bit thin, his midsection spreading just a trifle, but his mind and soul aflame with energy and devotion to a cause: alerting Chileans to the enveloping danger of a regime that preached democracy while dismantling it, irrevocably.

Early in October 1970 he made his first attempt at roiling the country's impassive and traditionally detached military men. Each commanding officer in the Santiago area received in the mail three white feathers in envelopes with a mock wedding announcement emblazoned on the back: the marriage of Salvador Allende to the armed forces. He gave as the return address that of a retired general of known leftist sympathies. To add insult to injury, he arranged to mail the envelopes from the Defense Ministry. The feathers were, of course, chicken feathers, and the symbolism of the message unmistakable.

In another of his columns a few days after Allende's inauguration, he wrote: "The armed forces are giddy with democracy." (To make his point especially biting, he used the word *chochas* for giddy, a word dripping sarcasm.)

For the first two years of Allende's government Puga watched with growing dismay the country's descent into a political and economic quagmire, but he confined his opposition to verbal sniping. It was the nationwide strike of October 1972, a volcanic eruption of frustration and wrath at Allende's nation-pretzeling policies, that pushed Puga to take more positive steps.

"Carlos Ashton [Radio Agricultura's general manager] had scads of navy contacts, of course [Ashton was a retired navy officer], and so did I— [Vice Adm.] Carvajal, [Rear Adm.] Sergio Huidobro, [Comdr.] Hugo Oppazo, and [Capt.] Arturo Troncoso. I also had some good air force friends: Sergio Arellano, Nicanor Díaz, Hugo Castro, Julio Tapia, Juan Soler [all then colonels]. In the army, Col. Sergio Redondo and I had been friends since boyhood."

Gradually, the circle expanded, but there was a permanent risk of its contracting, too. "It was a little," Puga said, "like a case of malaria: alternating spasms of fever and chills and interludes of normality. Our job was to keep temperatures up, to motivate, push, pressure, prod."

The "they" included a small coterie of civilians implacably opposed to Allende. Besides Ashton and Puga, the group included Gonzalo Prieto Gándara, Rubén Díaz, and one or two others thrown together during the tempestuous days of the October strike. Their military contacts expanded to include at least half a dozen other key men: Gen. Sergio Nuño, Gen. Arturo Viveros, Col. Julio Polloni, Col. Pedro Ewing Hodar, Col. Morell, Gen. Javier Palacios —all army—and Carabinero Gen. Arturo Yovane. Polloni and Morell [then director of the Army War College] were among Pinochet's "inner six" of the most trusted plotters; Ewing was then secretary-general of the Defense Ministry, a job that gave him easy access to pivotal people in all of the armed forces; Yovane, former Carabinero chief in Valparaíso, had developed close contacts with Admiral Merino and other navy commanders; Nicanor Díaz was Carvajal's deputy chief of staff of the Defense Ministry; Huidobro, another staunch anti-Communist, commanded the Marine Corps; Troncoso was Merino's most trusted go-between with the other services.

"At the beginning, the talk was mostly grumbling," Puga said. "But as the situation in the country got worse, our talk became more explicit too: how to get rid of Allende. We realized, of course, that so long as Prats remained as army commander in chief, there was nothing we could do, but by May many of us were drafting plans, just in case."

There was practically unamimous restlessness among officers in the armed services because of Allende's maneuver in bringing service commanders into his Cabinet as a device for ending the October strike and restoring order. But it was another Allende move, in March 1973, that, more than anything else, alarmed and angered the officer corps: his proposal to overhaul the country's educational system along Marxist-Leninist lines, under a program known as ENU—Escuela Nacional Unificada [United National School system]. The public outcry was so loud and so menacing that Allende was forced to scrap the plan just one month after it surfaced, but not too soon to draw the fire—and lasting enmity—of officers who would tolerate almost anything except what they perceived to be a direct threat to their children.

"You've got to understand we never were a formal group or organization or anything of the kind," Puga added. "And we met at different places: often in the library of the [very posh, very baronial] Club Unión [in downtown Santiago, just one block from La Moneda, and diagonally across the street from the Defense Ministry]; at different homes, usually of civilians. The big challenge for us, the civilians, was to get the military to trust each other, to open up to each other, to bring them together."

So it was not surprising that as the plot finally thickened, catalyst Puga should be in the middle of it. He left home that Monday night without revealing he was on the threshold of deliverance from the nightmare that had tormented him for the past three years.

At the Defense Ministry he went right to the office of the Armed Forces Operations Center (COFA). About twenty officers, mostly assigned to the Joint Chiefs of Staff, were on duty. By then all of them had been clued in. Yet to the casual eye—or even the prying eyes peering anxiously across the way from La Moneda—there was nothing special about the Defense Ministry that night. In fact, they had not yet even beefed up the guards outside the building—yet.

They called it "Operation Seaweed," and, in its own way, this routine-looking plan in the red folder was a "best seller." Admiral Montero, then top man in the navy, read it and thought it was so good he had it copied and sent to the commanders of the two other naval districts, as well as to the fleet commander. Orlando Letelier read it when he took over the Defense Ministry, and complimented the "author" on it. Copies were also made available to the high command of the air force and army.

"Seaweed" was the anti-insurgency plan for the Province of Valparaíso, and it was drawn up under the supervision of José Toribio Merino, the feisty admiral lately responsible for so many headaches in Salvador Allende's life. Merino wore three hats: governor of the province, commander of all military forces (around 5,000 men) stationed in the province, and commander of the Valparaíso-based First Naval District, the most important.

There was really nothing new about the idea of having an anti-insurgency plan: the navy had been drawing up such plans since 1945. This one had been given its latest update July 16, 1973. The latest plan took into account the spread of bastions of armed civilians—armed, trained, and protected with government connivance. Chief among them: the Las Habas shipyard and the dock area of the big port.

"Many had seen the plan," Merino said, "but few, very few, knew how to put it into effect, how to activate it. And the plan had a built-in —but not very obvious—reversibility about it. With just a few changes, a plan that was defensive could become a plan that was offensive, almost as simple as striking out the prefix 'anti' before insurgency, and what do you have? Exactly what we had intended once we gave up all hope that Allende would change his course. I had just about given up all hope myself after we got the results of an independent analysis the armed forces did of the March 1973 congressional elections. What we found was fraud—fraud everywhere, on a staggering scale. When we brought the results to Tohá's attention [José Tohá González, then Defense Minister] he did nothing."

The changes needed to convert the defensive plan into an offensive one were made on Saturday, September 8. They covered two pages: establishing chain of command, command post procedures, a who's who of civilian authorities, the highway and electric power networks, and similar details.

As of late Monday afternoon, only Merino and five other officers of his General Staff knew of Seaweed's new nature. Other officers assigned to First District headquarters in downtown Valparaíso had been ordered at five Monday afternoon to shift operations to the Naval War College, situated in the port area, and hub of the navy's communications network. The stated reason was to avoid being in the middle of the Altamirano-related disturbances expected the next day. Merino also ordered troops under his command confined to quarters that night, again on the pretext of preparing to meet any emergencies created by the thousand known extremists in the area.

At nine the admiral left his downtown headquarters and went home for a quick dinner—and to put his own house in order. He told his wife, Gabriela (full name: Gabriela Margarita María Riofrío Bustos de Merino) to take their three daughters—María Angélica, Ana Carolina, and Teresa Trinidad—and "hide."

In twenty-one years of marriage Gabriela Merino had come to expect almost anything of this unpredictable man who was her husband, but "hide"—hide where?

"I don't know," he replied. "Just anywhere that's not here."

Merino then removed from safekeeping and gave his wife his life's savings: $135. (He confessed to having in the bank at the time another 3,000 to 4,000 escudos, worth about $100 at the official rate, which practically nobody observed any more.)

"I didn't tell her why—just that there could be trouble and even an attack on the house, so I thought it best for her and the girls to be somewhere else. She finally went over to Admiral Weber's house, and two of my daughters to a sister's house."

(Weber, by then well out to sea aboard his flagship, the cruiser *Prat*, had opened his orders at about that time and learned the electrifying news. At dawn tomorrow the armed forces were rising up to remove Allende from the presidency. His orders: plot a course that would take him, at 18 knots, back to the coast. The *Prat* was to put in at Valparaíso, the destroyers *Cochrane* and *Orella* at Quintero, just a few miles up the coast, and home of the air force's main antisubmarine base; and the *Blanco Encalada* at San Antonio, where the army commandant, Col. Manuel Contreras, had requested navy help in neutralizing that important port city.)

About 10:30 P.M. Merino left his house and drove alone to the Naval War College, a drive he made in seven or eight minutes. There, he summoned the entire general staff together—some thirty officers in all—and broke the news. Now, in his newly assumed role as commander of the entire navy, he also dispatched orders to the other bases around the country: "Execute Subversive Plan Seaweed at 0600 Tuesday."

José Merino was no stranger to battle. During World War II he had weaseled an assignment as observer aboard the U.S. light cruiser *Raleigh.* He spent a year (1943–44) aboard that ship, finally serving as a regular officer on it—the sort of rule-bending that had characterized the entire life of this remarkable man.

It took just a few minutes for Merino to issue his orders. He then served a glass of whiskey to each of the officers with him.

"There is nothing worse," he told them, "than the wait before battle."

The small ceremony completed, Merino retired to his wardroom— and soon was sleeping soundly.

For Sergio Huidobro, the day and night were almost too calm. The Marine Corps commandant was so anxious to preserve appearances that he even made a few "unnecessary" telephone calls through the day.

"I also managed to read a book," he said. "In fact, I finished it that night at headquarters."

For César Mendoza it was a day and night for catching up—while honoring tradition.

The next day, Tuesday, September 11, was General Mendoza's fifty-fifth birthday. For more years than he sometimes cared to remember a group of twelve to fifteen friends got together on the eve of his birthday for a dinner celebration. As tormented as the times were, 1973 was not going to be an exception, and César Mendoza dared not arouse suspicions, even of such a trusted group of friends. And so he played out the charade.

"At midnight, I invented some sort of excuse and made my apologies. My friends howled and protested about my leaving so early, but I went ahead."

Mendoza had very good reasons for leaving. He was, for all practical purposes, a general without an army. As of that moment, no more than a handful of the more than 4,000 Carabineros stationed in the Santiago area recognized him as their chief. He was about to remedy that.

The first stop: the home of Col. José Sánchez, director of the 700-man School of Carabineros, the "West Point" of that paramilitary organization. Sánchez lived behind the Italian Stadium, just a few blocks from the place where Salvador Allende was, at that very moment, meeting with his ministers in the presidential palace, Tomás Moro.

"I drove alone, went up to the door and rang the bell. You can imagine Sanchez's surprise, seeing me at that time of night. He was in his bathrobe."

Once inside, Mendoza told him what was happening, and said he should arrange to have his men confined to quarters and ready to move out the following morning, with full combat gear, when Mendoza gave the word.

"The news just bowled him over. Naturally, he was hesitant."

Sánchez could be forgiven his hesitation. Mendoza was then the fourth-ranking Carabinero general, and here he was, usurping the authority of those above him and ordering Sánchez to get ready to go to war against the government—all this in an organization slavishly committed to doing everything strictly by the book. At last, however, Mendoza succeeded in persuading him it was not some sort of lunatic scheme, but a revolution involving the combined will and power of all the armed forces. Sánchez agreed to join the fight. The meeting was over in ten to fifteen minutes.

Mendoza was not the only one rallying Carabineros to the cause that night. Yovane, the Carabinero chief most deeply involved in the plotting, was calling on the chief of the 600-man Special Services force —the elite group charged with protecting the president, breaking up riots, controlling subversive activity. More than any other segment of the Carabineros, the men of Special Services had reason to hate the Allende government. First, because they had repeatedly been obliged by their civilian masters to repress demonstrations by men and frequently women of the opposition. Next, because increasingly they had found themselves pushed around, mocked, and humiliated by the toughs of Allende's private army, the GAPs. By September 10, 1973, Special Services were a legion of avengers waiting to be unleashed. Yovane had little difficulty convincing Col. Carlos Hendrickson, chief of Special Services, to join the revolt.

Yovane had also done "missionary" work at still another important post: the Noncommissioned Officers School, an 800-man garrison.

"Special Services and the NCO school had the best armament," Mendoza said. "It was important for us to be able to count fully on them." (Carabinero armament, because of the corps' dual role as an urban police force and rural border guard, runs the gamut, all the way from standard police organization sidearms, rifles, shotguns, and the like to small tanks, helicopters, and light artillery.)

Before leaving his office that afternoon, Mendoza had talked to three Carabinero generals to alert them and assure himself of their loyalty. One more detail remained. From Sánchez's house he put in two telephone calls, to the key Carabinero troop commanders in the Santiago area (there were 1,500 men scattered among the twenty-four stations in the metropolitan area).

"I didn't tell them why I was calling," Mendoza said, "and the reason I did call them was just to make sure they were at their posts, because we were going to need them the next day. They were."

That done, Mendoza climbed into his official blue Torino sedan and drove home, arriving sometime between two and two-thirty in the morning. His wife was sleeping. He did not disturb her: sleep was too precious that night for those able to get some.

III. The Sleepers

In all of Chile that night, it is unlikely that sleep spread a more merciful mantle than it did over Patricio Guijón. Merciful for what his life had been, merciful for what his life was about to become.

There is a temptation to see in this man's past a sentence of futility, to pity him for the "weakness" of those who allow life to defeat them.*

September 10 was a long and trying day for Dr. Patricio Guijón. It began, as most days did, with him leaving the one-story red brick house at the end of a small cul-de-sac (2238 Luis Carrerra Street) at

---

*See Appendix for the story of Guijón's background as told to the author.

seven-thirty. He first headed about a dozen blocks south to the gleaming, modern German Clinic to see one of his private patients, and then on to the German School, in the heart of Providencia, where he dropped off his twelve-year-old son. From there it was just a few short blocks to the Salvador Hospital.

Since late August doctors, nurses, pharmacists, and hospital workers throughout Chile had been engaged in almost constant strikes, interrupted briefly when new "settlements" or "agreements" were announced. The latest "settlement" was reported over the weekend. Doctors loyal to the government—by then no more than 10 or 15 percent—continued working, as did leftist nurses and attendants. That day the doctors at Salvador Hospital were to meet to review the situation in light of the new "settlement," but the chief physician boycotted the meeting, and matters remained in flux. Short-handed, the staff still on the job struggled to maintain essential services, a job complicated by the appalling shortages plaguing hospitals.

By the time he made it home that night, Patricio Guijón was a weary man. Still there were the ceremonial rituals that were the inescapable responsibility of the father of three ebullient boys: have you done your homework, did you take your baths, keep the noise down, do you have your books ready for school tomorrow, and, finally, making boys twelve, ten, and eight understand it was time to go to sleep.

It was all a blur in Patricio's mind, a night like so many others. But it was, of course, a night like no other.

There were twenty-five women and a stowaway there that night of September 10. The stowaway was a baby one of the women had smuggled in.

The place was the Hall of Honor of the National Congress, and the women were wives of striking truck drivers. The women were on strike, too, a strike without precedent in the history of Chile.

On August 15 a handful of them—more out of rage and frustration than by design—drifted into the Congress, seeking new means of dramatizing their protest against increasingly harsh treatment of their husbands, who had been on strike since late July. Once inside, an even smaller group decided to stay. By day their numbers would occasionally swell to hundreds, by night never fall below a dozen, and as the days and nights of their protest wore into weeks, they came to symbolize the fury and frustration of women all over Chile.

One among them bears special mention. Her name is Silvia Galarze de Díaz. She is a slender woman with an angular face and red hair. She was then forty-three years old. Twenty-seven years earlier she had met and married a handsome fellow named Exequiel Díaz Guzmán, a man eight years her senior, at that time a small shopkeeper. Many years later he would turn to truck driving, and eventually occupy a place of some importance in the ranks of the Santiago branch of his union.

Silvia Díaz was part of the pioneer group to enter the Congress on August 15. In all that time she left for only one hour, but was otherwise the only woman to keep a constant vigil there, night after night. It was a vigil the women had vowed to keep until Salvador Allende left the presidency. Wrapped in a blanket and huddled near the kerosene stove in the cavernous cold chamber on the night of September 10, Silvia Díaz wondered just how long they would have to wait.

There were a couple of things about that night that were, come to think of it, downright strange in the world of Iván Ayala.

For one thing, when Corporal Ayala got to his girlfriend's house in San Bernardo, they started in on him just as everybody else did these days. "So what are you guys in the army going to do about this guy Allende, how long are you going to put up with him, when does it all end?"

"Tomorrow," Ayala said. "We move tomorrow."

What made that strange was the fact that Ayala, when he said it, had no more idea that tomorrow would be the day than, say, Salvador Allende.

If it had all ended there, then it might have been no more than a familiar case of the young soldier playing big strategist to impress his girl's folks—or get them off his back. But it didn't end there.

Ayala was due back at the Military Academy on the other side of Santiago at nine the next morning. So the sensible thing to do, the usual thing to do, would be to enjoy this last day of pass freedom and sleep in, until seven or so. But he didn't.

"I don't know quite what happened to me," he said, "because I'm the world's soundest sleeper. But for some reason I woke up in the middle of the night. Instead of going back to sleep, I decided to head back to camp. I got there at six-thirty—and found everybody dressed and ready for combat."

It was the dawn of D-Day.

three

DARKNESS BECOMES A DAY FOR DYING

I. In the Still of the Night

I t was a solemn image that met "Caco" Sepúlveda in his mirror, and so man and mirror-man dispensed with the usual daybreaking ritual: "Dime espejo lindo; quien es el hombre más lindo de Chile?" (Tell me, pretty mirror, who is the handsomest man in Chile?) Instead, Eduardo Sepúlveda, Colonel, Chilean Air Force, shaved in thoughtful silence.

"Will it be bloody? Will the cordones fight? How long before it's over?"

Not even the man who had left his house a few hours earlier, Gustavo Leigh, a man with his finger on the very trigger of Chile's destiny, could answer those questions, and so Sepúlveda meditated alone and moved quietly so as not to waken the women and children asleep in the darkened house.

It was 4:00 A.M., a scant three hours after Sepúlveda had fallen into a fitful sleep. Not pausing for a cup of coffee, he slipped on a jacket to conceal his uniform, as Leigh had suggested. He then went out and climbed behind the wheel of the Chevelle provided him by the air force for a drive that would take him from the longest night in the country's history to its most cataclysmic day.

Sepúlveda did not need to go far to be reminded how that day had become inevitable. Since, at that early hour, the streets were deserted, instead of taking his usual route along the Costanera, he opted for Apoquindo Avenue. As he eased into Apoquindo, he saw in the distance a small fire, and as he neared the Almac supermarket, he discovered, huddled around the fire, a group of men, women, and children in what had become one of the most familiar—and pathetic —tableaux in Chile: housewives, and often their men and children, forced to spend the night on sidewalks outside stores, to have first crack at mostly barren shelves when the doors were opened in the morning to customers.

A mile or so farther along, beyond the point were Apoquindo blends into Providencia Avenue, he saw another cluster of overnighters huddled around a fire of burning apple crates, waiting for a bakery to open.

Arriving at the Defense Ministry, Sepúlveda encountered the first abnormal event of the day: a guard shooed him away from his usual parking place and directed him to park on the small, alley like street behind the ministry. The clearing of the battleground had begun.

Once inside the building, Colonel Sepúlveda joined a fellow officer who had arrived minutes before, Col. Eduardo Fornet, secretary-general of the air force, the man who had alerted Leigh a few hours earlier that Allende was trying to track him down. Sepúlveda had his first cup of tea of the day, Fornet, a cup of coffee. Neither knew it then, but they would share many, many more cups in that second-floor office; it would be nightfall of the following day before they would leave.

In this modern world of institutionalized indifference to work, Vincente Adrian Garrido González is one of those rare specimens who still sleeps with his boots on, figuratively speaking, to be ready for the job. At forty-four, Garrido was chief pressman for the morning newspaper, *La Prensa.* In physical terms, the newspaper was situated only half a block up Moneda Street from the presidential palace. Politically speaking, it was located an unbreachable abyss away. *La Prensa* was the official organ of the Christian Democrat Party (PDC).

For years the Christian Democrats had been locked in a trancelike fascination with the ideology, programs, and slogans of their spiritual brethren of the Far Left. That began to change late in 1972 when Eduardo Frei Montalvo, Chile's former president, sometimes referred to as the Kerensky of modern Chilean politics, overcame his lifelong disdain for infighting and led his party on the path of accelerating confrontation with Allende. In November 1972 Frei yielded to strong party pressure and agreed to run for the Senate. A month later, the same day Allende was addressing the United Nations, Frei accused Allende of "injecting the cancer of hate among Chileans" and creating "a catastrophic situation for the country." It was a theme he would hammer away at. On January 13, at a rally in Rancagua, the copper-mining city 70 miles south of the capital, he said that Chile was living in an atmosphere of "fear, hatred, persecution, and divisiveness."

Adrian Garrido was aware of the finality of that split. Yesterday's editions (September 10) carried the thunderclap report on the survey of provincial presidents of the party. The verdict: Allende must go and Congress be dissolved.

For Garrido, the days in that turbulent period were long and the nights all too short. It was close to 3:30 in the morning before he was ready to head home to his wife and three sons. Because of the late hour, he hailed a taxi, which he shared with three fellow workers. The ride was uneventful—nothing unusual on the streets—and, for the most part, each of the three men was silent, lost in his own thoughts.

"We were so fed up with politics, we had practically nothing to say on the way home," Garrido remembered in an interview in Miami in 1975. "I went right to bed, because I knew anything could happen, and I wanted to be as ready and rested as possible."

No amount of rest could, of course, prepare him for what lay but a few hours ahead.

Another newspaperman, of a different sort, had ended his day's labors, only a short time earlier, at La Moneda, just down the street from *La Prensa*.

At 2:30 A.M. OIR radio chief Farías spoke again to Joignant, director-general of the national plainclothes police force, Investigaciónes. Joignant, like Farías, had spent a fretful two hours on the telephone, trying to detect a pattern in the reports of mysterious troop movements.

"Don't worry, chum," he told Farías. "Those troops are loyal, and they're coming here to defend the government against any possible disturbances tomorrow."

It seemed to make sense to Farías. After all, Allende was scheduled to speak on nationwide radio later that morning from the State Technical University (UTE), itself a storm center, and the National Party youth movement planned a parade to demonstrate in favor of the striking truck drivers. Still, it was with a lingering doubt that Farías decided to call it a night. He told the two newsmen, Pepe Echeverría and Sergio Jaque, the radio monitor, Alex Sarmiento, and a driver that they could go home, and he locked up the office.

As he made his way out the south door of La Moneda and headed for his house on Alonso Ovalle Street a few blocks away, he noticed an unusual number of cars outside the Defense Ministry across the street.

Arriving home, he told his wife, María Cristina: "I don't think we will get to celebrate the National Independence holidays."

Those holidays were to begin the next day and be climaxed one week later on Independence Day, September 18. Farías was right; he would not get to celebrate that year. But others would.

An unusual number of persons were already arriving at the Defense Ministry. But all was not activity. Alvaro Puga, general manager of Radio Agricultura, had finally dozed off in the hall on the fifth floor. Maj. Jaime Herrera, the officer of the guard, slept peacefully too. Like most of the others in the ministry, he still did not know there was anything special about this chilly September morn.

It was, in fact, a night for unusual sleeping arrangements, and eye-rubbing interruptions.

Gen. Sergio Arellano did not manage to get to bed at his house until three in the morning. Thirty minutes later Carabinero General Yovane put his head on a pillow—and it wasn't even his own. As a security precaution, Yovane decided to spend the night, or what was left of it, at the house of a friend.

At four in the morning, Salvador Allende's daughter Beatriz was awakened by a phone call to her husband, Luís Fernández de Oña. The message: the revolution Salvador Allende yet believed he could ward off would explode at 7:45 A.M.

The tip was uncanny, closer to reality than any report to reach Allende until it was too late to react. But then intelligence was Oña's specialty. In his native Cuba he was known as Captain Fernández de Oña of the General Directorate of Intelligence, the Cuban KGB, and was the man who organized in Cuba the "Neighborhood Committees," the infamous system for weaving every block of every community in the country into a gigantic web of spies and informers.

The new day invaded the night at that same hour for the 1,200 men of the Noncommissioned Officers School at the southern fringe of downtown Santiago. "Diana," the Chilean reveille, sounded at 4:00 A.M. Colonel Canessa had ordered the school *acuartelado* (confined to barracks) late the previous afternoon, after picking up his orders at the Defense Ministry.

"There was a lot of grumbling as we fell in," Pedro Mora Pizzarro, corporal, second class, remembers. "But then they ordered us to break out all of our combat gear, and we knew this wasn't just another drill or false alarm. This was it.

"After breakfast we all went back to the barracks to make sure our gear was in order. And then we waited."

II. At the Edge of Day

Ever since midnight the ships of Chile's prime naval squadron—the cruiser *Prat*, the destroyers *Cochrane, Blanco Encalada,* and *Orella,* the oiler *Araucano,* the submarine *Simpson,* and two escort craft— had lazed through fair seas just over the horizon from the Chilean coast. They had been assigned stations three miles offshore along a 55-mile stretch of coast, from the copper port of San Antonio in the south to Quintero, site of an air force base just north of Valparaíso. Not one of the nearly three thousand men aboard those vessels could have failed to suspect that something was afoot when, after heading out from port Monday on a northwest bearing, they had suddenly, just after sundown, reversed course and returned to their present stations.

The captains had opened their sealed orders at midnight and discovered the stunning dimensions of their mission. Shortly after 5:00 A.M. the cold night air rang with the fateful "now hear this" from the public address systems of each of the ships: The armed forces have united in a movement to overthrow the government of Salvador Allende, and these ships of the line will take up battle support positions along that strategic stretch of coast. Although it was estimated that as many as 10 percent of the crew and a number of officers were pro-Allende, there was no breach of discipline then or later.

The scraggy silhouettes of the returning ships through the inky darkness were the first electrifying signal, to anyone who happened to see them, that the dawn that was about to break would bring a different kind of day.

At 5:00 A.M., from the army's Communications Center on the eighth floor of the Defense Ministry, a coded message was transmitted with few precedents in the history of the country. Drafted by Pinochet the previous afternoon, it instructed garrison commanders to seize control of the country.

The following is a copy of the message removed by Pinochet himself from his own copy of "Operation Dawn" and delivered to the author on October 22, 1974:

EJERCITO DE CHILE
COMANDANCIA EN JEFE

SECRET.GRAL. DAG.

SANTIAGO, 11 de Septiembre de 1973.

RADIOGRAMA

ASUMIR INTENDENCIAS Y GOBERNACIONES DE IN-MEDIATO Y OCUPAR coma EFECTIVAMENTE, PRO-VINCIAS Y AREAS JURISDICCIONALES coma TRANSMITIDO SIMULTANEAMENTE A COMANDO UU.OO. Y CDTES, GUARNICIONES pto. ACTIVAR CAJSIS pto. ATTE.

CDTE. EN JEFE DEL EJTO.

POR O. DEL COMANDANTE EN JEFE DEL EJTO.

RIGOBERTO RUBIO RAMIREZ
CORONEL
Secretario General de Ejercito

("Assume control and occupy immediately and effectively municipal and provincial seats of government, provincial offices, and dependencies; [order] transmitted simultaneously to commanders operational units and commandants garrisons. Activate Internal Security Plan. Respectfully, Commander in Chief of the Army. For the Commander in Chief of the Army, Rigoberto Rubio Ramírez, Colonel, Secretary-General of the Army.")

The CAJSIS in the message refers to the nine Internal Security Jurisdictional Area Commands (Commandantes de Area Jurisdicciónal de Seguridad Interior), six of them under the six army divisions, at Antofagasta, Santiago, Concepción, Valdivia, Punta Arenas, and Iquique; two corresponding to the two naval zones, at Valparaíso and Talcahuano; and one to the air brigade at Puerto Montt. Set up originally to take control of the country in times of presidentially declared emergency, the CAJSI were subordinated to the civilian-controlled Interior Ministry, but received their orders through the Defense Ministry. It was this mechanism that enabled the General Staff of the ministry, under Vice Adm. Carvajal, to assume such smooth coordinating control of all military units on the eleventh, and it was the existence of this mechanism that explains why Carvajal's office became the keystone of revolutionary planning in the days leading up to the eleventh.

Thirty minutes after that laconic but bold command had gone forth, the man who had authored it, Gen Augusto Pinochet Ugarte, ended the pretense of sleep and prepared to take command of the revolution. As he would any other day, Pinochet began Tuesday, September 11, with a vigorous, forty-five minute regimen of exercises. He had barely finished when the telephone rang.

"General," the caller said, "stand by, the president wishes to speak to you."

Pinochet remained on the line for a few seconds until the voice came on and told him the president was unable to pick up on that line at the moment, but would call him later. It was a call that would never come.

The family man in Pinochet would assert itself once more before he would become the military man, leader of a revolution. Pinochet resolved to leave his house at 6:50, ten minutes earlier than usual, to be able to swing by the house of a daughter (one of five children) and see his still sleeping grandchildren. As he left his house, dawn was just breaking over the city.

Others were up early that morning, some even earlier than Pinochet. One, a few miles to the east at the Air Academy was Gen. Gustavo Leigh. His first act was to order Operation Thunder put into effect as of 0600.

"The order was transmitted verbally," Leigh said, "so that everyone went to work normally, but when they got there, they discovered they were garrisoned."

After a quick breakfast (coffee and plain toast) Leigh inspected the academy and pronounced himself satisfied with the arrangements.

"We had a helicopter there and automatic weapons for defense and, what interested me most of all, the communications facilities so that I could contact any air force unit in the country, as well as having constant communications with the other commanders of operations on the eleventh. Not one unit failed me that day."

Of the four military commanders, none faced a more difficult and delicate mission than Gen. César Mendoza Durán. At 5:50 A.M., just twenty minutes after the alarm went off, he took the wheel of the official white Torino automobile parked outside and drove alone to his downtown office.

Mendoza—in common with the other commanders—is a devoted family man, and he invested part of those twenty minutes in a personal matter.

"I woke my wife," he said, "and told her not to go out that day— no questions, just don't go out. Then I woke my son (Carlos Albert, a twenty-four-year-old engineer) and daughter (Alicia Cecilia, twenty, a student at the University of Chile's School of Veterinary Medicine) and told them that because of the general strike and the danger of disturbances they should stay that day with their mother. It was my birthday, and my wife told me she had planned a cake for me. I told her it would just have to keep."

There was still the bite of cold in the air (41°F) when Mendoza went outside and started off alone for his office at the Norambuena Building. Because he had carried out a judicial order in December 1972 in defiance of official wishes (he had dislodged a mob from a supermarket they had illegally seized), Allende fired Mendoza as Carabinero chief in Santiago and "exiled" him to a job heading the Social Welfare Department of the corps.

"My 'troops,'" he said, "consisted of one aide and two or three orderlies."

En route to the office Mendoza had time to reflect on just how difficult and delicate was the challenge he faced. Difficult, because the Carabineros were the very last to be brought into the plot, and only into the fringes of the plot at that. This was for a variety of reasons: the high proportion of pro-Allende generals (seven of sixteen) in the Carabinero high command; the direct political control over the corps through the Interior Ministry; and the prejudice among many military men that the Corps of Carabineros was a "second-class" military force, despite the fact that all 26,300 Carabineros (unlike the other services) were career men, from top to bottom, exceedingly well trained, armed, and equipped, and that their 1,200 posts gave them unmatched geographic saturation coverage of the entire country. Still, they were excluded until the last minute, even from the secret radio network linking command posts, and that meant Mendoza had to direct his revolution on the run.

His mission was further complicated because his own position was so delicate. Mendoza was then fourth-ranking among the Carabinero generals, and the only other general actively involved in the plotting, Gen. Arturo Yovane Zuñiga, was ninth. Furthermore, the director-general, José Maria Sepúlveda Galindo, and the deputy director, Gen. Jorge Urrutia Quintana, were "unconditionally loyal" to Allende, and the number three man, Gen. Alfonso Yañez Retama, who might have been counted on for support, was sick in a hospital. By contrast, General Pinochet and General Leigh already commanded their branches, and Admiral Merino had emerged as the de facto boss of the navy several weeks before. Since there could be no "laying on of hands" by the other armed forces chiefs in advance of H-Hour, Mendoza was really on his own when it came to rallying others to his side —as he had discovered a few hours earlier, on his midnight ride. He quickly discovered again just how precarious his situation was.

"Arriving at Norambuena," he said, "the first thing that caught me off balance was to find my office open and one of the orderlies cleaning up.

" 'What's going on?' " I asked him.

" 'I don't know, sir,' he replied. 'All I know is we got an order a little while ago putting us on alert and confining us to quarters.' "

"This," Mendoza added, "troubled me greatly, so I began to wonder whether someone had squealed. I called the Carabinero school, then the prefect of Santiago, and there I learned that the order for garrisoning had come from General Urrutia.

"Sepúlveda, you see, had practically turned over command to Urrutia when he joined the Cabinet in August," Mendoza said. "Then I learned that Urrutia had given the order because of the report that the fleet had returned to Valparaíso."

At that point the Norambuena Building had a meager eight-man guard. But then, the Norambuena Building was really nothing special: Carabinero headquarters, theoretically the nerve center of the corps, were situated half a dozen blocks to the north.

"And," Mendoza said, "the only ones who knew I was there that day were those already in the building—and those running the revolution."

(Still, Mendoza would beef up the guard to sixty men around eight that morning.)

The Norambuena Building possessed, in fact, one very special quality. On the tenth floor of that building, a floor below Mendoza's office, was the control point for communications, with radio patrol units throughout the country. The Carabineros's excellent communications system was part of a six million-dollar modernization of it undertaken by Gen. Vicente Huerta Celis, who also modernized Carabinero weaponry, organization, and training during the six years (1964–70) he ran the corps. Half the communications money came from the U.S. Agency for International Development (AID), part of that agency's public safety program, a perennial and emotional target of extremist groups throughout the hemisphere. (The program was finally ended in the early 1970s because of incessant leftist pressure.)

"My first job," Mendoza said, "was to make sure everyone would pull together. With the number one and two guys sidetracked and the third man in a hospital, someone had to take charge, had to know what to do and be known. Fortunately, I was widely known, both because I had served as prefect of Santiago and because of the years I spent on the staff and faculty of the Carabinero school, so that many of its officers and noncoms had been my students."

While Mendoza was applying a mixture of persuasion, rank, and personal magnetism to winning recruits for a revolution still not declared, his sidekick, General Yovane, was off on another crucial mission: making sure that the Noncommissioned Officers School would side with the revolution, not only because it represented a force of eight hundred seasoned men, but because that unit, together with Special Forces, possessed the best armament available to the Carabineros in Santiago. By the time the fighting started, the two men had, in fact, managed to extend an invisible and decisive hand of authority over the entire Carabinero command apparatus, without the two generals who still believed they were in command ever even knowing it.

José Toribio Merino is a man of such iron resolve that it did not desert him even in the shadow of the most momentous day of his life.

"I slept like a log," Merino said.

In fact, of the four commanders, Merino was the only one who did allot a full night's rest for himself—and took it. He was asleep about 11:00 P.M., and awoke refreshed at 5:30 A.M., ready to spring into action almost immediately.

"I slept fully dressed, except for my jacket and shoes," he said.

His first act that dawn was to set a trap with far-reaching implications he would shortly spring: he ordered a single telephone line to Santiago left open. That line belonged to the Carabinero prefect of Valaparaíso, Col. Luis Guitérrez, a man known to be loyal to Allende.

"We left the line open so that he could call out from his home, but it was tapped," Merino said. "At 6:11 I got the word: he had telephoned Santiago to report the return of the fleet, and that troops were occupying strategic sites around the city."

With that Merino ordered the line cut, and continued his breakfast calmly. Valparaíso was now completely sealed off from contact with the rest of Chile, leaving Allende and his cohorts with just enough information to worry them, but not enough to know what was really going on.

Gutiérrez's report stampeded Allende into speeding off to La Moneda.

"We needed badly for Allende to go to La Moneda," Merino reflected. "If we had been forced to try to take him at Tomás Moro, in the middle of a residential district, it could have been a slaughter."

That maneuver accounted also for the earlier start of overt action in Valparaíso. Shortly after 5:00 A.M., a full three and a half hours before troops would hit the streets in Santiago, truckloads of marines, soldiers, and sailors were seizing potential flashpoints, such as the Customs Bureau, the dock area, the Las Habas shipyard, a traditional extremist stronghold, and the two railroad stations.

At the Puerto Station, a Marine detachment told the switchman: "All movement of trains is suspended."

"But the express is due at seven-fifteen" the bewildered railroadman replied.

"I repeat," the officer told him, "all trains are canceled." When the man continued sputtering that the express was due, the officer unloosed a familiar Chilean epithet:

*"Huevon!"** the officer exclaimed. "I said the station has been captured."

---

*Rough translation: "Big balls."

With that the startled switchman lowered the barriers. As the first trains began arriving, each was stopped. At Las Habas the day shift reported, and, as they did, known extremists were immediately arrested. By the end of the day about 260 prisoners had been taken—Merino's only regret.

"I wish," he would say afterward, "we had taken more. At that point we controlled the industrial strongholds, the cordones, and I wish we had rounded up more activists, especially the leaders. That would have been the opportunity to head off a lot of trouble later."

Simultaneously, small teams of troops, each with a noncommissioned radio technician, were striking at the twelve radio stations in the area, removing key crystals, according to carefully rehearsed plans, to knock those stations off the air. Others were doing the same with radio transmitters of private and governmental companies.

"We used the same people we had used for the past two months on arms raids on those stations," Merino said. "It went off like clockwork. By 5:145 there wasn't a station left on the air, and since we had already taken over the telephone company, the communications blackout was complete. Except, of course, for our own green navy phones—and that one line we left open."

So it was that an eerie dawn awaited early-rising residents of the city: static on their radios, streets devoid of traffic, and, off in the distance, the silhouettes of the fleet that wasn't supposed to be there.

There was one other fleet to be disposed of. At dawn on September 11 the American squadron was just entering Chilean waters off Arica, 893 nautical miles north of Valparaíso. They were steaming south for the rendezvous with the Chilean squadron for the deferred start of the annual Unitas joint naval exercises.

For them Merino had a laconic message of his own. At 6:00 A.M. he ordered a six-word signal radioed to the American flagship: "Motivos inesperados, imposible realizar Operación Unitas." (Unexpected reasons impossible; hold Operation Unitas.) The American ships—three destroyers and a submarine—promptly set sail for Peru.

That left one other ship to keep an eye on, the Cuban freighter *Playa Larga*. The *Playa Larga* had been unloading a cargo of sugar at a pier in Valparaíso when it was moved Monday afternoon a few miles north to Las Salinas to make way for another ship. For a dozen uneasy hours the Cuban ship would ride at restive anchor under the guns of Fort Vergara.

III. The Puppeteer

"It was from the start our plan—and our hope—that (1) there would not be a civil war, with all the bloodshed and death that would imply; and (2) he would give up, would realize it was all over, and give up too, the violent ones and the ones responsible for bringing the country to this state of ruin."

The speaker was Admiral Merino, the catalyst of the revolution, and the "he" was, of course, Allende.

Except that Salvador Allende was not a man about to surrender—for two important reasons. The first was that his entire adult life had been one long, relentless climb to power. The second resided in his style. Allende fancied himself as *la mejor muñeca de Chile* (the country's best manipulator), and so he would behave, to the tragic end as a man who was confident he could talk himself out of even the most final trap of all, a death trap.

Minutes after Colonel Guitérrez sounded the alarm, his boss, Carabinero General Urrutia, roused Allende from a sound sleep and gave him the news: "The navy has seized Valparaíso. The fleet is back. I don't have any details."

Allende didn't need more. When the telephone sounded a minute later, it was Carlos Briones, who had just been tipped by Joignant.

"I'm going to La Moneda," Allende told him. "I haven't been able to reach Orlando, but I want him to get into the Defense Ministry as soon as possible and find out what's going on."

Allende evidently had not yet tried. The first call Isabel Letelier received in the darkness before dawn was from Salvador Allende. The voice of the president on the other end startled her awake.

"There's been a navy uprising in Valparaíso," he told her. "Some marines are in the streets. Wake Orlando and tell him to get in touch with the commander in chief of the navy and get back to me."

Still groggy after having been awakened from such a short sleep, and the pain of the dental work still throbbing in his mouth, Orlando Letelier began dialing the telephone of Adm. Raúl Montero, the bewildered man at the eye of the hurricane about to hit Chile. Allende's delay in removing him as commander in chief of the navy was the final factor spurring the navy to act—but under Admiral Merino. There was no answer at Montero's house. Nor was there at the home of General Prats, the recently retired army boss. Theirs were among the first telephone lines to be cut during the night, phase one of "Operation Silence."

"We had two telephones," Isabel Letelier said, "and so while Orlando was on one, I was on the other. Finally, he got through to Briones, who filled him in on what had happened."

"Some time later—it must have been around six forty-five or seven —Orlando got through to the ministry. A general answered, or at least I thought it was a general, and I thought that was strange, too, at that hour."

Actually, as Mrs. Letelier, listening on the extension, would quickly realize, the calm voice at the other end belonged to Adm. Patricio Carvajal, Chief of Staff of the Defense Ministry.

"What on earth is going on?" Orlando asked him.

"Nothing, Minister," Carvajal replied. "Only the operations you ordered."

"How about the movement in Valparaíso?" Letelier asked.

"No, nothing special," Carvajal answered. "Only Operation Unitas. Will you be coming to the ministry today, Minister? You know we have a number of meetings scheduled for today."

"Of course," Letelier said.

Mrs. Letelier remembered that he winked at her and was chuckling as he hung up the telephone.

Her husband's immediate impulse, she said, was to go join Allende at either Tomás Moro or La Moneda, but neither of their two cars was available. Their station wagon had been loaned to her driver, an army enlisted man, who used it to go home. He was not due to report until 7:00 A.M.

"If this is an uprising," she told her husband, "we'll never see that station wagon again."

When Letelier got through a few minutes later to Allende, the president gave him different orders.

"I want my Defense Minister in the Defense Ministry," Allende told him. "See what can be done there."

Salvador Allende had been experiencing similar problems on the telephone in those first confused moments. On his first call to Carvajal's house, the admiral's wife answered and told the president her husband was showering. The second time he called, he was told the admiral had gone to the office, in the belief that it might be something urgent. There, on the third try, Allende located him.

"The troops in Valparaíso are on routine arms control raids," the admiral reassured him. Allende was not reassured.

He called General Sepúlveda, the director general—or so both still thought—of the Carabineros, and ordered him to triple the guard around La Moneda and meet him there shortly.

One call Allende did complete was to Carlos Altamirano Orrego, the fire-breathing head of the Socialist Party, who only two days before had warned that Chile would become another "heroic Vietnam" if the "enemies of the people" moved against Allende. In that same speech he heaped scathing abuse on the "scum"—he used the vulgar Spanish word *carajos* (pricks) and "cowards" of the Right who "hide in embassies, and seek asylum so as to flee from Chile and not have to face in a manly way the consequences of their acts. They hide behind the skirts of women, and they hide behind the rifles of soldiers," he said. (The cock would barely crow on the dawn of that day of destiny in Chile, a destiny Altamirano's fiery oratory and implacable politics had helped to forge, when he would be burrowing underground, and later seeking asylum in embassies.)

To that vitriol Altamirano added a ringing warning.

"It is absurd to speak of conspiracy," he said, "when the conspiracy is already afoot ... there can be no dialogue with terrorists and saboteurs. The conspiracy of the Right can be met only with the invincible force of the people united to the soldiers, noncoms, and officers loyal to the [legally] constituted government. The Socialist Party will not allow itself to be crushed by a seditious and oligarchic minority."

His wife of just over a year rememberd that night well.

"Carlos arrived home at ten, very fed up, his nerves on edge. We went to bed, and about eleven the telephone rang, and someone—I don't know who—told him that the Supreme Court had ordered the Court of Appeals in Valparaíso to take up his case, and he said something to me about that never before happening in Chile.

"After that, the telephone was ringing all night long. Around 6:00 A.M. the president called. Carlos didn't tell me what they talked about."

Altamirano dressed hurriedly and telephoned Carlos Lazo Frías, who lived nearby, and asked him to pick him up as soon as possible, since his driver had his car and Altamirano could not locate him.

The man who vowed he would make the streets of the city run red with blood in case of an uprising said a hasty good-bye and vanished.

His wife would not see him again. Chile would not hear of him again. The "revolutionary fighter" ran for cover.

The morning newspapers were on the stands as dawn broke over the city (at 6:51 that morning). They would be useful mainly as mementos of an historic day—or relics of another era—because none warned their shivering readers of the thunderclap only two hours away.

One Chilean newspaperman, however, was ready to cover the country's story of the century. That man was Mario Carneyro, editor of *La Segunda,* the afternoon tabloid and the brawler of the *El Mercurio* group in Santiago. Carneyro, one of the civilian gadflies of the military —and one of the sharpest thorns in Salvador Allende's side—got a call Monday night at home from a military friend who told him the next day was it. Without telling them the real reason, Carneyro ordered his entire staff to report first thing the next morning to handle an "emergency" story. In those troubled times emergency had become the routine, so few of his staffers were prepared for the story they would soon face. By 7:00 A.M. they had all arrived in the rickety and improvised newsroom quarters of the paper, pigeon-holed on the second floor of the aged *El Mercurio* building just three blocks west of La Moneda. But as things turned out, it was a story they would have to read about in somebody else's paper.

It would remain for the city's twenty-six radio stations to break the story that day, those of them still on the air, that is. For, starting at 5:30 A.M., the two hundred army, air force, and navy men assigned to "Operation Silence" began fanning out around the city in groups of twenty to thirty. In each group there were radio specialists who knew exactly what they were looking for. Florencia Varas described one such raid, on one of the most virulent of the approximately twelve stations loyal to Allende: Radio UTE, the station of the Marxist-dominated State Technical University.

"An army jeep and truck stop on a poorly lit street. An officer and four combat-uniformed men armed with submachine guns get out of the jeep. On a signal, soldiers do the same from the truck. . . ."

"From the door of the building the night watchman watches with alarm as they approach. 'Soldiers again!' he exclaims. 'They're all over the place these days.' He is careful not to open the iron door until they are near. Behind the door he hides the carbine he has no intention of using. It would be insane, he says to himself, against all of these armed men. Nor does he dare use the intercom to alert his comrades. The fact is that they have caught him completely off guard, arriving so swiftly, so silently.

"The officer is brief, preemptory:

" 'Open the door. This is a raid.'

" '. . . How many people here now?' the officer asks.

" 'Just six, the night shift,' the watchman stammers.

" 'Where are they?'

"The watchman motions with his head . . ..

" 'There are no arms here,' he complains. Out of the corner of his eye he notes with relief that no one has thought to look behind the door.

" 'Shut up,' the officer interjects. 'That we'll see for ourselves.' "

For the next hour the soldiers searched the station carefully, searched the personnel. Nothing. After they left, the staff exploded in laughter. Jerks. Not only did they miss the cache of submachine guns and grenades, they didn't even see the carbine!

In fact, the soldiers got exactly what they had come for: a small set of crystals. Radio UTE was off the air that day even before they began broadcasting.

At television Channel 7—the one directly controlled by the government—the military technician "did his job like a good surgeon, removing just exactly the right output tubes."

In those predawn raids the soldiers concentrated on the smaller Popular Unity stations known to be the most dangerous, yet where resistance would be lightest. In some, careful advance "casing" had disclosed there would be twelve to sixteen persons inside at that hour, many armed with submachine guns and other automatic weapons. Storming them not only would have been bloody, it would also have sounded the alarm. For those stations the plotters had a different remedy.

There was one other station that could not be silenced immediately: Radio Corporación, the Socialist station, regarded as the most virulent of all, tucked away in the honeycomb of the Bank of the State Building just across the street from La Moneda. Silenced once, it would later sputter to life again with the Popular Unity's last audible gasp.

International communications were Polloni's second priority—and biggest headache. Foreign companies, he said, were "sounded out" in advance, and "helped me visualize the problem." Those companies included ITT World Communications (overseas telex messages), ITT's All America Cables and Radio (international telegrams), RCA Communications (overseas telex). Through most of the daylight hours of September 11 those arteries to the outside world were choked off. Even more nettlesome was the problem of ENTEL, the state-run overseas telephone service, especially since the bulk of their traffic moved in and out of the country via a satellite ground station (the first in South America). During the night, troops occupied ENTEL's main offices and two relay stations (Batuco and Golondrinas). Taking the main tower downtown, Santiago's highest edifice, would prove even more nettlesome, and bloodier. What might have been another thorny problem, the former ITT Telephone Company, was made easier by the fact that the government-appointed administrator of the company was a military man.

"That," Polloni said, "enabled us to do our advance homework carefully and occupy the company early."

Shortly before seven that morning the newscasts began to blare out reports of the "rumors" of a naval uprising in Valparaíso. Communist Senator Julieta Campusano Chávez went even further. In a 6:45 A.M. interview she said a coup was "imminent."

But what Chávez did not know Alvaro Puga did, and so he was already busy even before first light of day making sure that when the revolution did begin, its voice would boom across the land. At 6:30 A.M. he called Francisco (Gabito) Hernández, then production manager of Radio Agricultura, and alerted him that the long-awaited moment was at hand: an air force detail would arrive at his house shortly. Hernández was then alone in the house with his mother and an aunt, both septuagenarians, both emphatically anti-Allende.

"Are you don Gabito Hernández," the officer in charge asked when they arrived.

"Yes, I am," Hernández answered.

"Lieutenant Calderón, at your service," the officer said.

Hernández quickly discovered that the "detail" included twenty-four men, armed with five 50-caliber machine guns and seven 30-caliber machine guns. Firepower in spades. But then, this house on Julieta Avenue had, as of then, become one of the most important military installations in the revolution, its long-waiting secret transmitter the voice of revolution in case the main system should be knocked out. Silently, Lieutenant Calderón deployed his men on the rooftop and around the one-story house, but not so silently that Hernández's mother wouldn't hear a strange noise.

"Did you hear that," she asked her sister Teresa.

"Must be mice, Francisca," the sister answered.

"No, too heavy for mice," Teresa answered. With that, the two women went back to sleep. The "mice" was a machine gun being fixed into place.

Another soldier was reporting for duty at 6:30 that morning. After a restless night at his fiancée's home, Cpl. Iván Sáez Ayala decided to report back to his base at the Military Academy two and a half hours before he was due. The scene that greeted him was startling.

"Everybody was in combat gear," he said, "and there I was in sports clothes. Colonel Floody [Nilo Floody, commandant of the academy] happened by just then and asked me what I was doing there. I told him I was heading for the gymnasium to work out for the games scheduled for that week.

" 'You pentathlon guys make the best combat troops, you know,' he said, and then went on his way. Nobody had told me yet what was going on, but I could guess."

And so Sáez quickly suited up for war.

The alarm went off at 6:45 A.M., as usual, in the modest house on Luis Carrera, and Patricio Guijón silenced it quickly. As always, he shuffled into the bathroom, stretched, and then entered the shower. The sound of the shower was the customary "alarm" for the couple's children. While Patricio shaved, Silvia prepared the Spartan breakfast customary in the Guijón household: Tea, with just a few drops of milk, and toast, chocolate-powered milk for the children.

Normality ended at 7:15 when the telephone rang.

"Pachi [the nickname he had used since childhood], you've got to get to La Moneda—pronto," the caller told him.

"But Pelado [the nickname he used for his friend and colleague, Dr. Alejandro Cuevas], the meeting isn't until Wednesday. Today is Tuesday."

"Don't ask dumb questions, and get going," Cuevas answered.

Silvia, listening in, said nothing, but told their twelve-year-old to hurry. Part of the family rites consisted of father Patricio dropping the boy off every day at the Colegio Alemán—the German school where he himself had studied as a boy—while Silvia took the other two children to their school at the eastern end of the city. The Colegio

Alemán was situated only a few blocks from the Salvador Hospital, where Patricio Guijón was a staff surgeon. Before leaving, he took a quick look in the mirror: sky-blue shirt, striped tie, gray woolen vest, gray trousers, black jacket with white pinpoints. The image of the proper Santiago professional.

As usual, Patricio took the family's Fiat 125, their one and only luxury. Silvia drove off a few minutes later in the battered station wagon to her job at the hospital. If either sensed the drama that was about to invade their lives, neither expressed it. Their parting was brief, the sort that couples married a dozen years tend to exchange in the waking hours of a winter day.

Patricio was only halfway to the school when the brakes of the car suddenly jammed. It was an irksome—but familiar problem. As luck would have it, Silvia that day happened to be driving a short distance behind him. He flagged her down and asked her to return to the house for a tool he needed to adjust the brakes. She did. Half an hour later he was on his way.

Fate had already frowned on Patricio Guijón that day, but the cruelest trick was yet to come.

It fell to an infantry general to lead the army's top armored unit. The general was Javier Palacios, the army's training chief, given the job the day before of commanding the support troops in the downtown area. Chief among them, Armored Regiment #2, still nursing the wounds of the war that wasn't, only a scant seventy-five days earlier. On June 29 their commander, Col. Roberto Souper Onfray, led them on a surprise morning attack on La Moneda and the Defense Ministry in what was to have been the spearhead of a nationwide "colonel's' rebellion." The revolt was, however, hastily improvised when army intelligence got wind of it, and the other units that were scheduled to act failed to do so. Instead, the massive weight of the entire military machine fell on Souper's marooned men, to such an extent that the regular units did not even need to open fire to subdue Souper and his men. Most of the shooting came from Allende's corps of window warriors, the snipers suddenly bristling in the windows of government office buildings overlooking La Moneda. The final toll that day was twenty-two dead, thirty-two wounded, and fifty arrested. The court-martial of Souper and the entire officer cadre of the regiment was still under way on September 11, so it was a leaderless and skeptical force that rallied around when Palacios arrived at seven that morning.

Palacios ordered the regiment to assemble in the main courtyard, where he told them that by order of Augusto Pinochet, commanding general of the army, and Herman Brady, commandant of the Santiago garrison, he was assuming command of the regiment—to finish the job they started on June 29.

There was an instant of silence. Then an officer stepped forward, saluted, and said: "Are you sure of what you are saying, my general?"

Palacios answered with action. Climbing aboard a tank, he shouted: "Now I run this show."

The entire regiment moved out with him.

Orders were going out to others in that era-ending hour.

Also at seven that morning Gen. Nicanor Díaz of the air force, Carvajal's number two man as deputy chief of staff of the Defense Department, summoned the guard detail assigned to the Defense Ministry.

"We are at war," Díaz informed them. "The armed forces have resolved to depose the government. Anyone not in agreement is free to leave."

There was but one question.

"Has anything been done to protect our families?" a soldier asked.

The general said that was not possible.

"Mine has no protection either," he added.

Almost on the dot of of seven o'clock the first armed "action" of the day took place. Engineer Jorge Nuñez was seated at the control panel next to a ninth-floor window of Radio Agricultura in downtown Santiago when a bullet shattered the glass, narrowly missing his head. Nuñez ducked as several more bullets came pinging into the room. The shooting, almost certainly, came from Communist Party headquarters, diagonally across Teatinos Street, a permanent nest of armed guerrillas, by then on full alert. Fellow workers helped a badly shaken Nuñez into an emergency control room deep inside the station and Agricultura continued to bring to tens of thousands of Chileans the electrifying news of the navy revolt.

Roberto Mason was sleeping peacefully when he got a call from his office.

"Something funny going on down here," Luis Muñoz told him. "There are an awful lot of military trucks on Nataniel Street and a tremendous amount of commotion around the Defense Ministry."

Mason thanked him and hung up. Mason was the news manager for the United Press International in Chile, a post he had occupied for a number of years. The caller was the news agency's early morning man, reporting on what he saw from one of UPI's ninth-floor windows in a building directly across the Plaza Bulnes from the Defense Ministry and diagonally across the Alameda from La Moneda.

Long years in the business had taught Mason that there are two kinds of crises: those that can wait and those that can't. He decided that this one was still in the more familiar category of those that can, and so he went about enjoying a leisurely breakfast of eggs and café con leche, coffee with milk. It was well he did.

Since he was stranded, Orlando Letelier enjoyed a leisurely breakfast too. The household staff, at that point, consisted of a cook and steward, both navy men. He was still at the table when his regular driver arrived from the ministry, a strapping man over six feet tall named Jiménez. Jiménez usually arrived with a bodyguard, but that morning came alone.

"Where's your companion?" Mrs. Letelier asked him.

Jiménez's answer brought the shadow of trouble closer to home for the first time.

"Funny thing," he said. "When I got to the ministry, my wife works there, you know, they said they were taking all the wives out because something was going on. So my friend took his wife home too."

"What is going on?" she asked him.

"I don't know," he said.

It was enough to trip an alarm in Isabel Letelier's keen mind.

"Orlando finished his breakfast calmly," she said later. "And then we said good-bye as if we knew it would be forever, because we knew it was something serious. I went to the kitchen—the staff was eating then too—and I said to Jiménez: 'You take care of my husband and make sure that nothing happens to him.' He flushed, got very red in the face, and then said, 'Señora, why do you say that? Nothing is going to happen.'

"So I told him, 'I know why I say that,' and the other three looked at me with the biggest eyes.

"My husband and I held each other very close at the door, and then I said to him: 'Orlando, be sure to call me,' and he said he would and told me not to worry. And then he was gone."

Allende and the man who was becoming increasingly his boon companion and confidant, Augusto Olivares Becerra, worked the telephone feverishly from Tomás Moro, trying to determine the dimensions of the revolt. Repeatedly they collided against the twin barriers of the invisible curtain of silence—telephones that had been disconnected—or, what was in devastatingly misleading ways more infuriating yet, someone who feigned innocence. One who was called upon to play the role repeatedly, beginning with Allende's first call to him shortly after midnight, was General Brady. Finally, Brady complained to Carvajal. Carvajal did not hesitate in getting Brady off the hook. He ordered the direct line linking Tomás Moro with the ministry cut.

That other, and shadier, adviser, Joan Garcés, caught the president during a pause in his telephone frenzies close to seven o'clock.

"The navy has rebelled," the president told him. "Marines are headed for Santiago. Carabineros are with me. As to the others, I just don't know. . . ."

Minutes later, at 7:20 A.M., Allende decided the time had come for action. Wearing a gray tweed jacket, a woolen turtleneck sweater of the same color with dark gray geometric designs, a sport shirt, dark gray trousers, and black shoes, he prepared to leave. Always the dandy, he tucked a blue silk handkerchief with red dots in the upper left breast pocket of his jacket. On his wrist was an expensive Galga Coultro automatic watch.

Allende quickly organized the caravan that would escort him to the palace: four Fiat 125s and a station wagon loaded with 30-caliber machine guns and three bazookas, and two *"tanquetas,"* armored car-type vehicles used by Carabineros as rubber-wheeled minitanks. Allende himself rode in one of the tanquetas. He took with him twenty-three GAPs, leaving more than double that number behind to guard the walled estate where his wife still slept on the second floor of the Moorish-style manor house, blissfully unaware that her world was about to end.

The caravan careened through the already bustling city streets at speeds of 50 to 65 miles per hour, screeching up to the Morandé 80 side entrance of La Moneda just a little over ten minutes after leaving Tomás Moro. With an automatic rifle in hand, Allende alighted to a reassuring sight: more than a thousand Carabineros posted around the huge palace, as well as five strategically placed tanquetas, looking more Martian than menacing with their four peepholes and pyramid shape. But menacing they were, highly maneuverable, fast, and armed with two heavy machine guns. The sight of such a show of force was the first soothing experience of a nerve-jangling morning for Allende: he could count on the Carabineros, after all.

From his eleventh-floor window Gen. César Mendoza saw the presidential convoy speed past, and wondered whether *he* could count on the Carabineros.

"Coming after those other surprises that morning," Mendoza said, "I wondered whether there hadn't been some betrayal, after all. But in any case, the cards had been played, and we couldn't back out then. I don't know which was worse, the tension or the anguish of not being able to tell anyone.

"A little later I did tell my aide, Major Blu, that he was going to have to make certain connections, contact various units, so that they would act. I myself called the Carabinero Academy to confirm the order for them to withdraw the presidential guard [at Tomás Moro] when I gave the command.

"General Yovane arrived a little afterward and said the noncoms' school was ready to move. He then called the prefect of Santiago on the intercom. At first it was a little difficult to convince them we weren't kidding, but then they reacted well."

Less well, but predictably so, was the reaction of the general who had under his command the 1,500 Carabineros in twenty-four posts around the urban area. His immediate mission was to arrange to withdraw the troops around the Moneda and garrison the rest of his men to have them ready for action, especially against the paramilitary commando groups around the city. Two lieutenants would move boldly into the vacuum created by their vacillating general.

The arrival of the tanquetas and the show of force around La Moneda caught the eye of the night manager of the Carrera-Sheraton, the city's biggest hotel, situated diagonally across the Plaza Constitución from La Moneda, and so he decided to brave waking his overworked boss, Miguel Gallegos Dubost.

"That coward S.O.B." Gallegos muttered, "must be getting ready for the students." Gallegos referred to a demonstration planned for that day by the Federation of Secondary Students, one of an almost monotonous series of protests those days demanding that Allende quit. The "S.O.B." was, of course, His Excellency, the President.

As he was dressing, Gallegos learned that the navy had seized Valparaíso.

"Then," he said, "I knew it wasn't just another demonstration."

Gallegos hurried down to the huge main lobby of the hotel, checked quickly what staff were in (240 of the full complement of 465 employees) and ordered the main doors opening onto the Plaza Constitucíon closed. (Later, when the shooting started, he would order steel shutters drawn over all windows from the second through fourth floors. The ground floor was solid wall except the door.)

"Mike" Gallegos was then rounding out twenty-three years in the hotel business, rising through the ranks with three international chains (InterContinental, Hilton, and Sheraton), returning to his native Chile at the outset of the Allende regime as resident manager of the very hotel where he had begun his career. Along the way he had developed a reputation for being as meticulous as he was affable. But nothing in his past would prepare him for what he was about to face that day. Few, either, would face it better.

Once inside La Moneda, Allende went directly to his office on the second floor. His first act was to call his wife.

"The situation is grave," he told her. "I will stay here. It is practically impossible for me to leave the presidency." He told her to be calm and remain at Tomás Moro.

Next, he took a quick inventory of the weapons available, and raged that they were hopelessly inadequate. He ordered a second group of GAPs to report to the palace from Tomás Moro, leaving about twenty-five defenders there, and for further arms to be brought to the Carabineros in the palace from their headquarters, a few blocks away.

Then he returned to the telephone, speaking briefly with Altamirano, and later with his two top labor leaders, the Communist Luis Figueroa and Rolando Calderón, president and secretary-general of the Communist-dominated labor federation, the CUT (Central Unica de Trabajadores). His orders: mobilize the factory shock troops, get people moving downtown (as he had done during the June 29 pocket revolt).

While Salvador Allende was preparing his defenses, another meeting was going on across the street in the Defense Ministry. The generals and admirals and colonels and captains who would command the revolution that day were learning, for the first time for most of them, about the bold step that was about to be taken.

As they began the meeting, they learned that the battle had, for all practical purposes, already been narrowed to Santiago. At 7:30 A.M. Admiral Merino sent word to Admiral Carvajal in the Defense Ministry: "Valparaíso is ours." Not a shot had been fired.

Col. Julio Canessa, one of the key troop commanders, got the call to report to the Defense Ministry at 7:15 A.M. Half an hour later he was there, together with other unit commanders, being briefed by Gen. Sergio Arellano, picked to command operations in the downtown area. Canessa made the short drive to the ministry in a Toyota station wagon with an escort jeep. Behind the wheel of the station wagon was twenty-eight-year-old Cpl. Pedro Mora Pizzarro, who had spent the past four years of his ten years in the army driving for the commandant of the Noncommissioned Officers School—and grown philosophical in the process. "The army's not a bad job," he remarked. "If you behave yourself, it goes well for you; if you don't, then it's a bad life." He would shortly have another opportunity to philosophize.

"There were two of us in front," he said, "a bodyguard and me, and the colonel in back. While we were parked outside the ministry, the guard took the colonel's .636 pistol from the seat to put it in the glove compartment. With that, it went off. The bullet lodged not five centimeters [less than two inches] from me. I knew right then and there that no matter how bad it might get that day, I wasn't going to die."

Canessa emerged from the meeting at 8:15.

"We told him what we had heard," Pizzarro went on, "and then he said, 'This situation has gone far enough. Now everything has already started.' I answered, 'If we have to move out, then move out we will.' "

Canessa still had not told them the details of what "everything" was. That happened when they got back to the school and he ordered the eight hundred students and four hundred cadre to fall in. He then broke the news to them. Although they had been up since four that morning, and had been confined to quarters many times before ("being garrisoned had become our daily bread," Pizzarro commented), the men were keyed up this time because of the news reports trickling in. Within minutes the four battalions were ready to move out. Their armament: light and automatic arms, 30-caliber machine guns, rocket launchers, and jeep-mounted recoilless rifles. The school's mission: control an area of fifty-odd blocks around La Moneda.

"I told the men we had tried to the very end to avoid this situation," Canessa said, "but that there was now no other way out. I said I expected each man would do his duty. Then the chaplain gave a blessing, and we moved out.

"There was great, visible happiness among the men. I had wondered whether we would have any defectors or subversives. There were none."

The school was situated just a kilometer from the downtown area. Canessa divided his men into two groups, one advancing north along Dieciocho Street, the other via Coquimbo, six blocks to the east, and wheeling north there. The two columns were thus advancing on parallel tracks straddling La Moneda.

Canessa's parting instruction: keep a close watch for snipers. On June 29 seven of his men were wounded by snipers convinced that his troops were rushing to support Colonel Souper rather than join in putting down the minirebellion.

Corporal Pizzarro, as it turned out, was one of the last to get the official news of insurrection.

"I was in the colonel's office getting his gear while he was speaking," Pizzarro said.

"The colonel took the group moving along Coquimbo toward Nataniel, where we doubled north toward La Moneda. We were in two columns along each sidewalk. The colonel was in the middle of the street, just as he had been on June 29. His whole staff was with him. Reaching the Plaza Almagro, five blocks north of Coquimbo, Canessa again divided his men, one to cross the Alameda a long block east of La Moneda on San Diego, the other to advance directly on it via Nataniel.

"The one crossing the Alameda was to link up with units from the Infantry School and converge on La Moneda from that side. The one approaching via Nataniel was to form up facing the palace frontally across that great gorge of subway construction."

The hope—as General Arellano had told the commanders that morning—was that when Allende saw he was not only surrounded but massively so, he would cave in rather than risk a bloodbath.

By 7:30 that morning Santiago's two and a half million inhabitants were divided into two groups: those who knew, approximately, what was going on and those who, blissfully, still imagined it was a day like any other, give or take a little agony more, a little agony less. The radio made the difference: either you listened, or you did not; and if you did not, the question then was whether some friend or relative within reach of a telephone did.

So it was that around seven that morning eighteen-year-old Jaime Grove Kimber was awakened by his father, who told him that the boy's great-uncle—and godfather—Salvador Allende, was faced with a military insurrection.

"I got up, and we all went to listen to the radio," Jaime recalled.

"All" included his mother, Allende's niece.

"We didn't talk much, just listened. That's how we happened to hear his last speech. I stayed in all day."

So it was, too, that Vincente Garrido, the tireless pressman, heard the news.

"I woke up at 6:30—I'm always up early," he said, "and, as usual, turned on the radio. After hearing about the occupation of Valparaíso, I got up—it was around 7:15—and tried to get Luis Carrasco, the news editor of the newspaper, who lived across the street. He wasn't in, and so I started to the office alone. At the beginning, everything seemed normal."

Navy Commander Jorge Grez was in his bachelor quarters on Avenida Bulnes, about five blocks from the ministry when he heard a radio commentator remark about the unusual turnout of Carabineros around La Moneda.

"When I had gone off duty at 9:30 Monday, I was supposed to be off for the rest of the week," he said. "My family was in Valparaíso, but I decided to stay in Santiago, because I expected something to happen that week. After hearing that radio report, I called the aide-de-camp on duty that week at Tomás Moro. A GAP answered and said the president had left for La Moneda sometime before 7:30 and that the aide had gone with him. Then I called the Officer of the Guard at La Moneda, and he told me the president had been there since 7:40. It was after I heard the president speak that I decided to go, and notified my driver to pick me up."

The news caught Sen. Juan de Dios Carmona Peralta while he was en route to the airport for a 9:00 A.M. flight to Caracas. One of the few conspicuous moderates among the top leadership of the Christian Democrat Party, Carmona was also the party's principal contact with the military. His contacts with them went back to his four years as

Frei's first Defense Minister (1964–68), reinforced in 1971–72 when he authored and guided to passage the Arms Control Law, the weapon the military had used increasingly to neutralize the power of Allende's underground paramilitary forces.

"When I got to the airport," he said, "I asked them to change my flight for the afternoon. At that time everything was normal at the airport—they hadn't heard anything. It was as I was leaving the airport that air force trucks arrived to close it down."

Eduardo Arriagada Moreno heard the news of the fleet around 7:00 A.M, and said to himself, "this must be it."

Arriagada was president of the Chilean College of Engineers, a professional federation embracing 8,000 of the country's 9,500 engineers. They were overwhelmingly anti-Marxist. In their last elections, in May, those against the government polled 92 percent, those for, 8 percent. The engineers were, in fact, the first organization of any importance in Chile to call, flat out, for Allende's resignation. In a resolution passed at a general assembly August 17, they said the profession faced the "gravest problems" in its history, and called for Allende to quit "for the good of the country." Next, they resolved, on September 6, to begin a nationwide strike as of September 10 to continue until Allende had changed course altogether or submitted his resignation.

Arriagada continued to listen to the radio as he rode to the college's offices on the ninth floor of a building flush against the Defense Ministry. At the wheel was a neighbor, Francisco Langlois.

They reached downtown without incident and parked on Avenida Bulnes, a block behind the building. As they alighted from the car, they saw soldiers advancing slowly along the avenue some 250 yards back—Canessa's men.

"As soon as I got in the office," he said, "we sent all the staff home. Nine of us—directors of the college—stayed. The first thing we did was call the General Staff next door to tell them we were on duty and standing by to advise on the defense of basic installations. We then started checking around—the waterworks, electric power company, and so forth—checking on the security arrangements, then relaying it on to the military. That was a day to remember."

James J. Halsema had his first brush with battle in 1919. He was then three months old, on an army train rumbling through Siberia carrying Herbert Hoover's war relief supplies, as well as passengers.

Halsema's father was a U.S. Army major, recently demobilized and heading back to the Philippines. In the years ahead Halsema would witness violence often, and usually by the luck of a bad draw. In 1936 he was to meet his sister for a holiday in Spain. The rendezvous was set for July 1936, when civil war erupted. He was a young reporter on the Manila *Daily Bulletin* on December 8, 1941, the morning the Japanese staged their second air raid of World War II on American territory. Four years later he would be back to witness the three-week Battle of Manila, when the city was liberated. Two years later, as an Associated Press correspondent, he covered the fighting at Batavia in the Dutch East Indies (later renamed Jakarta, Indonesia). In 1956 he strayed into Cairo, en route to the U.S. from Beirut, on the day the Suez war broke out. After that a modicum of calm entered his life, and bullets and bombs became a fading memory. In fact, his luck seemed to have changed. On June 29, 1973, he even missed a battle, the brief but intense one, in downtown Santiago. Instead, he read about it half a world away, in the Teheran *Times,* during a pause en route back to Santiago from an inspection trip to Saigon.

Halsema was the public affairs officer at the U.S. Embassy in Santiago. What he heard on the radio that morning did not arouse him nearly so much as what he had read in one of the newspapers: students would be staging a demonstration that day.

"And so," he said, "I asked my wife to fix me a sandwich, because I knew that demonstration means traffic would be all snarled up, and better to stay put in the office."

She forgot to do it. When his driver called for him at 8:00 A.M., Halsema went off empty-handed. He wouldn't get to return home for three days.

Frank Tonini, the peppery press attaché at the embassy, was in the front seat of the car, having been picked up first, and was spinning the dial of the radio as they started off. The first sound that caught his attention was the voice of Salvador Allende. In midsentence Allende was suddenly cut off.

"Something obviously was up," Tonini said. Their suspicions were reinforced as they reached the Parque Forestal, the pie-shaped sylvan area wedged between the Mapocho River and a line of luxury apartment buildings at the edge of the downtown area.

"The traffic was jammed—with the strike, we hadn't seen a traffic jam for a month. Furthermore, most were buses, which normally should have turned off at the diagonal there. Spinning the dial, we heard Gabriela Piderit on Radio Agricultura interviewing someone who had just come back from the area around the Moneda, describing the scene there. We kept trying to turn left, toward the office, but at every corner a Carabinero was waving traffic on. We got all the way up to the La Vega market, and I was about to tell the driver that at the next corner he should tell the police who we were when suddenly there was a corner with no one there. So we turned there and drove through the Plaza de Armas—there wasn't a soul in sight—and then on over to Agustinas and on to the garage. Just as we were about to go into our building, we looked down the street, and there, half a block away, was an army Six-by-Six with soldiers climbing out in full battle gear. [The American Embassy is situated in an office building half a block from the northwest corner of the Plaza Constitución; the west side of the Hotel Carrera is a dog-leg left across the street.]

" 'Frank,' I said, 'this must be it.' Frank said, 'I'm going to take a look,' and I told him I'd go on up to the office.

"A couple of minutes later he came up and said it was all quiet. There were a lot of soldiers in the plaza, forming up, but other than that, they weren't doing anything, just looking at each other. He also said he saw the tanquetas across the way, in front of the palace."

Meanwhile there was another veteran of violence trying to make his way to work from that same eastern sector of the city, the sprawling area of tony residential neighborhoods and posh suburbs stretching up to the Andes Mountains a dozen miles from downtown. That man was Carlos Urrutia, Colonel, U.S. Army, and chief of the much-diminished U.S. Military Mission in Chile. Only Urrutia's office was not in the embassy—it was on the eighth floor of the Defense Ministry, at the far end of the corridor from army headquarters. Like so many other people working in that drab maze, Urrutia was not in on the secret, and so he set off for work concerned, but not overly so.

"As was my custom," he said, "I turned on Radio Agricultura when I got up that morning and heard the news about the fleet. I dressed in civilian clothes—my uniforms were at the dry cleaners, who, like almost everything else those days, worked in fits and starts —and started driving in alone. I was abeam the American Consulate (in Parque Forestal) when I heard Allende speak, and there I diverted my route and began weaving through back streets. But the traffic got thicker and thicker, and finally, about three blocks from the office, I decided that if this was it, there wasn't anything I could do anyway, and if it wasn't, then I'd just wait for the traffic to clear, and so I headed back home, listening to the radio all the way. That is when I heard about the revolution.

At nine, I got home, told my wife what had happened, and stayed there until they lifted the curfew a few days later."

The voices most of Chile heard that morning, as they did every other morning during those crisis-freighted days, belonged to the men and women of Radio Agricultura. A visitor to the ninth-floor aerie of the station at 449 Teatinos Street that morning would have been impressed first by the clumsiness of the massive steel security door looming in front of him as soon as the elevator doors opened. It took two days just to get that door upstairs, and it was, of course, a testimonial to the station's reputation as a valiant and, for Salvador Allende, vexing voice of protest, so much so that he once told "Gabito" Hernández that if his government should ever fall, "Radio Agricultura will be to blame."

On the morning of September 11, as hope verged into reality, Radio Agricultura brought its listeners more than just news of the impending coup. By seven all was in readiness. Four hours earlier "César," still working feverishly in the Defense Ministry to finish connecting the shortwave command network, roused a Radio Agricultura engineer from sleep with a telephone call, telling him to be at the station at six so they could begin testing the "patch" linking the station with the Defense Ministry. Within an hour that "patch"—and a backup line to Radio Minería—were tested and working.

The regular morning broadcast was suddenly interrupted at 8:10 A.M.

FLASH: HERE WE HAVE THE VOICE OF SALVADOR ALLENDE, ON A PARTIAL RADIO NETWORK: THE PRESIDENT OF THE REPUBLIC HAS JUST SAID THAT THE NAVY HAD ISOLATED VALPARAÍSO. HERE ARE HIS TEXTUAL WORDS [Allende's voice followed]: "SPEAKING TO YOU IS THE PRESIDENT OF THE REPUBLIC, FROM THE PALACE OF LA MONEDA. CONFIRMED REPORTS REVEAL THAT A SECTOR OF THE NAVY HAD ISOLATED VALPARAÍSO [pause, and hum on the line] AND THAT THE CITY WAS OCCUPIED, WHICH SIGNIFIES A REBELLION AGAINST THE ARM . . . AGAINST THE GOVERNMENT, THE LEGALLY-CONSTITUTED GOVERNMENT, WHICH IS SHIELDED BY THE LAW AND THE

WILL OF THE CITIZENS. IN THIS CIRCUMSTANCE, I AP-
PEAL, ABOVE ALL, TO WORKERS TO OCCUPY THEIR
PLACES . . .

At that point, his voice trailed off with the words "of work" barely
audible in the background. Allende had been cut off just as he was
about to continue with an appeal for the one force he believed could
yet save him, to rally to his support: the paramilitary worker groups
in the cordones. The appeal did go out on the three government-
controlled stations still on the air: Allende's own station, Radio Portales; Radio Corporación, surliest of the Socialist Party stations; and
Radio Magallanes, the Communist Party station, which, in keeping
with their superior organization, was the one that would give the
rebels the most trouble. All three were still busily broadcasting cryptic
code phrases ("safari salvaje," or "the weather: Easter Island and
Santiago, torrential rain"), together with stern warnings to "sedition-
ists." (The first-quoted phrase means "savage safari," and, as to the
second, to lump Easter Island, a couple of thousand miles out in the
Pacific, with the capital city in a "weather forecast" was obvious code.)

Allende had barely finished his speech than a pair of Hawker
Hunter jets screeched low over the western sector of the city, and, as
they approached Avenida San Martín, let loose rockets. One flattened
the tower of Radio Magallanes, and a second took out Radio Portales,
in a direct line with that of Magallanes. A third destroyed the small
transmitter shed (roughly 70 square feet) of Radio Corporación. Portales was out for good; Magallanes switched to a hidden emergency
transmitter; Corporación was able to continue broadcasting on FM,
but with a very weak signal. For all practical purposes, Allende was
down to a single outlet to the nation he was still trying to lead.

That air attack—the "surprise" element in Operation Silence for
the big stations too well guarded for direct assault—almost backfired.
One of the rockets impacted close to the cable connecting Radio
Agricultura's transmitter shed to the tower. The cable was damaged,
but not put out of commission.

For many in Chile the radio droned too heavily on nerves already
too taut, and so they did not listen. Others had news enough in their
jobs, and so they did not bother either.

Esther Hinojosa belonged to that category. Mrs. Hinojosa, mother
of three children, was an executive secretary at Radio Agricultura,
and she had worked there for such a long time (thirty years) that she

said she was "part of the station's inventory." Together with tens of thousands of others in the capital city that morning, she had no clue whatever, when she boarded the bus near her house in Providencia, that a civil war was already raging in her country.

"As we got to the Plaza de Armas," she said, "someone on the bus remarked, 'You know, there's something happening at La Moneda.' Just then, we heard shots, but we didn't see anything."

In another city, or in a Santiago of another time, Mrs. Hinojosa and the others might have fled in fright. But this was Santiago of September 1973, and so she continued stubbornly on her way, leaving the bus five blocks north and one block west of La Moneda, at the corner of Catedral and Teatinos, and walked the remaining block and a half to her office without incident. Although it was already after nine, there was no sign of anything unusual—no special security outside the building, nor troops in the streets there.

"When I got to the office, someone said to me, 'Esther, run, they're bombing La Moneda.' "

She did not believe it, and the report wasn't true, anyway—yet.

Jorge Figueroa said he usually listened to the radio in the morning, but for some reason did not do so that day as he made his way downtown from his house in the El Golf section in a car with two friends. Figueroa, a short, compact man in his late forties, thinning gray hair, trim moustache, father of six children, was, at that time, production manager of Guías y Publicidad and a commercial adviser to *El Mercurio*. He was heading that morning for Guías y Publicidad, the former ITT company seized by the government a year earlier, which published telephone directories in Chile. They were housed in an office building on the Alameda, just a block west of La Moneda, where the Christian Democrats also had their national headquarters.

"We got as far as the Plaza Italia," Figueroa said, "when we discovered that all the streets were blocked. I decided to set out on foot. So I walked along the Alameda, right past the Defense Ministry and across the street from La Moneda. People were scampering and scurrying around, but I really didn't see anything unusual.

"When I got to our building, I discovered it was locked, and realized that something important must be happening. So I doubled back to the branch of the Bank of Chile on the corner, thinking I'd need some money to get through whatever crisis this was. But it was shuttered, too. So I crossed the Alameda, and walked up Teatinos, past [the west side of] La Moneda and on to *El Mercurio*. The streets were teeming with people. When I got to the newspaper, I heard the news: the junta had seized power."

Later, Figueroa would muse: "We Chileans do foolish things. You know, I was wandering all around there just five minutes before the revolution started—right there."

It takes more than mere gossip of war and revolution to divert Hugo Ravera from his appointed rounds. For one thing, Ravera is a man of iron will. A former soccer player in his native Italy, former opera singer (bit parts), and physical culturist (he exercises a minimum of an hour a day and, in his forties, had the thin, hard physique to show for it), Ravera was, in the ripeness of his middle years, a mountain climber. But no ordinary mountain climber: he already held one or two speed titles for dashing up and down 18,000-foot peaks around Santiago in record time, and was planning as assault on the Aconcagua, the hemisphere's highest peak, with an eye to setting a new speed record there. Besides his iron will, Ravera was a man beset with the problems of running one of the toughest businesses in Santiago in those times of scarcity: a supermarket (on the Plaza de Armas), as well as one of the country's leading egg, butter, and cheese suppliers.

So he attacked that day early, at 5:30 A.M., as he did most others, and by 7:00 was motoring in from the lovely mountainside home he designed himself in El Arrayán, at the eastern end of the valley.

"As we passed the Military Academy, we saw a number of buses loaded with troops, and I remarked to the young man who was riding with me, 'They must be on maneuvers.' "

Ravera continued on to the Central Station, where he made his first sales call of the day.

"My customer said to me 'You know there's been a military coup.' I answered, 'What coup? You must be kidding.' And so I continued on my way, because I had a lot of calls to make that day."

For the next five hours Ravera weaved his way in and out of side streets throughout the mostly poorer neighborhoods of the western end of the city, in an out of bakeries and small grocery stores, without incident.

"The coup, I said to myself, "must have been crushed."

All fourteen stools were filled with the usual regulars breakfasting at "Sandwich al Paso," the extremely popular short-order restaurant tucked into a sliver of space at the corner of Estado and Alameda, three blocks east of La Moneda. For twenty-one years, Vincente

Terreros Fernández, a slight, unfailingly courteous man of sixty-eight had run the place with his wife. They were there that morning, with their daughter María, three employees, and the ubiquitous cat "Puso."

It was close to 8:30 A.M. when someone glanced up and saw the tanks—a double row of them—moving west along the Alameda on both sides of the street.

Traffic was blocked when Pedro Toro A. was nearing the Casa Hidalgo, the electrical appliance store where he had worked as a salesman for the previous eight years. So he decided to get off the bus and walk the last three blocks, a walk that took him past the national headquarters of the Communist Party. Casa Hildago is at the corner of Compañia and Teatinos, on the same side of the street as Radio Agricultura, across the street from the Communists.

"I hadn't heard the radio, either, so I had no idea what was going on," the twenty-four-year-old salesman said. "I got there at 8:15, and was there a while when the shooting suddenly started. I saw a girl hit. I tried to telephone my boss, but couldn't reach him, and decided to lower the metal curtain. After awhile, I decided to close and go home."

They call him Juanito Caamaño, "Little Juan," because of his huge bulk. It happens that he also has a wry sense of humor to match such a name.

Despite his experience driving for newsmen—including chasing Fidel Castro over much of Chile during the Cuban dictator's visit— Juanito skipped listening to the radio that morning, too. Besides, the talk in the car as he drove his wife to work that morning was much too animated for any additional voices. The two women accompanying his wife were both Popular Unity loyalists, and the four of them were locked in spirited debate. When they reached their destination, the main office of the Chilean Telephone Company, Caamaño said good-bye, and the three women went inside.

"If I had only looked up," Juanito said, "I would have known something big was brewing. I learned later that the roof was teeming with soldiers."

But he did not look up. He drove west on Alameda a few blocks, finally joining a long line of cars waiting for gas. All of a sudden someone shouted, "The military is taking over," and the next thing he knew people were pulling out of line, he heard shooting, and he decided to pull out of line too.

On the theory that man does not live by fear alone, Caamaño
decided he had better restock the family larder before retreating to sit
out the war. He swung by the big "La Vega" farmers' market. Only
a single stall was open, but as its owner was a friend, Juanito managed
to stock up on eggs, chicken, and apples before heading home. He
almost did not make it.

When he flew into Santiago Monday, Jorge Alberto Braña's lug-
gage contained several items that anywhere else would have been
bizarre: six big loaves of bread, powdered milk, and butter. Braña, a
forty-seven-year-old former major in the Argentine Federal Police,
was the area security chief for Esso Standard Oil, based in his native
Buenos Aires. His territory included Chile, Peru, and Uruguay, as
well as Argentina, and this was a routine business trip for him. The
foodstuffs were for hard-pressed Chilean friends.

Braña left his hotel, the Carrera, at 8 A.M. Tuesday and cut across
the Plaza Constitución in front of La Moneda, heading for the Esso
offices on the fifth floor of the same building, next to the Defense
Ministry, where the College of Engineers was situated. The walk over
was uneventful. The walk back would be the longest of his life, because, unwittingly, he had strayed into his second revolution.

Fate was dealing Patricio Guijón still another chance as he drove
alone to his date with destiny. There was no radio in his car, but as
he neared the downtown area, he was several times forced to detour
because Carabineros were blocking traffic on so many streets. If he
had stopped to investigate, perhaps he might have realized the futility
of going on. Yet, being the kind of man he is, he probably would have
done exactly as he would do later when he would be confronted with
a choice, and go on, because that was his duty.

At the corner of Agustinas and Amunátegui, behind the Hotel
Carrera, Guijón "did the only intelligent thing I had done all morning. There is an underground garage there [the same one serving the
U.S. Embassy] where spaces were reserved for the El Teniente Mining
Company, formerly the U.S.-owned Braden Copper Company [Ken-
necott's Chilean subsidiary]. Guijón had been on the medical staff of
the nationalized company for some time, and so he decided to leave
his car there, with the keys in the ignition.

"Once inside La Moneda," Guijón said, "when I discovered what
was really happening, one of my greatest concerns was to let Silvia
know where I had left the car. I was finally able to reach my father.

Silvia was already at the hospital, and it's very difficult to get through to anyone there." Having assured at least the survival of "the family fortune," Patricio Guijón was ready to face the ordeal ahead. Or so he thought. Others were streaming into the palace at the same time: seven detectives from Investigaciónes, to join the defense forces; four Carabinero generals (Sepúlveda and Urrutia, photographed as they arrived together in a Fiat 125, followed by Generals Rubén Alvarez Oyarzún and Orestes Salinas, the latter, ironically, the head during the Frei years of the Grupo Mobil of Carabineros, the highly effective "SWAT" group so much despised and vilified by Marxists; Jaime Barrios, the Communist head of the Central Bank and former adviser to Che Guevara when Guevara reigned as czar of Cuba's economy, accompanied by his wife, Nancy Julien, which made them perhaps the only married couple in the palace that day; Carlos Briones, followed a few minutes later by the Foreign Minister, Clodomiro Almeyda; Edgardo Enríquez Froeden, the education minister and father of the head of the MIR, Miguel Enríquez, who appeared briefly, then left, saying he planned to return to his office and work as he would any other day; Agriculture Minister Jaime Tohá, who followed his Cyrano-like brother, José, the former Defense Minister. As José Tohá was about to enter the palace, he told newsmen clustered outside the heavily guarded portals: "we have not yet evaluated the situation. But we will not turn over power until 1976"; Daniel Vergara, Under-Secretary of the Interior throughout the Allende regime and a man who became famous for telling newsmen, no matter what the crisis: "No pasa nada" (Nothing's happening).

At the far eastern end of the palace, the part housing the Foreign Ministry, a single employee remained to work that day. Ernesto Espinoza made it to the office, only to find himself trapped there. For three ministers it was Providence that sent him.

The sentimental detour—to see his still-sleeping grandchildren—caused General Pinochet to report for duty ten minutes past his self-imposed seven-thirty deadline at his secret command post, the bucolic and isolated Peñalolén Signal Corps headquarters. He assembled his staff and broke the news to them, for many the first official explanation they had of their sudden "transfer." Pinochet was ready at eight; his communications team was still sweating to install the link between Pinochet's headquarters and Leigh's several miles to the north.

"Mario" had reported for duty at eight as he and Major Valdivieso agreed, He still did not know exactly what to expect, but as he drove out, he saw the tanquetas from Tomás Moro and the rest of the convoy speed past, "and everyone armed to the teeth." A Corporal Caimán helped Mario raise a telescopic antenna, in the hope that that would do the job. As they worked, a general walked past. "Turned out it was Pinochet," Mario said. "I didn't know it, though. I have a hard time distinguishing these military types. Besides, I was worried about my own problem, so I didn't pay much attention to him."

Meanwhile, across town at the Military Academy, his sidekick had reported for duty forty-five minutes earlier.

"There was no one at the gate," he said, "and so I went upstairs, and discovered the door [to the clandestine radio center they had just installed] was locked. So I started scrambling to find a key; time was running out on us. But, then, others began to arrive, and when the time came, we were ready, except for one small detail. I couldn't find anyone to man the microphone, and we couldn't do it—our voices were too well known to the other ham operators. With that, a cadet —an eighteen-year-old boy—wandered by and I grabbed him. Within a few minutes this scared cadet at the bottom of the military ladder would find himself chatting with generals and admirals."

Just as he was reporting to the Military Academy, another finishing touch was being put on the secret radio plans. A military patrol pulled up at "Gabito" Hernández's house and Major Meza of the air force arrived bearing two tape recordings and a typed text. It was a package very similar to the one Federico Willoughby had left at Radio Agricultura a few minutes earlier.

The lieutenant, who had set out that morning believing he was going on a mysterious arms raid of some kind, asked the major what was happening.

"From here," the major told him, "we are moving out to war."

"Now?" the lieutenant asked.

"Right now," the major answered.

Another officer was reporting for duty at that time. At 8:00 A.M. the hapless Colonel Gutiérrez, chief of Carabineros in Valparaíso, reported for "duty" to Admiral Merino.

"I told him," Merino said, "there was really nothing for him to do, so he could go home."

Also at 8:00 A.M. the bus bearing the day watch of Carabineros pulled up in front of Tomás Moro. The night watch boarded the bus. The day watch remained aboard. The orders given hours before by General Mendoza in the uneasy dark had been obeyed. Much later, the GAPs on the parapets realized the defense of the presidential residence was in their hands—alone.

Radio Agricultura engineer Ricardo Alarcón was trying desperately to honk, cajole, and weave his way the four miles separating him from "Gabito" Hernández. Hernández had called him at eight and asked him to rush to the station, two blocks from his house, pick up a certain recording and get it to him as fast as he could. He had to have it by eight-thirty. Alarcón coaxed and pleaded his way past several roadblocks, and, with the minute hand edging toward eight-thirty he handed the recording to Hernández.

The world would little note it, but the "fall" of Salvador Allende was "reported" at 8:15 A.M. "Before leaving the house," Eduardo Arriagada, of the Engineers College said, "I told my wife that the return of the fleet, as far as I was concerned, meant that Allende was finished. I told her to call her mother in Buenos Aires.

"So, at 8:15, she called her mother and told her that Allende had been toppled. My mother-in-law couldn't believe it, but she had no chance to call back. After that, the international circuits went dead."

IV. Por la Razón o la Fuerza*

Force entered where reason had failed at 8:32 A.M. in the still frosty (44°F) morning Tuesday, September 11, 1973.

"Economic Panorama," a program that had come to resemble in recent months a chronicle of delirium, was nearing an end, when, in the middle of the word "recommendations," the national anthem suddenly resounded over the air waves.

A pause, perhaps fifteen seconds. Out of earshot of listeners, a command and a curse. And then the resonant, vibrant voice of a man anonymous before then, anonymous thereafter: Army Major Guillár, speaking from a secret and hastily installed studio on the sixth floor of the Defense Ministry..

---

*"By Reason—or By Force": words on the national emblem of Chile.

SANTIAGO, September 11, 1973. In consideration of:
(1) The extremely grave social and moral crisis afflicting the country; (2) The inability of the government to control the chaos; (3) The constant increase of paramilitary groups trained by the parties of the Popular Unity which will lead the people of Chile to an inevitable civil war, the armed forces and Carabineros of Chile resolve:

1. The President of the Republic must proceed to the immediate handing over of his office to the armed forces and Carabineros of Chile.
2. The armed forces and Carabineros of Chile are united to begin the historic and responsible mission of fighting for the liberation of the fatherland and to preclude our country from falling under the Marxist yoke, and the restoration of order and institutionality.
3. The workers of Chile can rest assured that the economic and social conquests which they have achieved to this date will not suffer fundamental modification.
4. The press, radio, and television pledged to the Popular Unity must suspend their informative activities as of this instant. Failing to do so, they will receive air and land punishment.
5. The people of Santiago should remain in their houses so as to avoid unnecessary victims.

(Signed) AUGUSTO PINOCHET UGARTE, General of the Army, Commander in Chief of the Army

JOSÉ TORIBIO MERINO, Admiral, Commander in Chief of the Navy

GUSTAVO LEIGH GUZMÁN, General of the Air, Commander in Chief of the Air Force of Chile

CÉSAR MENDOZA DURÁN, General, Director-General of Carabineros of Chile.

Thus, in two minutes and twenty seconds did an old order end and a new one begin.

Along the Costanera, the overburdened artery bordering the Mapocho River, drivers began to honk their horns, and from the windows of apartment buildings on Providencia Street, Chilean flags began to flutter wildly.

At Peñalolén, Mario was about to move his car from the general's space where he had parked it when he noticed everyone listening to small transistors, and so switched on the radio in his car.

"Everybody in the battalion started cheering and slapping each other on the back and shouting 'Viva Chile,' and 'shit,' and I want to tell you that then, at least, it was the most beautiful word I had ever heard in my life. A minute later I heard a call on the shortwave: 'Mobile 5 from Position 5, come in Mobile 5,' and then it all came to me what I had done, and I was never prouder in my life."

Inside the Capitol the truck wives listened in silence, then burst into the national anthem, crying as they sang.

In the U.S. Embassy, Halsema, just a minute before 8:32 A.M., turned to Manuel Bravo, one of the Chilean aides in the press section, and suggested they tune in the radio. That is how he happened to hear the proclamation.

"I rushed upstairs to tell the ambassador [Halsema's office was on the fifth floor, the ambassador's on the eighth] and find out what he wanted us to do. 'Monitor the radio,' he said. I asked him whether he wanted any special security precautions started, and he said nothing more than the routine at that point, which, for the most part, meant taking sensitive files to the communications room [for quick destruction if need be]. My secretary, Lois Knoll, did that in a few minutes flat."

For one man, finishing his morning ablutions, the news came first in a telephone call, next when he turned on the radio to catch the tail end of the proclamation. Pelayo Figueroa Toro immediately remembered the day, nearly three years before—October 28, 1970—when he rode with a driver to Salvador Allende's offfice to deliver to him a very special document. Figueroa was the secretary-general of the Senate, a post he had occupied then for ten of the thirty-four years he had spent as a Senate employee, and the document was the one formally notifying Salvador Allende that the Congress had elected him President of Chile. Before television cameras in place for the occasion Figueroa had said:

"Mr. President, I have an important document to deliver to you."

"Don't call me 'Mr. President,'" Allende interjected. "Call me friend, as before. And that will demonstrate to you that democracy continues in Chile."

"That," Figueroa responded, "is my hope and the hope of all Chile."

Listening to the proclamation of revolution, Figueroa said to himself that despite the reassuring banter, he had felt, even as that exchange took place three years ago, that "democracy in Chile was in danger."

The scene in La Moneda was pandemonium. GAPs and others brandished submachine guns and glowered at the special palace guard of Carabineros, still busy setting up their own defenses. The high and low of the regime scurried through corridors and the two interior plazas. And, in his second-floor office, a soldier's helmet on his head, the 1,200-round-a-minute AK submachine gun Fidel Castro had given him on his desk, his jacket pockets bulging with machine-gun clips, the President of the Republic was attempting to stop the inevitable. Even after the infuriating words of the broadcast, he had yet to be convinced that the rebellion was widespread, and he continued to expect the militia to rally massively. Furthermore, Allende still counted on the loyalty of the Carabineros. The man who believed he commanded them, General Sepúlveda, had tried several times to get General Parada, the Santiago commandant, to declare himself unequivocally. Allende grabbed the telephone and shouted obscenities at Parada.

Allende persisted in his efforts to reach one of the top commanders of the rebellion. An aide told him General Arellano, in charge of the downtown sector, was on the line.

"Shit on General Arellano," Allende shouted.

On the streets around the palace the sights and sounds of imminent war clashed with the slapstick of a city in which many could not, or would not, take it seriously. The Terreros were still serving up breakfasts at "Sandwich Al Paso" as fast as their hands and dwindling supplies permitted when someone glanced up and saw the tanks, a double row of them, moving west along the Alameda, on both sides of the street.

"It is crazy but true," their daughter, María, said, "but someone cracked, 'They must mean business this time. They're not even stopping for the lights.' " (One of the oddball curiosities of Colonel Souper's June twenty-ninth revolt was that the tanks, on their way to lay siege to the presidential palace, actually stopped for the traffic lights.)

But even the sight of tanks would not intimidate Santiaguinos, battle-fatigued already from so much contention and conflict, especially those, like the Terreros, who still did not know the news.

"From across the way," María said, "someone shouted that we'd better lower the metal curtains, it was something big, and so we did."

From behind the shutters they would watch, minutes later, when the shooting began, how even then, crowds of curious would edge forward to get a better view. (*El Mercurio* would later publish an incredible photo of a crowd pressing against a police line, as if at the edge of a parade rather than, as they were, at the edge of a battle.)

"We saw one man fall," don Vincente said, "then another across the way at the corner of Serrano Street. When a third was hit, the crowd ran. . . . "

Less stubborn—but stubborn all the same—a group of schoolgirls intercepted by a newsman as they made their way downtown from the north. "Turn back, turn back," he shouted. "There has been a revolution." It took some persuasion to convince the girls that their planned demonstration had been canceled; it was no longer needed.

Manolo Bravo's wife decided she wasn't needed, either, when she reported for work at the Third Carabinero Precinct. Mrs. Bravo was a lieutenant in the Carabineros.

"The situation was so confused," she said, "and I saw there was nothing I could do." With a large coat over her uniform, she made her way to Agustinas, and there joined her husband at the U.S. Embassy, helping him to transcribe broadcasts the rest of the day.

Another "visitor" arrived at the embassy: Louise Crane of the Voice of America. She had been feeding the news by telephone to VOA headquarters in Washington on the developing crisis in Chile when she was suddenly cut off. Still she was luckier than most of her colleagues in Santiago that day. Few reporters would manage to get any word out at all for days.

Allende's confidante-companion, La Payita, heard the reports of an uprising early and decided immediately that her place was in the palace. She made it there on the shirttails of a military officer.

When Allende's naval aide, Commander Grez, reached the palace, he discovered that the Carabineros had orders from the president himself to let no one in. Grez persisted, and asked for an officer to identify him. When one appeared, he was waved on.

"Mrs. Ropert," he said, "followed right behind me." So did Hernán del Canto.

Two other women in Allende's entourage were on their way: his daughter Beatriz, who crashed through a police barricade and rushed into the palace, pistol in hand (according to her own version), and his sister Laura, who, politically and emotionally, was closest to him of all his family. Laura had not listened to the radio that morning and was about to set out for Congress when a friend called and told her to tune in immediately. Hearing that La Moneda was surrounded, she decided to head for the palace anyway, but quickly collided with the first obstacle of the day: her car wouldn't start. She lost half an hour while a neighbor helped her connect a battery cable that appeared to have been disconnected intentionally. When she finally reached the city's second railroad terminal, the Mapocho Station, just eight blocks north of La Moneda, traffic was tied in knots. A Carabinero, armed with submachine gun, shooed her away as she attempted to pass the barricade.

"I am Laura Allende," she shouted. The Carabinero either did not hear—or it did not matter. He motioned again for her to turn around. She remembered her brother's advice: if anything like this should ever happen, she should join with other members of the party as quickly as possible. Realizing it would be impossible to reach the party's national headquarters on Alameda, she decided to head for the Con-chalí district headquarters in a working-class neighborhood in the northern sector. The place was deserted. Next, even farther north, in Batuco, she found a few disoriented members at the party's headquarters. They all decided to head for the larger and better-organized Cordillera regional headquarters, famed as a bastion of resolute fighters. There the scene was similar to the one at Batuco. With growing desperation, she drove to the homes of five party leaders. All had fled. It was during this odyssey that she learned of the ultimatum. She switched off the radio and drove on.

With supreme nonchalance, UPI newsman Roberto Mason drove right up to the door of his office, flush across the Plaza Bulnes from the Defense Ministry, and at a 45-degree angle across the Alameda from La Moneda, and parked his Citroneta outside. He found the usual two messengers, newsman Tomás Guitiérrez, and one or two administrative employees on duty. They were joined shortly afterward by Steve Yolen, over from São Paulo to sit in for the vacationing bureau manager. Yolen had walked over from the Carrera Hotel, arriving in the nick of time. Bullets were not far behind him.

Following the reading of the proclamation, eleven seconds of awkward silence intervened before the new armed forces network sputtered back to life with a repeat of the national anthem and some martial music. Then Guillár was back, reading the proclamation again—live, with even more emphasis, more emotion, and an extra word or two (the presidency now became the "high" office). Guillár then went directly into the reading of instructions he said had been imparted by the government junta, the first clue that the four military commanders had already decided to constitute themselves as a "government." The word "provisional" did not occur in the statement. Nor would it. The instructions expanded the ban on broadcasting to include *all* unauthorized stations in Santiago Province, and held managers responsible for removing key components and turning them over to local military commanders so as to assure that their stations could not return to the air until the all-clear was given; they also ordered all private radio systems off the air, "under pain of military reprisal."

Those who had made it to work that day, mostly government employees, began a frantic rush to flee the downtown area. A few decided to continue on their way to the center.

Vincente Garrido was one. With an increasing sense of tension, the pressman finally reached Bandera and Moneda Streets, just half a block from the newspaper. There it took his pass as a newspaper employee and persuasion to cover the last few yards. He might have spared himself the trouble, and the danger ahead. *La Prensa* would not publish again for two more days.

Hector Humeres was a government "employee" who decided that his place was at his desk. Since 1967 Humeres had headed that unique institution, the Contraloría, the eleventh man to hold the job since 1927 (on the advice of an American, Edwin Walter Kemmerer, whose portrait hangs now in the office of the secretary-general of the Contraloría). Humeres looked and acted the part of the austere, suprapolitical position he held: balding, serious, proper, yet a man with an easy smile.

"I was with my driver at Mapocho and Bandera [eight blocks north of La Moneda] when I heard the military proclamation. I decided immediately that I must be at the office because Allende would need me as an adviser on legalisms, or as an intermediary of confidence [Ministro de Fe] should he agree to hand over power."

So Humeres continued through streets already bristling with the warriors and weapons of war, through the no-man's-land that the Plaza Constitución had become, directly past the south facade of the ticking time bomb La Moneda had become, and on to his ninth-floor office directly overlooking the palace below.

The call he had steeled himself to handle never came. But a series of unforgettable scenes did await him.

The man who headed the larger and sturdier of the two pillars of Chile's juridical system was Enrique Urrutia Manzano, the seventy-three-year-old Chief Justice of the Supreme Court. As such, he also presided over the entire judiciary. He learned of the revolution in a telephone call from one of his children. The experience of the past three years had convinced Urrutia that Allende had led Chile into a wilderness of hatred in which the legal, social, economic, and political vitality of the country had perished. When he switched on the radio he seldom used and heard that momentous proclamation, he felt only undisguised relief.

Sergio Poblete Garcés, a retired general, listened with anything but relief. Poblete was then number two man in the Government Development Corporation (CORFO), one of two generals implicated in the plotting to subvert the air force. Around 9:00 A.M. someone poked a head into his office and said "soldiers and Carabineros are surrounding La Moneda." Poblete found no executives in the neighboring offices and few employees at all, nor was there news on the teletypes in the communications room. So he went up to the top floor to take a look for himself (CORFO is situated across the street from the Capitol, four blocks from La Moneda). What he saw was enough to convince him that it was serious. He called his wife and told her not to come to town to open her shop, and later he remembered files he would rather not have found, and so he instructed his secretary, Eugenia Victoria Díaz, to burn them. The real bombshell came when he heard his name among ninety-five ordered to surrender by 4:30 P.M. or face "consequences easy to foresee." He told his secretary to go home, but she said she was too worried about him to leave him there. She persuaded him to wait, at least until the "heat" was off, in an apartment-office several blocks away. There the hunted general and his faithful secretary remained in seclusion for the next forty-eight hours.

His code name was "Galeán," but his air force buddies knew him as First Sergeant Belarmino Constanzo Merino. A died-in-the-wool MIRista (member of the radical MIR), his days as a plotter went back to the middle of 1971. His contacts had included the elite of the elite of the MIR: the "hero" Luciano Cruz, before he died; Miguel Enríquez, the commander in chief; Pascal Allende, the president's nephew, and heir-apparent to command of the MIR. Constanzo's job was to recruit others for a conspiracy they called "Plan September," aimed at seizing the Air Academy—of great symbolic importance because it was the birthplace of the air force—and the adjoining El Bosque Air Force Base. That conspiracy was to have exploded in September 1972. It was later aborted, and another developed. The new and expanded plan included the infiltration and neutralizing of the Cerrillos Air Force Base in Santiago, as well as the Quintero Air Force Base near Valparaíso. Those plans included taking anti-Marxist officers and men prisoner, blowing up airplanes, turning over arms to MIRistas and other Allende "combat" forces. General Poblete was to assume command of El Bosque Air Force Base. When the time came to act, Sergeant Constanzo, in common with other plotters, found himself "scared to death." Instead of joining in blowing up airplanes and fuel depots, Constanzo stayed in his office all day, wondering how he would get out of the hole he was in.

The message to "Mario" in his Mobile Unit #5 was a test. It was the first formal message transmitted over the secret shortwave network linking Leigh, Pinochet, and the Defense Ministry. It was also the last to Mobile Unit #5.

Thereafter, the stations on the network were:

> # 1—Pinochet
> # 2—Leigh
> # 3—Military Academy
> # 4—Unused
> # 5—Defense Ministry

Why the Military Academy was included is a mystery. No significant operations were conducted from there. But it was also a stroke of luck. All efforts to repair the link between Leigh and Pinochet had failed. The Military Academy—via the voice of eighteen-year-old plebe cadet Dante Pino (there is irony in the fact that the cadet picked at random should have a name that appeared as a diminutive of the big boss, Pinochet)—became the bridge connecting the two.

Merino communicated directly with Admiral Carvajal via the navy's private "green telephones." That left the Carabineros's new boss, General Mendoza, out. In the first, confused moments after the ultimatum, he was unable to get through to Leigh to find out just when in hell the bombs would fall.

"Later an aide of mine managed to talk to one of Leigh's aides and get it straightened out," Mendoza explained. Also, he was later able to establish a regular communications link to General Brady, the Santiago commander in the Defense Ministry.

But if Mendoza was momentarily in the dark about the actions of the other three, so too was Pinochet in the dark about what was going on at Carabineros headquarters those first moments.

"Station One [Pinochet] to Station Five [Carvajal, in the Defense Ministry]: Is Yovane working on Carabineros?" (Evidently Pinochet meant to say Mendoza rather than Yovane.)

"Position Five to Position One: Yes, he commands the forces surrounding the Moneda," Carvajal answered, and made it clear he was talking about General Mendoza.

The military began tightening the noose around La Moneda. The tanks of Armored Regiment #2 once again were in enfilade position facing the south facade of La Moneda, as they had been nearly three months before. Troops of the Infantry School took up position at the corner of Agustinas and Teatinos. Facing them perhaps 300 yards away, across the plaza, was the fidgety, reinforced guard of Carabineros. Facing them, as yet unseen from dozens of windows—the Bank of the State, the Ministry of Public Works, the Treasury, the offices of the government newspaper, *La Nación,* over the shoulders of the tanks below, and from dozens of the preselected vantage points—were the snipers, the fanatic "kamikaze" units of Salvador Allende's *vía chilena.*

Across the way the Tacna Regiment—the one General Viaux had led in bold rebellion four years before—deployed around the northern approaches to La Moneda. With them were Colonel Canessa's men of the Noncommissioned Officers School.

"When we got to the Plaza Almagro," Corporal Pizzarro said, "the colonel sent Captain Cardemil, Corporal Tolosa, and me on ahead to the Plaza Bulnes, chasing people off the streets, telling people to close their shops, to get off the balconies. Traffic was chaos, cars and buses going every which way, running traffic lights, everybody rushing to get out. When we got to Plaza Bulnes, there were some jeeps there with 30- and 50-caliber machine guns mounted on them, their guns pointed at La Moneda. But still no shooting. In fact, Captain Cardemil had to chase away a couple who were walking along Alameda holding hands and kissing. It was eerie."

The arms and reinforcements Allende had summoned, and so badly needed, arrived from Tomás Moro shortly before 9:00 A.M. The small convoy swung into the presidential garage, beneath the Public Works Ministry, directly across Morandé Street from the side entrance to the palace.

Among those who saw them arrive were two Carabinero lieutenants, Patricio de la Fuente Ibar and Juan Martínez Maureira, the one about to relieve the other as duty officer in the Capitol of Santiago Province, situated at the corner of Morandé and Moneda, a stone's throw across the street from the palace. The lieutenants commanded a detail of a dozen men. On the two floors above them were two men who far outranked them, but only one whose mind was definitely made up. He was Julio Stuardo, who, in five months as governor of Santiago Province, had developed a reputation for iron-fisted repression. On June 14 he personally commanded a force of Carabineros with tanquetas and bulldozers to round up five thousand striking copper miners who had marched 70 miles to force the government to negotiate their demands. On July 29 he joined Jaime Faivovich—the man he had replaced as governor after Faivovich had been impeached by the Senate, only to be named at once by Allende Under Secretary of Transportation—in a head-cracking raid to seize two hundred trucks of striking teamsters. On August 12 he personally ordered Carabineros to use tear gas, billy clubs and nightsticks on two thousand trucker wives protesting in the Plaza Constitución. The man with Stuardo whose mind was not made up was General Parada, the prefect of Santiago. The two were accompanied by about fifteen GAPs.

Shortly after the proclamation was aired the lieutenants received radioed orders to pull out. Concerned about the safety of other Carabineros on the third floor, they were debating what to do when they saw a station wagon loaded with GAPs arrive and pull into the presidential garage, followed almost immediately by others. The lieutenants swung into action, ordering their men to follow them into the garage. There they surprised fifteen GAPs as they were unloading submachine guns, antitank mines, bazookas, and boxes of ammunition, all destined for the palace. The lieutenants ordered the GAPs to take the weapons back into the provincial Capitol building, locking the GAPs in the guard room on the first floor. Among the prisoners was a GAP known as "Bruno" wanted for the murder six weeks before of Capt. Arturo Araya Peters, Allende's naval aide-de-camp.

Stuardo and Parada watched the lieutenants marching their prisoners along the street as did others in La Moneda itself, across the way. The lieutenants were barely back inside the building than Parada and Stuardo were screaming at them by telephone to release the men forthwith. The young officers refused. They shortly had one other protest to contend with: Salvador Allende called them and told them that if they did not release the prisoners, he would have them sacked immediately. Allende had a special reason for wanting the prisoners released: the lieutenants had unknowingly taken one of La Payita's sons. From the window of the palace she saw him as the prisoners were marched out of the garage. She appealed to Allende for help. But he could not budge the lieutenants. Instead, they put through a call to Carabinero Special Services, the SWAT-type team Allende had raged about so much as a candidate. Once in power, he did not disband it, merely changed its name.

That episode had not yet reached its climax when Allende had an even more serious problem to contend with.

"Look out the window," one of the GAPs shouted. Allende, surrounded by about thirty persons, jumped up and made his way to the small balcony just in time to see the last of the tanquetas guarding the palace speeding away. With them went the thousand Carabineros who were his ring of steel around the palace.

"When I first arrived," Commander Jorge Grez, Allende's naval aide-de-camp, said, "I was shocked to see him with the helmet on and a submachine gun on his desk. But he was still in bold spirits. When I reported, he waved from his chair, and the first thing he said to me was: 'Once again, we have problems with your navy, Commander.' He had used those exact same words to me just two weeks before, and I was taken aback when he used them again."

"It was when someone on the OIR staff brought him the text of the proclamation that his mood changed." Grez said. "He had heard it, but now, reading it, he became much more somber, changed."

Yet bravado enough remained for a last public hurrah. Allende went back on the balcony for another look around the mostly deserted streets and plaza. As he did, a small cluster of persons ran toward the balcony from the main post office building. Allende waved to them, and the scene was captured by photographers in the group. It was his last public appearance.

Still another blow awaited him. Over the official radio came the words:

BANDO [Communique] #2: THE PALACE OF LA MONEDA MUST BE EVACUATED BEFORE 11 A.M. IF IT IS NOT, IT WILL BE ATTACKED BY THE AIR FORCE OF CHILE.

WORKERS SHOULD REMAIN IN THEIR PLACES OF WORK, IT BEING ABSOLUTELY FORBIDDEN FOR THEM TO LEAVE.

IN THE EVENT THEY SHOULD DO SO, THEY WILL BE ATTACKED BY LAND AND AIR FORCES.

THE CONTENTS OF BANDO #1 ARE REITERATED IN THE SENSE THAT ANY ACT OF SABOTAGE WILL BE PUNISHED IN THE MOST DRASTIC FORM POSSIBLE ON THE SPOT.

For Salvador Allende there no longer remained any doubt: it was surrender or fight—alone—to the finish.

He was, in fact, even more alone than he imagined. There would be resistance at three or four factories, but furious resistance never materialized, nor was there a mobilization of armed militiamen converging on the center of the city to save him.

Nor did he know that, at 8:50 A.M., Gen. Washington Carrasco had reported to Pinochet: "Concepción is ours, without a shot having been fired." Concepción was not only Chile's third city, it was also the birthplace of the MIR and a redoubt of terrorism. Carrasco had amputated them with surgical precision. Aided by an engineer and three telephone company technicians, he had managed, during the night, to disconnect 1,800 telephones belonging to top MIR and Popular Unity leaders. As dawn broke, all 1,800 were being taken prisoner, while other raiding parties seized government offices, the extremist-dominated University (of Chile), militia-manned factories, key installations. By noon, the 1,800 were on, or en route to, Quiriquina Island, in the mouth of Concepción Bay. (The next day, a lone sniper opened fire at dusk from a downtown rooftop on a crowd of civilians in the Plaza de Armas, the only "combat action" in that city.)

Shortly after Concepción was secured, armed "resistance" flared in Antofagasta, the country's fourth city and second port, 825 miles north of Santiago. Carabinero Guillermo Schmidt Godoy, an avowed Marxist, service revolver in hand, broke into the office of the commandant of the Fourth Precinct. He shot to death the precinct commander and deputy commander, Maj. Osvaldo Mario Nuñez Carrasco and Capt. José Hector Davila Rodríguez, both fathers of two children. Schmidt was court-martialed that day and executed by a firing squad the next day.

Inside La Moneda, Allende spun the dial of a radio, seeking in vain stations still proclaiming his fight. Only Radio Magallanes, broadcasting from an emergency transmitter, remained on the air.

"Next to his desk," Grez said, "he had three telephones with direct lines to the radio stations—Portales, Magallanes, and Corporacion. He was jiggling the crank when an operator came on.

" 'This is the president,' he said. 'I am going to speak to the nation.' The operator said, 'give me ten seconds,' and he waited, and then he went on." His voice was calm, his speech measured.

This will surely be my last chance to speak to you. The air force has bombarded the antennas of Radio Magallanes. My words carry not bitterness but disappointment. May there be moral punishment for those who have betrayed their oath: soldiers of Chile, commander in chief Admiral Merino, who has proclaimed himself commandant of the navy, as well as Mr. Mendoza, that drag-along general who only yesterday affirmed his fidelity and loyalty to the government, and who has now proclaimed himself director-general of the Carabineros. In the face of these deeds, I have only one thing to say to the workers: I am not going to resign!

Placed in this historic juncture, I will repay with my life the loyalty of the people. I tell you that I am certain that the seed we have given to the worthy consciousness of thousands and thousands of Chileans cannot be rooted out entirely. They have the force, they can crush us, but social processes are not held back by crime or by force. History is ours, and the people will make it.

Workers of my country, I have to thank you for the loyalty you have always had, the confidence you placed in a man who was only the interpreter of a great yearning for justice, who pledged his word that he would respect the Constitution and the law, and who has done so. In this definitive moment, the last in which I am able to speak to you, I wish to take advantage of the lesson: foreign capital and imperialism, united with reaction, created the climate in which the armed forces would break with their tradition, the one

Schneider would teach them and Captain Araya would reaffirm,* both of them victims of the same social class that waits today in their houses while other hands reconquer power so that they can continue defending their profits and their privileges.

I address myself, above all, to the modest women of our land, the farm women who believed in us, the worker who wanted more work, the mother who knew of our concern for children.

I address myself to the professionals of the fatherland, those who continued working against the sedition sponsored by the professional societies, the classist societies, which also defended the advantages of a capitalist society of the few.

I address myself to the youth, to those who sang and gave of their joy and their fighting spirit.

I address myself to the men of Chile, the worker, the peasant, the intellectual, to those who will be persecuted, because in our country fascism has already been with us for a long while: in terrorist attacks, blowing up bridges, cutting railroad lines, destroying oil and gas pipelines, in the face of the silence of those who had the obligation to act. They were implicated. History will judge them.

Surely, Radio Magallanes will be silenced, and the sound of my voice will not reach you again. It doesn't matter. You will continue to hear it. I will always be with you. At least my memory will remain with you: that of a worthy man who was loyal to the fatherland.

You, the people, must defend yourselves, but not sacrifice yourselves. You should not allow yourselves to be cowed or mowed down, but neither should you be humiliated.

Workers of my fatherland, I have faith in Chile and in its destiny. Other men will overcome this dark and bitter moment that betrayal would impose on us. Continue believing that, much sooner than later, once again the grand promenades will be opened on which free men walk to construct a better society.

Viva Chile! Viva the people! Long live the workers!

These are my last words, and I am certain that my sacrifice will not be in vain; I am certain that, at the very least, it will be a moral lesson that will punish felony, cowardice, and treason."

*Allende was referring to the army's Chief of Staff, Gen. René Schneider, murdered in October 1970 in a bungled bid to keep Allende from assuming the presidency, and Capt. Arturo Ayala, naval aide-de-camp to the president, murdered just six weeks previously, July 27, 1973.

Having conceded that all was lost, Salvador Allende then went about slamming the doors of escape behind him—but not without one more try at "puppeteering."

Allende had just finished speaking when the green telephone, the navy phone, on Commander Grez's desk started ringing. The time was 9:15 A.M. An aide picked it up and summoned Grez. It was Admiral Carvajal (the key link between Pinochet, Leigh, and troop commanders throughout the combat) ordering Allende to leave the palace immediately. If Allende stayed longer, Carvajal warned, it would be on his own responsibility. Grez gave him a quick rundown on the situation in the palace—which Carvajal promptly relayed to Pinochet.

"I have just spoken to the naval aide-de-camp," Carvajal told Pinochet, "Who tells me that La Moneda is being defended by around fifty GAPs and forty to fifty Carabineros, and that the president is running around with a submachine gun with thirty shots and saying the last two shots were going to be for himself."

"Pure fiction!" exploded Pinochet over the radio. "That lout wouldn't know how to shoot a tube of toothpaste!"

Carvajal laughed and told Pinochet he had instructed Grez to urge the Carabinero commander in the palace to pull his men out or risk being bombed.

Traffic on the secret radio network was already picking up. Pinochet, complaining that Radio Magallanes was still on the air, asked Leigh to "study the possibility" of knocking it out in an air attack. (As the day wore on, Pinochet's tone became more peremptory, his commands more unquestioned. Leigh, strong throughout, did not yield ground so much as it was preempted by Pinochet.)

Even Cadet Pino got in his oar in those early moments. Relaying a call from Leigh to Pinochet, the intrepid cadet said: "Gustavo wants to speak to General Pinochet."

At that point, he did not realize that "Gustavo" was a general too. (Minutes later, Pino was back on the air, complaining that he did not have a typewriter to copy traffic for relay between the two generals. Would someone please send him one?)

Leigh demonstrated his sense of "public relations" early in the battle, proposing to Pinochet that they issue another communique announcing not only their intention to fight to the end, but reassuring the population that their fight was "not against the people" but in defense of the rights of the majority, and that the majority backed them in their revolt. Pinochet assented, adding, somewhat excitedly, that the communique should emphasize they were fighting against "the hunger Sr. Allende is sowing, the lines, the misery, the poverty." Shortly afterward, almost verbatim, as the two commanders had drafted it with Cadet Pino brokering the conversation, the communique went out as Bando #5.

"Domínguez, Under Secretary of the Navy," Pinochet told Carvajal via radio, "has just called me, and, it seems, someone in La Moneda has proposed that the three commanders in chief go to La Moneda and ask for the president's surrender." The "someone" was Allende; it was his last *muñeca,* attempt to manipulate.

In his frenzy of telephone calls, he had put one in to the Defense Ministry. It was fielded by Gen. Ernesto Baeza, in seniority the number three man in the army. General Baeza had arrived only a short time before to attend a routine meeting and been given a quick fill-in on the situation from Generals Brady and Arellano. Allende said he wanted to speak with the commanders in chief, that they should come to La Moneda and negotiate with him. Baeza said he would relay the message, but he believed Allende should surrender, as he had been advised to do.

"Allende told me that under no circumstances would he accept the ultimatum," Baeza said. "He also said he didn't believe the air force would dare bomb La Moneda, and that, in any event, they could do whatever they wanted with him, he was not going to surrender."

"Mr. President," Baeza said, "your stubbornness will drag many to their deaths with you. You will be responsible for those deaths."

Once again, Allende refused to consider surrender, and said the commanders should come to him.

"He was neither abusive nor excited as he spoke to me," Baeza said.

Baeza relayed the message to Pinochet.

"General Pinochet's reaction was relentless: a flat no."

Relentless is a mild word for it. Pinochet, his voice rising and his speech speeding, shouted into the radio: "I told you that creep is tricky; he is a liar. If he wants, let him go to the Ministry of Defense and surrender. . . ."

Carvajal was quick to comply with Pinochet's decision; they would not go to him; Allende must come to them, the military commanders.

He picked up the phone and again called Grez. In stern tones he said: "Tell Allende I want to talk to him right now." The time was 9:25 A.M.

Grez went immediately to the president's office, next door. The GAPs, outwardly suspicious in their treatment of the military all morning, fingered their weapons menacingly. Grez told the president that Carvajal was on the "green phone" in his office. Without hesitation, Allende took the call. But it was not the reply he expected.

"There was no protocol," Grez said. "He went in and picked up the phone. The GAPs in his office did not follow. There were two or three of us standing around. Carvajal began speaking, but Allende interrupted him and began shouting and cursing at him. He was tremendously excited. When that flare-up passed, he quieted down, and Carvajal again spoke to him, but he didn't let Carvajal finish. He threw the telephone on the table and said: 'I am not going to permit them to speak to me in those terms. . . . ' "

"Those terms" were the military's first formal ultimatum given directly to Allende: surrender, or the palace would be bombed. Carvajal told Allende that a plane was standing by that would take him—and any members of his family—anywhere he wanted to go on the South American continent.

After that explosion, Grez decided he must consult quickly with the other aides to coordinate their moves. Tension in the palace was increasing notably. The army aide, Maj. Sergio Badiola, was the duty officer that week, and so had reported that morning at Tomás Moro and been with the president since. But the senior aide, Air Force Maj. Roberto Sánchez, head of the Military Household by virtue of the fact he had been with Allende throughout his presidency, had only then arrived, and he rushed right in to talk to the president. Sánchez brought instructions from Leigh about the arrangements for evacuating the president and his family from the country (a DC-6, fully fueled and crewed, was standing by at the old Los Cerrillos airport at the southwestern edge of town, still used for domestic flights). When he emerged, Grez asked for a huddle of the three.

Grez, meantime, had followed another instruction from headquarters: he had talked to the lieutenant commanding the Carabinero palace guard. The lieutenant agreed to withdraw his men at the right moment. They would leave at 10:30, discarding their weapons in the palace, and exit through the main door facing the Plaza Constitución.

Hands in the air, they ran across the plaza to the underground Carabinero station on the other side. Orders had already been given to the army troops not to fire on them.

Earlier, when Allende discovered the outside guard leaving, he vented his fury on the Carabinero generals he had believed would keep the corps loyal to him. How was it possible, he asked, that generals could not command the obedience of lieutenants and other junior officers? The generals had stood before him, unarmed and troopless, listening in silence. Now, he had not even that satisfaction.

"Afterward," Grez said, "they [the generals] talked among themselves. I did not see them again. They left the palace."

"We believed the Carabineros would be loyal," the Interior Minister, Carlos Briones, said. "It was a hard blow to him."

"It was about then he started to drink," the navy steward said. "Whiskey—Chivas Regal. By 10:30 he was pretty tipsy." (Another military man inside the palace said he saw Allende down four whiskeys within an hour's time. Briones said he saw the president drink only one.)

Carabineros were not the only ones abandoning La Moneda. After listening to the first military communiques, GAP Julio Hernán Soto said he was "afraid," and so he bolted out the Morandé door and across the street to the presidential garage, then up to the fifth floor of the Public Works Ministry, where he hid in an empty office. Soto contemplated suicide, but decided he "lacked the courage." He passed out when the shooting started. Along the way, he stashed the pistol and submachine gun he was carrying and destroyed his GAP identity card. He was captured when troops swept the building.

Allende was right about Radio Magallanes. At 10:00 A.M. it was silenced by a single rocket fired from a distance of two kilometers (1.2 miles) by an extraordinary pilot at the controls of a helicopter.

Squadron Commander Jorge Massa Armijo had won worldwide fame on December 22, 1972, when he piloted a helicopter to an unprecedented 16,500 feet in a daring rescue of the survivors of a Uruguayan air force plane that had crashed in the high Andes. Search parties had hunted them for seventy days; it would later be disclosed that they had resorted to eating the flesh of the dead in order to stay alive. For the thirty-nine-year-old major rescue missions were his stock-in-trade: he had rescued more than two thousand persons in his career. The son of a pioneer air force general, Massa went aloft for the first time at the age of three, and had since flown everything but kites. He was also, on and off, one of the official pilots assigned to Presidents Alessandri, Frei, and Allende—he had last flown Allende a month before.

In view of his credentials, small wonder that Leigh turned to him to solve the pesky problem of Radio Magallanes.

"We had gone up earlier that morning," Massa said, "but our detection gear kept pointing south, and everyone was convinced the transmitter must be north of the city." (For a time, the Communists used a mobile transmitter, which *was* north of the city; hence the confusion.)

The trail he followed finally led due south, through heavy cloud cover hard by the steep-rising Andes. Just north of Rancagua, 50 miles south of Santiago, he locked in on it.

"We broke through cloud cover, and I sighted the antenna at a distance. Because of the clouds and mountains, I couldn't get any closer without risking drawing fire, and so I fired a single rocket. That was enough."

Salvador Allende was now alone.

The Special Services bus had finished loading the prisoners across the street from La Moneda and was just pulling away when the shooting started. From all sides the air around La Moneda reverberated with the sounds of war. Jim Halsema, on the fifth floor of the American Embassy building, said he had not heard such intense small-arms fire since World War II. From the Ministry of Education, Colonel Canessa's troops came under heavy fire, and two of his men fell wounded. Corporal Pizzarro hit the dirt and began firing while lying on his back. Most of the gunfire raining down on them came at first from the Education Ministry and the big ENTEL tower two blocks south. Canessa and a major with him in the Plaza Bulnes suddenly found themselves under heavy machine gun and rifle fire from three sides. Eight men fell wounded around them, and the major kept blazing away with his gun until it was empty. As he described it, "Some of my men practically shielded me with their bodies" as they helped him get back to cover under the marquee of the Continental Theater. The worst of the shooting at them had come from that building behind them, the one housing the Continental Theater and, on the ninth floor, the offices of the United Press International. Canessa had already ordered a check of some apartments in the building (it was a combination office and apartment building); now he called for supporting fire from the Defense Ministry, across the way, against the rooftop snipers and those firing from windows of the building.

In the Plaza Constitución to the north, the tanks had opened up with cannon fire. One volley blew in the big double doors of La Moneda. Corporal Pizzarro was among those searching the building.

"I got as far as the fifth floor," he said. "We found one foreigner with a blank passport and a batch of photos, including one of Colonel Canessa and Captain Caldemil in a parade—he had practically a collection."

(It would take a while, but eventually troops would flush more than a dozen snipers from that building, including several Hondurans.)

Canessa, meanwhile, had pulled his men back 150 yards to regroup, with Pizzarro at his side. "I said to myself, this is my lucky day, so wherever my colonel goes, that's where I go," the corporal said.

Inside the Carrera-Sheraton the sounds of war brought the immediate danger of panic.

"People started screaming as soon as the shooting started," its manager, Mike Gallegos, said, "and people started rushing to the lobby. A few bullets came into the lobby area. My first job was to get everybody away from the windows."

It was not an easy job. Nor was it made easier by the presence of 37 foreign newsmen among Gallegos's 378 guests, most of whom were still in the building. Add to that the fact that a high percentage of his staff were themselves Marxists sympathetic to Allende, and potentially hostile to foreigners. Top it off with the traditional reluctance of civilians to submit to the authority of other civilians.

"My first job was to get the employees on my side," Gallegos said. "I appealed to their pride as Chileans, to be brave in this emergency, so we could all be proud of being Chileans. Then I took a quick look around for trouble spots. I found one at once: waiters were still serving breakfast in the Copper Room [situated on the street level, on the Agustinas side]. I stopped that right off." (The room was later a shambles of bullet pockmarks).

Next, Gallegos had his five telephone operators call all guests in their rooms and ask them to report to the lobby for a meeting.

"I told them I had talked to the authorities—bullshit, I hadn't talked to anybody, of course—and they had assured me they realized we were an international hotel and no harm would come to us. I told them anything that came to my head, but, most of all, pleaded with them to stay away from the windows.

"In all of this, the telephones never stopped ringing, friends and relatives of guests and staff. Between the telephones and some women whining and whimpering and the shooting, it was bedlam."

When the tanks opened fire, it got even worse.

"The whole building shook," Gallegos said. "Some people became hysterical and tried to run out. We had security at the door, blocking them, but it was a job. One of our younger telephone operators got really hysterical, and we had to slap her and give her a tranquilizer I happened to have in my pocket." (Gallegos called the telephone operators "heroines," particularly the chief operator, "who always stays right at the board, no matter what, earthquakes or whatever. She did that day, even in the worst of it.")

The worst was about to come. Around 9:45 A.M. Gallegos learned that the air force was going to bomb La Moneda. The Carrera was, as jets go, just a whisker away.

Gallegos had already ordered the hotel's emergency clinic moved downstairs from the sixth floor to the basement. The hotel's doctor and nurse did not make it that day, but among the guests were two doctors, a man and a woman. Gallegos recruited a crew of volunteers to patrol corridors on each floor to prevent looting and save the curious from themselves, keeping them away from windows. Meanwhile, he began evacuating guests to the basement—those who would go, that is. "Quite a few refused," he said. "I told each of them three or four times the danger they were in and that we could not be responsible for their lives. Many stayed in their rooms anyway."

Curiosity was a killer elsewhere. Former President Jorge Alessandri was dressing in his downtown apartment when snipers in the tower of the cathedral across the street opened fire on troops in the Plaza de Armas below. The abundance of trees in the plaza added to the confusion, and bullets flew everywhere. A maid in Alessandri's apartment could not resist the temptation, and peeked from a window. A bullet lodged in her head, killing her. "I had told her until I was sick of telling her, 'don't look out,' " Alessandri said.

Jorge Braña, as the senior authority present, had already ordered the five or six who made it to the Esso offices that morning away from the low windows when a soldier entered, checking for snipers. "He told us to leave the main doors open [to make control of the building

easier]. Normally, we would have had around seventy persons there
—we have two floors of space. When the heavy machine guns opened
up, the walls shook, and the building actually trembled. Most were
taking it pretty calmly, although the telephone operator was getting
nervous. When we heard about the ultimatum, the bombing of La
Moneda, we all got pretty scared."

During an earlier exchange Pinochet had remarked: "Killing the
dog puts an end to the rabies."

Now he wanted to know whether the vaccine was taking.

"Tell me, Patricio," he asked Carvajal on the radio, "with everything that has been done so far, hasn't that gentleman reacted?"

The answer: no, he had not.

Amid the sounds and fury of war, several still sought a peaceful way
out. Foreign and Interior Ministers Almeyda and Briones, and former
Defense Minister, José Tohá appealed to Allende with every argu-
ment they could imagine, trying to persuade him that to surrender
now was the only way to convert what was happening into a lost battle
rather than a lost war. " 'No, and that is final,' " he told us," Briones
said. " 'I will leave here dead.' "

"He was a changed man that morning," Briones, a man who had
known and admired Allende for a quarter of a century, said.

The other peacemakers were the three military aides. They requested a private interview with Allende, and he agreed. The president was then surrounded—as he would be most of the day—by a
group of GAPs and others. Several of them noisily protested that
milicos (the slang word for military) could not be trusted and they
would not leave Allende alone with them. Allende then ordered everyone out of the room, but several GAPs remained in a corner.

"With that," Grez said, "he got up and shouted: 'I want everyone
out of here because I am going to talk to them.' Some still stayed in
a corner, so we went into a small room. Altogether it took ten minutes
for us to begin the conversation, and once we did, it didn't last but
six or eight minutes."

"Each one of us gave him our estimate of the military situation, and
told him we each had a duty to fulfill in trying to persuade him. I
pointed out to him the futility of a few armed guys attempting to hold
out against the coordinated action of the entire armed forces, including an air force attack on the palace. I also told him that I, at least,

would not act against personnel of the armed forces, even if he should order it. Since I was the junior aide, I was the last to speak."

"He then told us he would not give up. He was not going to leave his office, and he was not going to negotiate with the commanders in chief on the conditions they demanded [unconditional surrender, with freedom to leave the country with his family]. He told us, as the only representatives of the armed forces present at that moment, that his final decision was to stay in La Moneda, he was going to defend himself, and for that he had this, pointing to his submachine gun.

" 'I will defend myself,' he said, 'until the end, and if it is necessary, the last shot of this machine gun I will shoot here'—and with that he lifted his index finger and put it inside the roof of his mouth. The gun was then on his lap."

"Major Sánchez, who had been with him the longest, tried again to persuade him. but he was adamant. He then authorized us to leave the palace and report to our respective institutions.

"Then he said a formal farewell to each of us. He shook hands with us, and then he got up and left. He called out, in a very loud voice, to those outside and told them of his decision to let us go."

Grez noted that before the meeting began, he had traced in his mind four possibilities: (1) Allende would order them arrested and used as hostages; (2) order them to stay under his command; (3) send them to the Defense Minister as negotiators; (4) let them go. "I never thought for an instant," Grez said, "that he would order us killed."

After that fateful meeting, each of the aides was on his own. Grez went to his desk and took some things from it, stalling for time to see how Allende's men would react. ("I wanted to be ready in case anyone should attack us.") Next, he summoned the six or eight navy personnel attached to the palace as stewards, plus his driver and his own aide, and told each of them to get out as best as they could. It was then 10:20 A.M.

"There was a tremendous amount of shooting outside," Grez said. "Sánchez and I made for Morandé 80 [the side door]. Badiola stayed back a little. When we got there, the Carabinero opened the door, and we ran out. We stayed pressed close to the wall as we ran out—it was difficult and dangerous. We got to Liberty Plaza [on the south side of La Moneda] just as two tanks rolled up. Then we crossed Alameda on that one catwalk over the tunnel. That was the most difficult part of all, because in our dress uniforms we stuck out like sore thumbs.

[Altogether, they had crossed perhaps 400 yards of an area completely enfiladed by gunfire.] At the ministry we separated. I went directly to Admiral Carvajal's office and reported.

" 'Tell me what happened,' he said.

" 'He's not going to leave La Moneda,' I told him."

"Conforme [O.K.]," said Pinochet when Carvajal radioed Grez's report. "At ten to eleven I am going to give the order to bomb. Consequently, all units should withdraw at that time two blocks from La Moneda. . . . "

Told that the Carabinero palace guard was then coming out, Pinochet also gave orders that they should not be fired on as they left. Carvajal told him too, that General Mendoza, by then in close contact with the ministry, had just reported that the general headquarters of the Carabineros had been neutralized.

In the palace, Allende summoned all but a few lookouts to the Toesca Salon, the elegant and spacious room used in normal times for State receptions. According to his daughter Isabel, he told them: "I have taken this decision, I will remain here until the end. They offered me an airplane to leave the country. I rejected that offer. That would be even more infamous than the behavior of those traitorous generals." He added that he would fight to the end, but did not wish to waste lives uselessly. So, he said, the women must leave, as well as any men who could not handle a gun.

Patricio Guijón did not hear that speech. In fact, he heard Allende speak only once that day, when the president came downstairs later on one of his rounds to cheer up his "troops" and check on supplies and defensive positions. But Guijón did not hesitate when they told him he could go. Although he and the other doctors had not yet treated their first patient, despite all the shooting, they agreed their place was there.

As Allende was speaking to those in the palace, two Hawker Hunter jets were preparing to take off from the air force base at Concepción, 400 miles to the southwest. Their pilots still did not know their targets. But they were prepared for almost anything. Shortly after the air force moved their precious Hawker Hunters several weeks earlier for safekeeping away from Santiago to more easily defended bases, the commander of one of those bases—at Concepción—had drilled his pilots on low-level missions over the coal-mining cities of Coronel and Lota. To the point, in fact, where the governor asked whether those noisy flights could not be stopped. The answer: they were indispensable.

Those forty British-made Hawker Hunters were a "gift" Allende had made to the air force. At the time Allende took office, the Chilean Air Force was down to a piddling twenty-nine combat planes, fifteen of them wheezing relics of World War II (B-26 light bombers). Neighboring Peru, meantime, had already dodged the U.S. ban on sales of sophisticated weapons to Latin America by outfitting themselves with a dozen French supersonic Mirage fighters. As part of his campaign to woo the military, Allende ordered two missile destroyers and two submarines, also from Britain, for the navy, the jets for the air force, and dangled before all services the promise of $300 million in Soviet military credits.

Streaking down the runway at Concepción, the jets were only one hour twenty minutes from downtown Santiago.

With time running out, former Defense Minister José Tohá decided to try once more. He put in a call from the palace to Carvajal at his Defense Ministry command post, and asked for ten more minutes to try to convince Allende. With a courtly manner matching Tohá's own, Carvajal said he would do what was possible to obtain a temporary cease-fire. But he noted that snipers were not paying much attention to "his orders." And, he reminded Tohá, those planes are already enroute.

Tohá protested that he had done all he could to convince Allende.

"Then take him by force," Carvajal urged.

Tohá reminded him that the president was armed with a submachine gun.

And indeed he was. His daughter Isabel carried away a memory of "my father, a watchful combatant, moving from window to window, cheering up the members of his personal guard [the GAP], keeping his sense of humor even in the most miserable moments, blasting away with a machine gun at the tanks of the rebels." Allende was hardly in a mood for "negotiations." The only ones that interested him by then were persuading his daughters and the other women in the palace to leave. The implacable clock was closing in on him.

He took aside his daughter Beatriz, the fighter and companion and confidante so close to his own ideals. Finally, he persuaded her: the fight must go on. You must carry the fight beyond these walls, beyond these borders. Finally she agreed. But time was running out.

There were less than twenty minutes left before the aerial bombardment was due to begin when Allende realized he must act. He again dialed General Baeza's number, but this time Baeza was not at his desk, but four floors above with Carvajal, on the ninth floor of the Defense Ministry. Precious minutes were lost as Baeza hurried back to his telephone. More excruciating seconds passed as he dialed and dialed Allende's number and the phone kept buzzing busy. At last he got through. Allende told him:

"General, I want you to tell the commanders in chief I need ten extra minutes so that the women can leave the palace. One of them is my daughter, and she is pregnant. [That was Beatriz, but Isabel was also there.) It is simple humanity. There are a great number of men here, but none of them will leave. Only the women."

"I'll do what I can," Baeza promised, "but it's going to be very difficult, because those planes are already approaching. Mr. President, I insist, you must lay down your arms. The armed forces will guarantee your safety, and that of the members of your family. You are risking too many lives."

Baeza said Allende clung "stubbornly" to his position.

In his bucolic headquarters, far from the scene of the fighting, General Pinochet asked repeatedly for assurances that the battle was being pressed energetically.

After Carvajal had given him the names of the units already in action, Pinochet replied:

"Good, because this cluck is not going to give himself up."

"We are attacking already," Carvajal told him, "we are surrounding and attacking with considerable intensity. Soon we are going to be able to take it [the palace]."

"O.K." said Pinochet, "and as soon as we do, we drop him off at the airplane and send him on his way."

Carvajal reminded Pinochet that Allende had refused the offer of the airplane and wanted the commandants to come to the palace.

"What he wants," Pinochet said, "is for us to get there so they can stick us in a dungeon . . . so the answer is no. For now, attack La Moneda—hard!"

A few minutes later Pinochet told the admiral. "This is final, that he give up and hand in his resignation. This is the last time we will address him as president. He will be guaranteed his life and physical safety and sent abroad. Ten to eleven: resign and there will be no more bloodshed. Otherwise, to the last consequences!"

Carvajal: "In other words, the offer stands to take him out of the country."

Pinochet: "The offer stands to take him out of the country. But if the plane should crash as it were taking off . . . " (Nervous giggling followed this flash of gallows humor.)

With the deadline rapidly approaching, the appeals for the time multiplied: Major Badiola, by then in the Defense Military, relayed one from Allende, General Baeza another. Allende himself called Carvajal, and Carvajal agreed, after a sharp exchange.

"Take care, Admiral, that the fascists don't kill them [the women]," Allende said.

"What 'fascists' are you talking about, Mr. Allende," Carvajal shot back.

"I know you," Allende said, "you are a sailor and not a fascist."

Allende went to the waiting women and a number of men who had decided to leave with them. He told them Carvajal had pledged a five-minute cease-fire so that the women could leave before the bombs fell.

"Papa," his daughter Isabel protested, "you still believe in the word of a military man!"

Beatriz protested that if they left, they would be taken as hostages.

"They'll kill us," she said. Allende said it would be better if the military killed the women, because "then history will judge them not only as traitors but as murderers of women."

He added: "Please, go. You have a mother to look after. You, Tati [Beatriz], you have your husband; your duty is to be with him." In the face of further protests, he said:

"If you don't leave, you'll force me to go into the street with you."

The girls broke down crying, kissed their father, and waited at the side door. As Carvajal promised, the military stopped shooting, but the snipers did not. The jeep sent from the Defense Ministry to pick them up was forced to turn back. Finally, Isabel, Beatriz, and the other women scurried into the streets. They were on their own.

The negotiations to delay the bombing provoked a brief crack in the facade of military unity. It happened when Patricio Carvajal reported that Tohá was on the line at that moment, asking for a cease-fire to get the women out, and that he and Briones and Almeyda were trying to get Allende to negotiate.

"This is Augusto," Pinochet broke in. "Confirm that you hear me, Patricio . . . this gentleman is buying time. He is trying to take advantage of us. I do not accept any negotiations. What 'conditions'? There are no 'decorous' conditions. What sort of crap is he trying to pull? Unconditional surrender! Is that clear? If he wants to go, accompanied by Sepúlveda [the deposed Carabinero chief], to the ministry to surrender, good. If not, we are going to bomb."

In one of the rare instances that day when he seemed to be seeking support for his decisions, Pinochet next called Leigh.

"Gustavo, Augusto is calling you," intermediary Pino said. The message from Pinochet was similar to what he had just given Carvajal, though calmer. Now it was Leigh's turn to lose his cool.

"Position Two to Position Three," he said, aiming his message at the relay station. "It is nefarious to give delays and accept negotiations. All this talk is turning things around. Tohá, Almeyda, all of them, let's send them anywhere—except Argentina."

Leigh then asked, "Do we or don't we attack La Moneda?" His pilots were already holding just south of the city. Static and cross-talk snarled communications in those crucial moments. To make matters worse, Leigh was unable to get through immediately to Pinochet. Pinochet was talking on the telephone and unable to come to the radio. Over the crackling came the voice of Leigh: "To hell with delaying tactics, jeeps, and women. I am going to attack now. Over and out." Then Pinochet came back on the line: give them three minutes to get out, three minutes, he commanded. It would take all of three minutes simply to relay the messages through Cadet Pino's "command" post, but the refugees they were trying to save had already fled anyway.

The air attack was halted, the planes ordered back to base to refuel.

Leigh told Pinochet: "The air attack is now scheduled for 11:40. Conforme?"

Pinochet gave his "conforme."

Battles, and the ghosts of them, were meanwhile breaking out elsewhere around the city, and around the country.

At midmorning Pinochet reported that he had just learned Socialist brigades were planning to attack the Defense Ministry. Pinochet told Carvajal to make sure the troops were ready, with automatic arms in the windows. The attack never came. Fortunately, for it would have been suicidal stupidity.

Far to the south, another kind of brigade was launching an attack that was anything but suicidal. The vaunted "Comandante Pepe," the swaggering scourge of landowners in the south of Chile for the past three years, was laying siege to a military garrison with a rough-and-ready force of eighty fellow MIRistas. Except that the "garrison" was a small Carabinero outpost, manned by a sergeant (Benito Carrasco Riffo), a corporal (Juan Campos Campos), two Carabineros (René Cáceres Aedo and Belisario Navarette Sánchez), and the sergeant's wife, Rosa García.

The real name of "Comandante Pepe," leader of that attack force, was José Gabriel Lliendo Vera. A thirty-three-year-old former agronomy student, he had lorded it over a "liberated" territory of 860,000 acres of farm and timberland in the mountain and lakes region south of Temuco. A force of over three thousand farmhands worked those expropriated properties. To rule his fiefdom, "Comandante Pepe" counted on a force of about four hundred MIRistas. Despite his obvious lawlessness, he was unmolested by officialdom, which denied he existed. It did not prevent a number of government people, including Laura Allende and the secretary-general of government, Jaime Suárez, from being photographed with the "mythical" bandit.

A small man, with medium sideburns, black hair, black eyes and black moustache, "Comandante Pepe" lived in a world of absolutes. He told British author Alistair Horne, as early as 1971, "Civil war is inevitable in Chile." A year later he went off to Cuba, but returned in time for his prophecy to be fulfilled. The target he picked out when war did come was a rustic wooden outpost, surrounded by log fences and vaguely suggesting a frontier fort. It was located at Neltume, in the beautiful forest region of Valdivia Province, on the shores of Lake Panguipulli.

Like figures in a Western movie, the defenders moved from window to window of the two-story outpost, staving off the attackers. Inside, Mrs. García loaded guns, distributed ammunition and water. The ending was also Hollywood: their ammunition running low, the defenders were saved when a relief column of Carabineros reached them. "Comandante Pepe" and his men scattered. Many, including their commander and his violent-talking consort, Valentina, were tracked and caught by an army rifle unit. "Comandante Pepe" was later executed.

North of Santiago, in the province of Antofagasta, a group of MIRistas from a nitrate mine attacked another isolated Carabinero outpost. A Hawker Hunter, patrolling along the mountainous frontier, was diverted to help. The pilot made one low pass over the attackers.

"They were so terrified," General Leigh recounted, "that they all started waving white handkerchiefs. End of attack."

In Santiago fighting broke out at several points as morning wore on, and groups loyal to the government had a chance to react. Students from the State Technical University and the Abelardo Nuñez High School, armed with submachine guns, attacked the 11th Carabinero Precinct. One Carabinero was killed and several wounded before the attack could be repelled. Another armed group shot up the headquarters of right-wing National Party in downtown Santiago.

The first international incident involved, almost inevitably, the Cuban Embassy. A group of civilians rolled garbage cans into Los Estanques Street, where the embassy was located, to block access to it. Officials of the embassy dismantled the barricade and fired shots in the air. An army unit moved up close to control the situation. Pinochet got a report from the scene:

"From the embassy of Cuba, which is surrounded," he radioed Carvajal, "they fired with machine guns on our troops. In consequence, you are to advise the ambassador, call him on the telephone, and tell him the following: they fired on our troops. In consequence, to avoid international problems, there is a plane available to take him to his country. Tell him that we break relations, that he should pack his bags and be ready to go within twenty-four hours. General Benavides gave me the information [about the shooting], and he would not lie to me."

Bullets would continue to fly around that embassy into the night; charges and countercharges for days afterward.

Leigh's premonitions about the vulnerability of his planes at Los Cerrillos were confirmed midmorning when snipers opened fire with machine guns on the base. They were firing from a tower of a factory, one of many in that area that had made the "Cordón Cerrillos" the most intimidating of the bastions in Allende's industrial Maginot Line. The defenders, a thousand yards away, had readied, however, a weapon of their own invention even Leigh did not know about. They maneuvered it into place now. It was an artillery piece, fitted to fire airplane rockets. It took but a single round from this explosive monster to silence the snipers.

Scattered resistance was encountered at other points around the city as morning became noon, but for all practical purposes Allende's hopes of any army of militiamen springing to his defense had been decisively dashed. Only the hardcore fought with him—the GAPs, the MIRistas, here and there, members of the sabre-rattling "brigades" of the Communist and Socialist parties. And since it was left to these "professionals," so it was that the most intense fighting of the morning away from La Moneda raged at precisely the spot where the largest number of them were clustered: Tomás Moro. The first army unit on the scene seemed to have wandered into the waiting circle of fire almost as if by mistake. As its men were arriving, Pinochet was on the radio asking whether Carabineros had occupied the estate yet. There were no Carabineros, only a few soldiers and a couple of dozen officer cadets from the Military Academy. Cpl. Sáez Ayala was aboard one of the buses that morning when they set out on what was supposed to be a patrol. And a well-armed one: they had with them, aboard those buses and a ¾–ton truck, bazookas, rocket launchers, grenades, .30-caliber machine guns; the men were carrying 20-round automatic rifles.

"We came under fire even before we could see the wall around the place," Sáez said. "They were shooting at us from an apartment building a little to the left of the place. We were approaching from Pehuen Street, from the northwest, and were about to round the corner onto Tomás Moro Street when it started.

"A lieutenant ordered us to break for cover on a side street directly opposite the front wall. Most of the shooting was coming from machine guns mounted on watchtowers over the main gate."

The "patrol" was aborted, and the troops pulled back to await help.

René Largo Farías, the vigilant radio-monitor who gave Allende the first alarm of suspicious troop movements in the now long-ago hours of the night of September 10-11, wandered alone through the halls of the palace, time running out on the postponement of the bombing attack. Someone offered him a gun, which he declined. He had never used one. Augusto Olivares discovered him and said he should leave, since he was useless to them there, but could do some good outside. Olivares practically pushed him out the door onto

Morandé Street. Alone, in a no-man's-land devoid of persons, filled only with the sounds of intense gunfire. Farías walked slowly, with his hands in the air. Incredibly, he kept right on walking . . . all the way to his house, a dozen blocks away. For Farías the war was over.

In the palace, Allende was waging a private war, against the memory of the country's past. "Let's give ourselves the pleasure," he told his companions, "of smashing the busts of all these old reactionaries." With a wave of the hand, he indicated the busts of the country's past presidents. "Respect only those of José Manuel Balmaceda [who committed suicide after his regime came toppling down in strikingly similar circumstances in 1891] and Pedro Aguirre Cerda, the only democratic presidents." [Aguirre Cerda had headed the first Popular Front government thirty-five years before.]

With that, he started knocking the busts off their pedestals himself. The scene was witnessed by one woman who had not left the palace with the others: La Payita.

"When he was pressuring the women to leave," she said, "I hid in a small cellar tunnel. I had decided to fight at his side to the very end. A little while later the president discovered me.

" 'I knew you would figure out some way to get around me,' he said.

"Soon after that, Bartulín [one of the doctors] asked me for the key to his car because he wanted to give it to a companion who had to go. [She offered no clarification of this mysterious incident.]

"A bit later I spoke again to the president. I asked him how he had convinced Beatriz and Isabel to leave. He answered: "I told them they would be in charge of taking a personal message to Fidel."

"Afterward, he called us all together in the Winter Garden. He gave new instructions, then spoke to his friend, Joan Garcés, asking him to go. 'This fight is not for you,' he said, 'because you are a foreigner.'

"At another point I heard Carlos Jorquera [the press chief] say to Allende as he greeted Lautaro Ojeda: 'You see, President, how your old friends don't let you down? Here we are, at your side, though a little afraid, right, Lautaro, old fellow?' "

Around 11:00 A.M. "César" discovered that the newly won "silence" had been broken: Radio Corporación was back on the air, this time on FM. An air force major, firing an automatic rifle from the fourth floor of the Defense Ministry, managed to knock out the antenna of the station on the roof of the State Bank Building across the street. Once again, the airwaves belonged to the junta.

Leon Vilarín, one of the men who had made this revolution happen, was in hiding at the home of a truck driver when it all broke out. For several weeks an order had been out for his arrest, an order he took delight in mocking. On August 12 he even turned up as a guest on the popular "A Esta Hora Se Improvisa" television program and defied the police to catch him when he left; Allende's own barber, Vilarín's personal "spy" in La Moneda, came over, helped to disguise him, and Vilarín left the studio the next day. His mission: to tell the truck drivers of Chile, via the network of the revolution, that the strike was over. They had won.

Others would do the same that day—shopkeepers, engineers, and other unions who had banded together in a fight to save a way of life. One who proclaimed the strike over with special satisfaction: Dr. Edgardo Cruz Mena, secretary-general of the Chilean Medical Society. Only the previous Thursday *Clarín,* as part of the campaign of vilification of him, had published a front-page taunt: "Dr. Cruz Mena, antipatriot: the people are going to hang you by the balls."

During that late morning lull the military command tended to some of the details of how they would manage the immediate aftermath of their revolution. It was clear, from the improvisations, that they had given little advance thought to it.

Leigh proposed declaring a state of siege, the constitutional device for giving the military complete control over the internal life of the country, and a curfew effective at 6:00 P.M. that day. Pinochet agreed excitedly. He said the communique should add that the provisions of martial law would apply, meaning that any person "caught with arms, or explosives, is going to be shot on the spot, without trial." Later, Carvajal proposed using the Chile Arena and the National Stadium —the first an indoor arena, the second the city's major outdoor stadium—for prisoners. Again, there was quick agreement.

Speaking of prisoners, Pinochet said to Carvajal: "Patricio, tell me: Altamirano, this Enríquez, and this other one, Palestro, and that crowd, any idea where they are? Have you found them, or have they gone underground?"

Carvajal: "I have no information on where they are."

Pinochet: "Give instructions to the intelligence services of the three branches to find them and take them prisoner, because they must have gone underground. They are real snakes."

Pinochet was worried about still another missing man.

"The problem of Allende," he said, "has me worried, because this *huaso* is running around in circles." (*Huaso* is a vulgar term for gaucho, the Latin American equivalent of cowboy.)

Leigh weighed in with still another suggestion: to issue a communique stating that the attack on La Moneda was going to be carried out because of Allende's refusal to surrender and to avoid further bloodshed.

With the possibility of a major uprising of Allende people still not discarded, Leigh told Pinochet he had two LAN-Chile planes standing by in Antofagasta, ready to transport troops to Santiago if needed. (In the days ahead, the LAN planes would be used frequently in troop transport and other military operations.)

Their interchange turned suddenly somber again on the secret network. A report was relayed to Pinochet that unknown elements were surrounding the Military Hospital, the main military medical facility in Santiago. He ordered the report checked immediately and defense measures taken (the report proved false), and added: "Those who dare go out in the streets to attack us, well, there isn't blood enough to save them."

He also received a report of the intense sniper fire from the roof of the State Bank building, and asked Leigh whether he could provide crews for two army U-H helicopters to "sweep" that and other rooftops with machine-gun fire. Leigh agreed, but there was a long delay, a fatefully long delay.

Before noon the only other major armed and trained organization in the country fell into their hands: Investigaciónes, the two thousand man detective force. Julio Rada, then prefect of Santiago and "attached to our cause" (that of the revolution), took control of the Investigaciónes headquarters.

An air of fatalism prevailed in the area immediately around "ground zero"—the squat palace of La Moneda—as the time of the new attack approached. Over the armed forces radio network warnings went out repeatedly to civilians to stay off the streets, and for those in or around the palace to seek secure shelter. Many, philosophically, decided to stay where they were. Many were unwilling to believe the attack would take place at all. Few believed it could happen without surrounding buildings suffering damage.

For some the damage had already occurred.

"I had been calling around to the various news media," the U.S. Embassy's Jim Halsema said, "and when I got the United Press International, there was quite a delay before Steve Yolen got to the telephone. When he did, he was huffing and puffing."

"What's going on?," Halsema asked. "Why all the panting?"

"You'd be huffing and puffing, too," Yolen shot back, "if you had had to crawl on your belly to answer the telephone."

Bullets began crashing into the UPI office shortly after Colonel Canessa came under fire in the plaza below. It went on for six hours, "the longest six hours of my life," Yolen said, "it was like the end of the world." More than four hundred impacts were counted on the walls of the UPI suite of offices. Not a plate of glass remained unsmashed in the long bank of windows facing Nataniel Street and the Defense Ministry across the way. At one point, Yolen said, it was so bad that the office was filled with concrete dust as the bullets pinged into the walls. To the din of their own hell was added the noise of the tanks booming away below.

Bad as it was, it might have been worse. Mason met one of the soldiers next day who was among those ordered to fire at UPI from the Defense Ministry. The soldier was a draftee and son of a UPI employee.

"I knew you were newsmen and not snipers," he told Mason, "but who listens to a draftee in the middle of a battle? So I pretended to shoot at you, but actually was aiming at the 'Yoga' sign next to you."

As good newsmen, the UPI men could not resist the need to know exactly what was going on down below, and so from time to time they peeked through the windows. Each time they did, they drew a new volley of fire.

When the shooting started, Yolen had ordered all the "support" people, including his secretary, to seek the safety of a lower floor. He, Gutiérrez, Mason, and one messenger, Mario Ibaca, remained. None of them was hurt. Furthermore, despite the siege, UPI managed to get their big story out. At 11:00 A.M. the agency's correspondent in Mendoza, Argentina, got through on a forgotten private line. The line was kept open for eight hours, permitting Santiago's UPI to dictate a story directly from the scene of the major action. Including the biggest story of all, then only minutes away.

Another civilian installation was also taking heavy gunfire by mistake. In the case of the Hotel Carrera, however, it was not gunfire coming from the building but a freak circumstance that triggered the frenzy of firing. Snipers were firing at the troops in the Plaza Constitución from all sides, including the offices of the Government Petrochemical Company (SOQUIMICH) directly across Agustinas Street from the hotel (and on the same sidewalk as the embassy). In the heat of the battle one or more of the soldiers believed the firing was coming from the hotel, and so opened fire at it. As the bullets thudded into thirty-five-year-old crusty concrete of the building, they raised smoke and sparks. From below that smoke and the sparks looked like the flash of guns, and so the more the troops below fired, the more it looked as though they were being fired upon. Round after round was pumped into windows of the hotel, and the facade of the building was stitched by patterns of machine gun fire. Altogether, seventy-nine rooms suffered damage. Hardest hit were rooms number 821 and 1121, the latter that of the manager, Mike Gallegos. (His wife Nena and daughter Danai, thirteen, were not in the suite during the shooting; they had left to help out as soon as trouble started that morning.) The suite took over 290 bullet impacts. In the window air conditioner alone, Gallegos later found nine bullets and perforations made by twelve to fifteen more. The shooting was so intense that the hot lead set fire to curtains in the suite. Altogether, the hotel suffered $200,000 damage, an absurd figure calculated on the unrealistic rate of exchange then in effect for the dollar. Actually, it was much higher, and the damage uncovered, of course, by insurance.

Thanks to Gallegos's cool-headed control over his guests, only one of the approximately 520 persons in the building was wounded: a newspaperman caught shrapnel in his shoulder and was treated in the hotel's clinic.

At the American Embassy, all offices facing Agustinas Street had been evacuated as soon as the shooting started. It was a prudent precaution. Windows on the two top floors occupied by the embassy (the ninth and tenth) were shattered by gunfire; those on the three lower floors (fifth to eighth) were not. The main concern at the embassy was that an enraged Marxist mob might attack. That fear dissolved when they saw the show of anti-Allende force clearly in command of the streets below. Their security needs having been abated, their thoughts turned to food. The operators of the small embassy snack bar did not make it in that morning. The problem of how to break into it was solved by a man whose usual job was to keep people out, the embassy security officer. The forgetfulness of Jim

Halsema's wife in preparing the sandwiches he had wanted to take along that day was solved. Although Halsema and a skeletal staff would remain in the embassy for three days, the food supply never ran out. Norma Price, a secretary in that captive skeletal staff, turned out to be a whiz of a snack-bar cook.

But the war was far from over for the embassy staff. Security once again became the uppermost priority when they learned of the impending bombing raid on the nearby presidential palace. Halsema and other officers herded everyone into the basement to sweat it out.

Through the morning Hector Humeres had watched the raging battle through a crack in the heavy metal blinds of his office. He could make out clearly the snipers in the Public Works Building directly opposite. He saw the tanks open up on La Moneda. Since there was no firing from the Contraloría, the one government building around La Moneda not infiltrated by snipers, only a few shots were fired at the building. One of them impacted near the entrance to Humeres's office. Otherwise, he and the fifty-odd Contraloría employees who made it into the building that day were awed spectators of a war being fought at their very feet. As the time for the bombing neared, Humeres and one or two others gave up their ringside seats and headed for what they hoped would be the safety of the basement.

"There was no panic," he said, "because I had seen demonstrations of rockets before." Brave words: no more than 50 feet separated the Contraloría from La Moneda.

Half a block up from the palace on the eastern side, Vicente Garrido and the others trapped inside the offices of *La Prensa* were debating what to do when about ten Carabineros came in and told them to clear out, pronto. Garrido and a few others were escorted half a block away from the palace to the corner of Estado and Moneda streets. "You're now on your own," a Carabinero officer said. Garrido set out to retrace his footsteps of only a few hours earlier. But this time he was a man alone in a city under siege.

"I was scared, plenty scared, especially of the snipers. Most of the way I was in and out of doorways and so close to the walls I almost became part of the masonry.

The time was approximately 11:30 A.M. Rising tension took its toll on the commanders of what was now, irrevocably, a fight to the finish that could be decided only by force of arms. As the moment for the daring air attack neared, communications apparently failed the air force commander, and he had to appeal over the secret radio network to General Díaz, at the Defense Ministry, for "urgent information, immediately" about the takeoff of the Hawker Hunters from Concepción.

"It is vital, he needs to know immediately," an aide told Defense.

Reassured that the planes had already taken off, Leigh went on the air with a message to Pinochet: there would be a slight delay, but the planes would be at the target shortly. Pinochet, jittery because of reports that arms were being distributed to Allende militiamen in the posh Vitacura and Las Condes sectors of the city, exploded:

"*Why* are they behind schedule? Armed groups are forming all over the place!"

Through the laborious relay system Leigh informed Pinochet that the planes had been forced to refuel at Concepción. Pinochet was only partly placated.

"If there is another delay," he barked, "I'll attack with infantry and tanks. That's my decision." In the ensuing confusion an order was actually given for the Second Armored Regiment to launch a frontal attack on La Moneda, but the order never reached the unit. The order that did reach the units surrounding the palace was the one for them to withdraw to safe positions—the air attack was imminent.

"We moved back 150 yards," Corporal Pizzarro said, "and even so, some of the guys were scared. But I wasn't, because I had seen air attacks before, in maneuvers, and besides we had already been under so much fire that morning. I was more concerned about what was going to happen after the air attack."

Inside La Moneda Allende led a group of GAPs and cronies to a small room in the basement, more like a medieval vault than a room. When Briones arrived with Almeyda, the Tohá brothers, and Aníbal Palma, they discovered there was no room there. Rank no longer mattered, only survival. In panic and confusion, they fled through the open courtyard at the south wing of the building. There, they were saved by a forlorn Foreign Ministry employee named Ernesto Espinoza.

"I arrived that day at about eight," Espinoza said. "When I realized how serious the situation was, I tried to leave, first by the Moneda door, then by Morandé, but sniper fire prevented me from doing so. So I decided to barricade myself in my office on the first floor. From there I called my family to reassure them I was all right and tell them what was happening."

Espinoza was still in his office, listening to a small transistor radio announcing the imminent air raid, when he heard voices in the hall outside.

"I looked out, and there was Almeyda, the Tohá brothers, Briones, and "el Pibe" [a nickname, which translates roughly as "the Kid"] Palma, and a newsman from the TV department of the Office of Information and Radio. They were all calm, and I invited them to join me in my office. We knew the bombing was coming, and each of them began telephoning their homes. They had come to be with Allende, and he had practically kicked them out of the basement.

"We debated where to take shelter, and first went to the vault of the Records Office. But I didn't know the combination, and we didn't even try to force that iron door. Luckily, I remembered the boiler room, located in the basement. We went downstairs and pushed the door in. There we waited, thinking we were more or less safe. In any case, we had all said good-bye to our families."

Carlos Briones waited with a different feeling.

"I thought we would die there," he said.

The atmosphere was less somber at the other end of the palace, where Allende and some thirty others waited for the attack he still seemed to believe was unthinkable. Allende had armed himself with a bottle of whiskey "to while away the raid," as one of those present would later put it. Among those with him: La Payita, Jorquera, Olivares, Joignant, Daniel Vergara, and Puccio.

Payita said that every time the subject of the bombing came up, Allende brushed it off. "Don't be afraid, they won't dare," he said. With time running out, he flirted with the idea of a desperate gamble: he would make a dash for the presidential garage across the street, to link up with the larger force of snipers in the Public Works Ministry. Someone suggested forming a flying wedge around him. That idea was discarded. Allende advanced another: they would ask for a five-minute truce and use the time to make a getaway. Jaime Barrios told him, "Mr. President, you can't ask for another truce."

"Don't you know, Jaimito," Allende answered, "that five minutes are sufficient to change history?" This idea, too, fizzled, and, finally, the group made their way to the basement shelter.

"A few compañeros [Allende preferred that term, meaning "companions," to the more polemic "comrades"] began arriving semiasphyxiated," Payita recalled. "The president took off his mask and gave it to one of them. A girl also came in. She was very faint, but she began to sing, softly, 'Cuba, how pretty is Cuba.' "

In the Congress building, three blocks away, the military aide-de-camp shepherded the wives of the truck drivers and the others who had made it to the Capitol that morning down to the basement of the Senate to sit out the attack. "We were singing and trying to cheer up those who were afraid. There was cheering and some crying, and we were all nervous, but somehow," one of them said later, "we weren't afraid."

"Station One, Station Three calling. Station Two advises that in seven minutes the Hawker Hunters will bombard La Moneda."

Cadet Pino's voice betrayed the excitement of his message as he asked Pinochet's headquarters to acknowledge the message. "Déme Roger [Give me a 'roger'], he said. "Recibido conforme" came back the laconic reply, that is, "Got it O.K."

The pilots of the two planes selected for the attack were then circling just south of the city when they learned the identity of their target: La Moneda. Until that instant they knew no more than that they were to fly to Santiago and await target instructions.

They came out of the northeast, circling the San Cristóbal Hill in screaming descent from 5,000 feet. Dr. Zoltan Bernath saw them from the patio of his home in the eastern suburbs, and reflected on how lucky he was: normally he would have been at his office on the seventh floor of the building at Valentín Letelier #96, just a short block north of the target, La Moneda. Bernath reflected, too, on the stubborness of Salvador Allende, a man he had never met but, from the window of his office had often seen entering and leaving that seat of power about to crumble in smoke and flame.

Jorge Braña saw them, too, from the fifth-floor window of the Esso offices just to the left of the palace. Not since the earliest days of Chilean aviation, June 4, 1932, had air force planes flown over the capital in anger and threatened La Moneda. That time it was to herald a leftist revolution and the birth of the country's brief but crucial Socialist republic, the first in the Western Hemisphere.

By the time Hugo Ravera glanced up to see what everyone was staring at, the planes had already released the first of their deadly missiles. Hurtling down at 480 knots (545 miles) per hour, each of the planes released a brace of rockets from a height of 500 meters and a distance of 800 meters, approximately, as they passed over the Mapocho railroad station.

Each of the planes carried eighteen rockets, some explosive, some penetrating. The pilot could fire two at a time, in groups of four or all eighteen at once. Once he lined up the target in a gyroscopic range finder, it took four to eight seconds from the instant he pressed the button until the rockets streaked out at supersonic speeds toward the target.

The first pass was at 11:52 A.M. The second plane was one minute behind. Over and over again they returned, four times, each of them, each time raining stunning destruction on the palace. In all, nineteen rockets blasted the squat palace. Not one missed the target.

At 12:13 P.M. it was over.

"First, there was dark smoke," Jorge Braña observed from the Esso offices on Plaza Constitución, "then white. Later, much later, I saw the flames begin to rise from the northeast corner."

Huddled in the basement of the office building housing the American Embassy, only a couple hundred yards away, combat veteran Jim Halsema said he never realized the attack had happened. "We didn't hear the rockets as such," Halsema said, "just more sounds of war."

Those sounds of war were unmistakable for Steve Yolen and his UPI cohorts crouched on the floor of the new agency's offices directly across the Alameda from the besieged palace.

"The planes passed directly over us and dropped their bombs," Yolen said. "I counted at least twenty high-explosive bombs. We all prayed the planes wouldn't miss, because we were on the top floor."

While UPI was relaying word of the attack to the outside world via the forgotten circuit to the Argentine city of Mendoza, Gen. Nicanor Díaz was reporting to his superiors, Pinochet and Leigh, on the results:

"Direct hit," Díaz said over heavy static. "There is a large fire in the center of La Moneda."

The attack on La Moneda completed, Leigh turned his attention to an unexpected target: Tomás Moro. Because of stiff resistance there, Pinochet had asked the air force to "soften it up." That attack only narrowly missed becoming a catastrophe.

First Leigh sent a helicopter to strafe.

"But," he said, "the shooting was too intense—there were GAPs everywhere, on the rooftops, everywhere, and they were shooting even at the pigeons flying overhead. So I ordered a plane to attack, reluctantly because Tomás Moro is, after all, in the middle of a residential area."

This time the pilot did miss. With a rapidly lowering ceiling and the needle-in-a-haystack problem of picking out one house among many, even an estate as large as Tomás Moro, the pilot sighted what he believed was the pathfinder helicopter. It turned out to be a helicopter that had moved away from the target area and was then hovering over the Air Force Hospital, only ten blocks northeast of the presidential estate on the direct approach path of the attacking plane. Three times the jet swooped over the "target," unleashing a total of twelve rockets.

Luckily, the jet blasted a partly finished new wing and not the main hospital building. Still, fourteen persons were wounded in the raid (no one was killed).

When the mistake was discovered, Leigh immediately ordered a new, "light" attack on Tomás Moro. This time the pilot did not miss: two or three rockets crashed into the residence from the north side.

By then Hortensia Allende had fled. Sometime around 11:00 A.M., Isabel Letelier, still trying to get a telephone fix on what was going on, got through to Mrs. Allende at Tomás Moro. "She was very annoyed," Mrs. Letelier said, "because they wouldn't let her go to La Moneda.

" 'I'm going to get in a car and go by myself,' she told me. 'I want to be at Salvador's side.' "

"Tencha" Allende had her chance to leave sooner than she imagined. Minutes after her conversation with Isabel Letelier, the shooting suddenly stopped. She did not know it, but the troops had been ordered to pull back to clear the way for the air attack.

Her driver, Carlos Tello, took advantage of the lull in the fighting to lead her out through a back gate in the wall into a British-run convent school, Sagrado Corazón, behind the estate. There, apparently aided by the nuns, the two obtained a car. Only she did not set out for La Moneda, but for the home of Felipe Herrera Lane, the first and longtime president of the Inter-American Development Bank. Herrera, who had quit the bank two years before and returned to Santiago to further his well-known political ambitions, was a lifelong Socialist and fancied himself an Allende confidant. He lived in a stylish house across town from Tomás Moro, at the edge of San

Cristóbal Hill. Once there, Tencha put in a call to the Mexican ambassador, Luis Martínez Corvalán, who only two days before had joined in welcoming her back to Chile from a junket to Mexico. That afternoon he picked her up at Herrera's house and took her to the embassy as his "guest." She insisted, in the days following the revolution, that she had not sought asylum in the embassy and had no intention of leaving the country. She would later change her mind about that, as suddenly as she would repudiate her own statement that her husband had killed himself, just as he had always said he would rather than surrender.

The attacking planes this time were coaxed onto target by a special spotter. Leigh had ordered his own helicopter aloft to guide the jets in. When he did, Lt. Col. Julio Tapia volunteered to serve as the spotter because he knew the neighborhood well.

"But, my friend," Leigh protested, "you are a bookkeeper and have no business buzzing around in helicopters. And do you have any idea of the risk you would run?"

"Yes, my general," Tapia said, "I know the risks, but I want to do it."

"You know," Leigh said later, "the pilot was a young fellow, young but very decisive, very aggressive. He and Tapia not only guided the planes, but also opened fire with the fixed .50-caliber machine guns on the chopper. I saw them from my command post. Later I saw them blasting away with the side machine guns.

Back at the base, Tapia reported matter-of-factly: 'Your orders have been carried out, my general. We guided the planes to the target.' But he said nothing about their own near disaster. The helicopter took a number of hits, one of them a bullet that went through the floor in the space between Tapia's feet and the pilot's back.

They did their spotters' job well: this time, there were no misses. Three rockets smashed into the north facade of the mansion. That was enough to break the fighting spirit of the GAP defenders. No sooner had the attack ended than they too fled. Before the regular army moved in under Col. Nilo Floody, another "army" swarmed into the mansion, an army of looters, from a nearby slum, who sensed the opportunity and, heedless of the danger, invaded the smouldering mansion to cart off television sets, radios, and other appliances—and a commodity even more valuable in the Chile of September 1973: food and drink from the estate's abundantly stocked storerooms.

The air attacks completed, it was Leigh's turn to be impatient.

"The air attacks on La Moneda and Tomás Moro have been completed," he reported to Pinochet. "I would like to know the results now of the ground attacks." He would soon have his answer—the blazing climax of the drama.

Within the rubble of the palace, Salvador Allende still clung to an illusory hope. The bombardment ended, he put in a call to Erick Schnake at Radio Corporación, in the sniper-infested State Bank Building, just a few yards away across that strip of no-man's land that was Morandé Street.

Schnake said it was an "anguished" Allende who asked him to appeal to the workers via the microphones of the station to converge on the center of the city and save their embattled president.

But the voice of Radio Corporación was dead. When finally it sputtered briefly to life again, it was too late.

four

DEATH
IN THE
AFTERNOON

I. "Still Standing—But Stooped"

For the two women and forty-odd men huddled behind the four-foot thickness of those ancient walls those twenty-two minutes were a terrifying eternity. Each sortie shuddered the stout walls, filling the air with choking dust and their hearts with the unspoken certainty that they were doomed to die there.

Suddenly, there was silence, a silence as unbelievable as had been the sound of the first rocket.

"Looks like it's over," someone cried out in the small vault where Allende and those closest to him crouched. Allende discovered he had been cut by flying glass; one of the doctors bandaged the cut.

Allende reacted quickly to the situation. Obviously the air attack was only a softening up. A quick head count revealed several GAPs missing, presumed lost in the air raid. Allende led the survivors back to the second floor to brace for the inevitable attack by ground forces. As he did, a thought crossed his mind: Almeyda, Briones, the Tohá brothers were missing. Perhaps they had escaped before the attack started. Perhaps they were at this moment negotiating with the accursed rebels. A chance, a slim chance, but a hope all the same. Allende grasped at that straw.

But Briones and the others were only a few hundred feet away, at the other end of the palace, emerging cautiously, disbelievingly, from the room they feared would be their tomb. As they did so, they discovered that the entire northwest wing—Briones's Interior Ministry—was a smouldering rubble. They made a dash through the Winter Garden courtyard for the Foreign Ministry, and in an office there found an intercom connecting with the Defense Ministry.

They identified themselves to the incredulous officer who answered and added that they wanted to surrender. The officer agreed to send a jeep. Minutes later he called them back: impossible to get through, the sniper fire was too intense. The men resigned themselves to wait, not realizing they were then in the prime target area of the embattled building.

They had another caller. The persistent Isabel Letelier somehow managed to ring through on the telephone in that office. Almeyda answered.

"He was coughing," she said, "apparently still suffering the effects of the dust from the bombardment. He asked me where Orlando was, and I told him at the Defense Ministry. He said they had been in the basement of the Foreign Ministry and had the impression that he was somewhere else—that something had happended to Orlando in La Moneda."

She reassured Almeyda that her husband was at the Defense Ministry, and Almeyda gave her reassurances.

"The president is all right," he said. "We don't know how the rest of the palace has withstood the bombing because we're at the other end, but the president is all right."

The now deposed ministers were not the only ranking politicians calling the Defense Ministry. The high command of the Christian Democrat Party had watched the bombing attack from the terrace of a secret hideout readied for such emergencies. Sen. Osvaldo Olguín, vice-president of the party, put in a call to the army commandant's office to plead for Allende's life.

"We have no intention of taking his life," the reply came back. "What happens to him now is strictly up to him."

Former President Eduardo Frei Montalva made a similar call. The answer was the same.

Suddenly the silence was no more. In its place, the infernal sounds of bedlam—machine guns and rifles barking, men screaming, and the whistle-boom of cannon fire from Sherman tanks on both the north and south exposed flanks of La Moneda and the 105-millimeter artillery pieces unleashing their lethal fire across the expanse of subway construction. Sgt. Alfredo Leiva Lillo, age thirty-five, father of four children, seventeen years in the service, watched from his post on

Avenida Bulnes as an artillery shell splintered the heavy wooden doors on the south side of the palace.

"Move out!" Colonel Canessa snapped the command as the 15-minute arilllery and tank bombardment eased up. Around twenty men of his command—the noncom school—followed him into the open spaces of the Plaza Bulnes.

They walked into an ambush.

"We had crossed there several times before that just before and after the bombardment to talk to General Palacios on the other side of the plaza," Sergeant Leiva said, "and there was no shooting. Now, suddenly, we were getting it from all sides."

For the next half hour—"I didn't look at my watch and it seemed like ten times longer than that, but they tell me it was around half an hour"—Canessa and his men took cover in the exposed plaza as best they could, mostly behind spindly scrub trees growing there. "It was a scene for the movies," Sergeant Leiva said.

Corporal Pizzarro, the man who knew he would live a charmed life that day, was one of the men trapped in the plaza.

"Bullets were coming at us from all sides," Pizzarro said. "Sergeant Mella and Major González and myself were crouched behind a small tree. A bullet hit not three or four inches over my head. I wheeled around and saw that the fire was coming from behind us, too, from the windows below the Yoga sign on the Continental Theater Building, and so opened fire against them."

"It would have been a slaughter to go on," Canessa said, "and so I ordered the men to pull back to the cover of the building."

Pizzarro covered as Canessa, Col. Osvaldo Hernández Pedreros, Sergeant Leiva, and two others—the only ones still in the open in the plaza—ran back to the building.

"There was a cadet next to me," Pizzarro said, "who also ran out of ammunition, just as Colonel Hernández had a minute before. So I covered for him also, and then, all of a sudden, I was out too, and so I ran like hell. The bullets were tearing up the grass all around my feet as I ran. I saw three men near me get hit."

Before pulling out, Pizzarro had a chance to avenge his fallen comrades.

"I saw a sniper pop out three or four times from a window below that Yoga sign. Finally, the third or fourth time, I got him. He fell with his arms through the Venetian blinds. He stayed there all day like that, his arms hanging through the blinds."

Canessa set up new headquarters in the fire station under the building. The wounded were dragged in there. Before the day was out, Canessa's men would suffer twenty casualties, eighteen wounded and two dead. In view of the heavy cross fire, Canessa decided to deploy his men on two looping tracks: one west on Alonso Ovalle and then north on Lord Cochrane to cross the Alameda there and converge on La Moneda from the L-shaped, alleylike street that was Letelier. The other moved with elements under General Palacios's command behind the Defense Ministry, then north on San Diego, alongside the colonial main building of the University of Chile, across to Bandera, then west to Morandé. Pizzarro went with the first group.

General Palacios, commanding the Second Armored Regiment, led a foot column along that route. They got as far as the corner of Moneda and Morandé, within a stone's throw of the northeast corner of their objective, La Moneda. But intense fire halted their advance, and they flattened themselves along the north wall of the Intendencia building. Seventeen of his men fell wounded. Intense as the shooting was, it did not scare off a bunch of irrepressibly curious bystanders crouched behind a newsstand across Moneda Street, in plain view of the desperate defenders of the palace.

No sooner did the western column of Canessa's troops emerge onto Alameda from San Diego than they came under heavy diagonal fire from the ENTEL (State International Telephone Company) tower to their left and Education Ministry to their right.

"That's where Sergeant Toro got it," Pizzarro said, referring to one of the most popular men in the cadre of the NCO School. "A machine-gun burst, probably from the Education Ministry. I hit the dirt and stayed there for probably five minutes, playing dead. Finally, a tank came rumbling up, and I got up and ran behind it."

Lt. Hernán Ramírez Jald, twenty-three-year-old son of an army colonel of Danish origin, was next to Toro when he was hit.

"The bullet caught him on the top left side of his head," the young lieutenant said. "He was in a kneeling position when he got hit. The bullet went through his helmet, right through his head and out the back."

Ramírez was second in command (under Captain Quiroga) of the 100 to 150-man detachment Canessa had sent to move against La Moneda from the west.

Ramírez had already crossed Alameda with some of the men and was making his way along Amunátegui Street when the shooting started behind him.

"We couldn't see where the shooting was coming from," Ramírez said, "and so we headed back across the street to Lord Cochrane. A soldier was hit on the way over and killed—his name was Castillo. Four or five others were wounded. The rest of the troops were on the other side. When we got there, I had a Toyota jeep pick up the wounded. It must have been hit twenty times when we swung out. The driver was hit in the right arm, but the corpsman wasn't hurt. Then I crossed from the south side again, bolting from behind a newsstand on Alameda. As I ran, I watched a machine gun rake up the sidewalk behind me."

Once on the other side, Ramírez rounded up the rest of the troops still there—about forty of the sixty to seventy men in his company, together with five or six engineers. Once he herded his men back, Ramírez went to Canessa and asked for helicopter support in clearing the rooftops. That help would be nearly an hour and a half in coming, but armored tanks did provide one piece of critical support. A tank took aim at the ENTEL tower and with a single fusillade wiped out the sniper nest halfway up the slablike concrete tower. Stranded again on the south side of Alameda, Ramírez used his jeep to rush the wounded to the military hospital until he was relieved by regular ambulances. At one point he had to change a tire on the jeep while under fire. Altogether, Ramírez's company lost two dead and several wounded in the fighting around that corner.

Ramírez was not alone in calling for air support. Pinochet, reacting to reports of murderous sniper fire from the roofs of the ministry buildings on the southern flanks of La Moneda, got on the radio to Leigh.

"Gustavo," he said, "they are firing from the roofs of the Public Works Ministry and the State Bank. I think it would be a good idea to stage an air attack against the roofs in that area. I am going to send a parachute unit and special forces, but, meanwhile, it would be a good idea to give them a going-over from the air."

"O.K.," Leigh came back. "Just as soon as I can, in a few minutes, I am going to lay down some fire on those buildings." Those "few minutes" would stretch into well over an hour before the two helicopters would finally appear, a delay with historic implications.

Nearly seven miles to the east four companies moved against

Tomás Moro. From the scene an officer reported to headquarters: "It is still standing—but stopped."

Cpl. Sáez Ayala sat out the aerial bombardment with the rest of the attack forces on buses parked a prudent distance away. The air raid ended, they got the order to take the target. Even four army years and twenty-two years of life had little prepared the chain-smoking soldier for what he would now see.

"People were still looting when we came through the gates," he said, "but they started to run when we appeared. The first thing I noticed was a pool with a stuffed crocodile alongside. That side of the house was half fallen down—it looked like maybe four rockets had hit the place.

"We saw maybe three or four bodies, and then two women, a telephone operator and a nurse. The place looked like a palace to me even with all the destruction. A funny thing, there was no fire of any kind.

"I was one of the first guys into his [Allende's] office. There was a big desk with maybe eight drawers. In one of the drawers at the right, a big deep one, there was practically an entire bar. In the middle drawer were a lot of documents. I saw a lot of figurines, gold and silver. There was a closet full of clothes, and a TV and a fireplace, and two jugs filled with marbles.

"In his bedroom, everything was disorder," the corporal added, "including elements that go against . . ." Here, Sáez Ayala hesitated, fumbling for words: ". . . well, you know, all kinds of deviate sort of things, pictures, but the pictures were the least of it. There were artificial penises and things like that, and all kinds of magazines with pictures.

"The artificial penises were on a glass shelf in the bathroom, not at all hidden or anything. There was also an exercise bicycle and some other things.

"Next to Allende's room there was a kitchen, and leading down from that a tunnel. Down there were not just bottles of whiskey but big carafes, and bottles of wine, hundreds of them—Casillero de Diablo and bad ones too. Behind the freezer we found a door. It was to a dark room, with armament in there, all kinds—rocket-launchers and grenades, all kinds of things, American, Russian, Czech. It was like a munitions dump."

Ayala said he also saw the rooms for the GAP garrison: six bunks to a room, five or six telephones in each room, weapons racks, television sets in the rooms. In the GAP dining rooms they found dishes with uneaten food.

"I didn't go upstairs to her [Mrs. Allende's] room," Sáez Ayala went on, "but I did see the strong box when they opened it—a notary, or whoever he was—and it was full of bills. I don't know whether they were dollars or what, but there were a lot of them. I was looking in through a window when they were checking that stuff. You can believe me or not, I don't care. I know what I saw, and that's what I've told you."

Laura Allende arrived at Tomás Moro minutes behind the soldiers. The soldiers barred the way. A neighbor took her aside and told her what had happened and that her sister-in-law had already fled. Overcome with rage and impotence and sorrow, she climbed into her car and headed home. Along the way she picked up an unknown hitchhiker. Her house was empty too. Certain that she would soon be arrested, she began packing a bag. The authorities would come for her that day. But not to arrest her.

It was a deadly war, but it was also a bizarre war, played out before spectators peering warily out of office windows overlooking the main battleground, and some, like those at the newsstand on Moneda Street, inching forward for a better look. That kind of curiosity would cost many their lives.

Such was the fate of a young man recently returned to his native Chile after spending six years in the United States. In the style of the times in the United States (less so in Chile), he was long-haired and bearded. During a gun battle near the apartment building where his family lived in a poorer section of town, the young man came downstairs to take pictures. Whether by accident or by design—because he looked "suspicious"—a bullet ended his life.

It was a war in which the spectators, and even some of the participants, took time out for lunch. At Radio Agricultura Esther Hinojosa cooked up plain noodles for the twenty persons there. Around 1:00 P.M. General Poblete, the central figure of so many conspiracies against his comrades-in-arms, sent his secretary to lunch in the cafeteria of the Development Corporation across the street from the Congress and just a few blocks from the shooting. She thoughtfully returned with a plate of lentils for him, but he hushed her as she arrived: the radio was announcing the names of ninety-five persons who should give themselves up by 4:30 that afternoon, or face serious consequences. Poblete said he could not believe his ears, and his faithful secretary, Eugenia Victoria Díaz, said she could not either, and so the two of them embarked on their forty-eight-hour tête-à-tête. At the Esso offices the wife of one of the managers found provisions in an office cabinet: crackers and jam, white beans, a typical "green sauce" dressing (parsley with garlic in a cream sauce), and coffee.

While so many others were lunching, Cadet Pino, in his unexpectedly pivotal relay station, was feeling his oats, though not having a chance to enjoy them. Through the morning and early afternoon Pino had progressed from the timid and scared occupant of a circumstantial hot seat to a cocksure and sometimes even slightly imperious "commander." On three or four occasions he "improved on" messages from Leigh to Pinochet or vice versa, adding an "urgent," subtracting an extra word or two. So it was not out of the lad's evolving character that he should be heard over the high command network complaining churlishly: "What happened to our lunch? We ordered half an hour ago," and later, after it apparently had been delivered: "How do they expect us to eat? There are no plates here. Wait downstairs in the mess hall. We'll eat there." (There were others that day who would forget altogether about food. Mike Gallegos, busy looking after his besieged charges in the Hotel Carrera, gulped a glass of water around 6:30 that afternoon, and realized it was the first sustenance he had taken all day—"unless you count the tranquilizers, and I must have taken fifty of them.")

But hunger gnawed at even the mightiest that day. President Allende asked his beloved Payita to whip up a snack for him. As she later described it:

" 'It's going to be a long day,' he told me. We found several chickens already cooked, left by the cooks before they took off that morning. I hadn't finished preparing the snack when the bombs began to fall. [She meant shells, but the confusion was eminently understandable.] One of them impacted in the kitchen, opening a huge hole. The air became unbreathable, both because of the rockets [again, a small confusion] and the tear gas. I saw the president firing from the windows with his AK, a gift of Fidel. We had to pull him by the legs to save him from being killed by the bullets."

Though he had long touted himself as a man of peace, Salvador Allende had become increasingly fascinated with violence. One of his proudest accomplishments was besting Fidel Castro during the month

Castro dawdled in Chile at the end of 1971. Early in 1971 a British historian noted that "the image of a gun-toting revolutionary was also obviously not repugnant to Allende personally." On this day of Armageddon he slipped easily into the warrior's role, so easily that even those closest to him were astonished. "He was another man that day," Briones said.

La Payita watched as he took a bazooka to fire on the attacking tanks. (Fidel Castro, "reporting" from Havana a month later, claimed Allende actually knocked out a tank himself with bazooka fire.) Allende was not the only "civilian" in combat: Jaime Barrios, former head of the Central Bank, also shouldered a gun at the windows of the palace.

To all but Allende and the few fanatics still fighting with him, these were, however, quixotic gestures in a battle whose outcome could no longer be in doubt. Dr. Oscar Soto, Allende's personal physician, did a head count and discovered that only eighteen to twenty GAPs remained alive in the palace.

The military commanders were, in fact, already occupying themselves with the aftermath of the battle. From his headquarters at the bucolic setting of the Air Academy, Leigh had weighed in through the day with a series of useful ideas. When the commanders agreed they would have to go through with the air attack on La Moneda, Leigh suggested a communique saying it was Allende's stubbornness that made the attack imperative, and that it was being done to avoid wanton bloodshed of a prolonged battle. Later, Leigh proposed a state of siege and curfew. Pinochet agreed, adding, "But we've got to say that martial law will be applied to anyone caught with arms or explosives, and they are going to be shot out of hand without waiting for a trial." Unverified reports, which the government of Chile sharply denied, claimed that 220 persons were summarily executed in the days martial law was in effect.

Still another detail remained, which Pinochet and Leigh had previously discussed, and which Pinochet now communicated to Admiral Carvajal: where to take the prisoners already being rounded up. The two commanders had settled on the National Stadium, an outdoor arena, and the air force's indoor Chile Arena. In the weeks following the revolt approximately six thousand persons were arrested in Santiago, a smaller number in the provinces, but by early October, four thousand of them had been released.

But concern about the aftermath of revolution was interrupted by the need to cope with still another Allende *muñeca*—his last maneuver.

Around 1:15 Allende got through by telephone to Carvajal and told him he wanted to send emissaries to discuss surrender terms. The emissaries: Daniel Vergara, Under Secretary of the Interior, perhaps the only man in Allende's official family who had survived the entire three years in the same job; Fernando Flores, secretary-general of the government; and Osvaldo Puccio, Allende's private secretary.

Allende's terms: (1) he would surrender and resign the presidency; (2) inclusion of a civilian in the new government junta; (3) a nationwide cease-fire; (4) negotiations between the military commanders and himself about the precise terms of surrender.

Carvajal ordered a cease-fire in the area and managed to get a jeep through the unremitting sniper fire to the Morandé entrance to the palace and pick up the trio.

The three were taken under heavy guard into the main hall of the Defense Ministry, facing on the besieged Plaza Bulnes. Flores had a small bruise on his cheek. Vergara looked all around him as he entered the dark and somber hall, but appeared calm. Puccio, the principal negotiator, appeared fidgety and nervous. The chief of air force counterintelligence took charge of the group, and they were practically pushed into the elevator for the ride up to Carvajal's office.

With his characteristic calm, Carvajal, seated behind his desk, lit a cigarette slowly and deliberately, took a puff, and then looked up at the men facing him.

"Well, gentlemen," he said, "what brings you here?"

"We come," Flores said, "at the behest of His Excellency, the President of the Republic, Salvador Allende."

"The ex-president," Carvajal interrupted.

". . . at the behest of the president," Flores repeated.

"Ex-president, I say," Carvajal repeated, the smile vanishing from his face.

"We are here to discuss terms of the surrender," Flores finished.

"There are no terms, only unconditional surrender," Carvajal retorted icily. Vergara said they would then report back to the president. Carvajal did not bother to challenge the title, but simply snapped: "No, you'll stay here. We'll notify Allende." The three were taken to the ministry basement, stripped and searched. They had reached the end of their "Socialist road to revolution." Carvajal then got on the radio to Pinochet and Leigh.

"Flores, Puccio, and 'Barnabas' Vergara are here," Carvajal reported. (He used the nickname hung on Vergara because his protuding teeth were suggestive of a vampire, and also after a character in a TV show then popular in Chile.) "Sr. Puccio comes with terms from Allende. I told him they were not acceptable. I told them that the only terms were unconditional surrender. The only guarantee they would be given is that we will respect their lives."

"How about Allende?" Pinochet shot back. "Has he or hasn't he come out?"

"No, he has not come out," Carvajal replied in his drawling calm cadence, "because, according to Flores, he wants to maintain decorous conditions for his surrender."

"What 'decorous conditions,' " Pinochet exploded. "There is no 'decorous condition'! What kind of a pipe dream is this? The only thing we offer him is respect for his life. In his entire life, he has never known decorum and now he comes around asking for it."

"Agreed," Carvajal said. "General Arellano is going to send an officer with a patrol to pick up the prisoners [in La Moneda]."

The end was in sight. But it would not come so tidily as Carvajal had imagined.

II. "At This Time, Some People Are Coming Out Of the Palace . . . I Suppose Allende Is Among Them . . ."

Back at the palace, Augusto Olivares, Allende's closest crony, brooded aloud. "We're lost," he told the president. "no one in the armed forces is with us." He did not say so, but there was another bitter disappointment crushing him. Only the night before he had told Allende: "President, the industrial *cordones* are the revolutionary reserve of your government. Only they would rush to La Moneda to defend you in case anything should happen." Ever since the aborted uprising of June 29, Allende's Socialist Party and their close allies of the Movement of the Revolutionary Left (MIR) had seized hundreds of factories around the country and stepped up the arming and training of the industrial militia. (Later estimates indicated the Allende forces were organizing and arming the equivalent of twelve to four-teen regiments.) These forces engaged in a few scattered battles that day, but made no massive move to rescue the trapped president.

Nor were the military buying Allende's terms, as Olivares was now to discover. He put in a telephone call to the Defense Ministry. Col. Pedro Ewing Howar answered.

"Has Daniel Vergara arrived?" Olivares asked.

"Yes, with Puccio and Flores," Ewing answered.

"Have they reached an agreement?"

"None worth talking about. Only unconditional surrender."

"Will Vergara, Puccio, and Flores return to La Moneda?"

"No."

The conversation ended, and with it any lingering hope that might have sustained Olivares. He went down to the first floor, into a bath-room, and, without bothering to close the door, began to urinate. Dr. Soto saw him and poked fun at him. As Soto walked away, he heard a shot. Returning, he found Olivares slumped over, dead. Soto smelled the pistol to make sure the bullet had been fired from that gun, that it was suicide. It was. Next to see him was Carlos Jorquera, the presidential press attaché, and a great friend of Olivares. Seeing him, Jorquera began crying uncontrollably.

La Payita remembers it was Jorquera who pulled himself together and ran to tell Allende. Allende, La Payita, and a few others went downstairs.

"We saw Augusto on the floor," she said. "It was a depressing sight. I will never forget the look of anguish on the president's face as he saw his dearest friend dead."

With the death of his closest friend, the fight went out of Allende. He decided to surrender.

The men directing the revolution were, of course, unaware of the scene inside the palace. And so they concerned themselves with mat-ters that seemed important, though they would soon be drained of all meaning. Herewith the text of their talk during those final moments:

Carvajal to Pinochet, immediately following the exchange about Allende's emissaries:

"The legal people and all advisers here, all of them, have recom-mended strongly that it would be advisable to give more thought to permitting him [Allende] the chance to leave the country, because they tell me that this man is going to go from one socialist country to another insulting us. So it would be more convenient to keep him here." (Carvajal was reflecting, among others, the opinion of his absent boss, Admiral Merino, who from the first instant the question was put to him, earlier that day, was unhesitating: don't let Allende leave the country under any circumstances!)

Carvajal did not have a chance to complete his "over and out" before Pinochet's voice boomed over the radio in rising fury:

"So this champion is going to insult us, eh! Let him go to socialist countries. In other countries they won't even receive him."

Carvajal attempted to interrupt:

"These are, they're the requests of. . . ." That is as far as he got. Again Pinochet cut him off.

"Let him go!" he shouted, his voice filled with more emotion than at any other time that day. Again Carvajal attempted to cut in, again he was interrupted.

"Let him go!" Pinochet said, his voice approaching a shriek.

At this point, Leigh, who could hear Carvajal but who could not hear Pinochet, joined the debate.

"If he is in the socialist countries," Leigh said, "we needn't care less. But if he stays in this country, he is going to be a center of attraction, and a focus for the masses, and he is going to be exploited and. . . ."

Once more Pinochet cut in, unaware that Leigh was talking.

"It's decided, then. We are going to concentrate now on military problems." His words were carefully spaced and emphasized. The debate was ended, and from that instant on, there was no longer any doubt about who was in charge of Chile.

A pause, and, still again, the methodical voice of Patricio Carvajal:

"Then we are going to proceed to arrest him, and his life will be respected, and he would be permitted to leave on the airplane with his family, and Mr. Puccio can accompany him. . . ."

Again, Pinochet:

"And that he gets out of here immediately!"

Leigh to Carvajal:

"The two helicopters are at this moment about to arrive. They are going to sweep the rooftops where the machine guns are, on the Public Works Ministry and the State Bank. These helicopters are going to open fire within a few moments."

(Pinochet acknowledged, then added: "Please tell those pilots to make sure they fire only on the rooftops and let me know when they'll be there so we can coordinate their fire from the ground." Leigh estimated it would be another ten to fifteen minutes, since the choppers were en route from Air Group 10.)

Pinochet or no Pinochet, Carvajal still had nonmilitary matters to decide.

"Second," he said, "that Fernando Flores and Orlando [apparently he meant to say Vergara, but gave the first name, instead, of the Defense Minister, Orlando Letelier, taken captive hours earlier] and that we send back as an emissary only Puccio, just Puccio. . . ." Once again, Carvajal was interrupted for an exchange between Leigh and Pinochet concerning the 'copter attack. When Carvajal resumed, it was with electrifying news:

"Augusto, they have just advised me they are ready to surrender unconditionally and have asked for a cease-fire."

Back came Pinochet's gruff reaction: "From La Moneda to the airplane for the mister and his family—and no other, no GAP!"

The final decision to surrender had been communicated to General Baeza, Allende's chosen pipeline into the top command.

"Here they were," Baeza said, "Puccio and Flores and Vergara, coming to us after the air attack, with a big part of the palace in flames and tear gas filling the air so as to force those still inside to leave without further destruction being done, and along they come with more or less the same proposition we had rejected that morning."

"Carvajal," Baeza continued, "naturally would not accept, and so Puccio was named to take our answer back and the other two taken prisoner. Our answer was the same as this morning: that the president should resign and surrender to the armed forces.

"Puccio was asking for paper and a pen to write the answer, and while he was writing, the telephone rang; it was one of Allende's men, saying he had resigned and asking for a vehicle to get out."

As agreed, the attacking army did cease fire. So did the defenders inside La Moneda. But the snipers, especially those on the rooftops, did not. Crucial minutes ticked past.

In fact," Baeza said, "we agreed to send a high-ranking officer to receive the president's surrender. But the fire was so intense that twenty minutes or more went by and they could not get through. So the attack on the palace was resumed."

Those twenty minutes would change the course of Chilean history.

The end so obviously near, Carvajal relayed another legal thought, but, curiously, he addressed himself to Leigh.

"Gustavo, Patricio here," he said. "Here in the command post of the garrison, we feel it would be convenient to demand of Allende, before he leaves, that he sign his resignation. I am in accord with that idea."

Then the news that caused even the unflappable Patricio Carvajal to speak with obvious excitement:

"Meanwhile, some people are coming out of Morandé 80. I suppose that Allende is among them. So for the moment, we are going to arrest all of them. I ask for your concurrence."

"Here, General Leigh for Patricio. Agreed, agreed. For me that is a detail. For me that is a detail that the Peruvians, when Belaunde left, gave no thought to whatever. But OK, if he signs, fine. But if he refuses to sign it, what are you going to do? The important thing is that he leaves the country, at least in my judgment. Over."

"Agreed," Carvajal replied. "We'll see to it that he signs the resignation and then—to Cerrillos so that the plane can leave. Good."

Leigh chimed in with another "Conforme."

Pinochet remained a silent partner as the dialogue between Carvajal and Leigh continued.

"I'm afraid," Carvajal said, "that the departure of the plane cannot be so quick as all that if he is going to be given the opportunity of leaving with his family, because from the time Allende arrives and gets together with his family, I would imagine it will be at least an hour. Over to you."

"Conforme, conforme," said Leigh. "I find we'll have to put a time limit on this, before night comes and we have problems. I can put a helicopter immediately at the Military Academy to embark all his people and take them to the airport. But let's not worry too much if, in the worst of cases, and in the end, if dark comes, this man gets aboard alone and the family stays in Chile. But with all this hanky-panky they can stall until dark to play whatever trick on us. I can put a helicopter in ten minutes, I can put a presidential helicopter in the Military Academy, and there the family can embark or he by himself immediately. Over."

"Agreed," said Carvajal. "I believe it would be convenient to set a limit in any case, because this is going to take a while. What time limit could we put?"

"I calculate, Patricio," Leigh answered, "that the outside limit to take off with him should be four in the afternoon. And not one minute more! Over."

"Splendid. That's the way we'll do it. Finished as far as I'm concerned."

Suddenly, Pinochet came back; "Do you read me, Patricio? Has Mr. Allende gone yet?"

"Some people are leaving now," Carvajal said. "I sent personnel of intelligence to find out the names of the principals who are leaving there."

There followed a series of verbal head-ons between Carvajal and Pinochet—with the usual "overs" or "rogers"—as Carvajal was saying those who were leaving were being taken prisoner immediately.

Pinochet: "Listen, Patricio, another thing. I think that the three commanders in chief and the director-general of Carabineros have got to get together to issue a joint declaration. In that case, Sr. Allende —out!"

"We are preparing the information," Carvajal said, "to give out both by military communications and by radio, saying that Allende has surrendered and the others who give up, the principal ones who give up. . . ." Pinochet interjected that it should add that Allende had requested leaving the country.

"Conforme," said Carvajal. "Gustavo, Leigh tells me that he was going to put a helicopter to take Allende's family to Cerrillos so that they could take the plane and leave before four this afternoon."

"Conforme, conforme," Pinochet said. "After four, I believe that around five or five-thirty, time for the meeting of the commanders in chief and director-general of Carabineros."

"What time do you want to hold the meeting?" Carvajal asked.

"I believe we should call it for four . . . around five or six—poof, old fellow!"

It was a rare incursion into humor for Pinochet that day, and Carvajal reacted appreciatively. Then back to business. "Good. We have a meeting of the commanders in chief in the ministry. Understood?"

"No," Pinochet came back. "It has to be up here. . . ."

Carvajal then slipped into what might have been a security lapse. "You mean the meeting there in Peñalolén?" he asked, the first time that day the location of any of the headquarters had been given. Pinochet confirmed that the meeting would be at his headquarters, and Carvajal said he would notify Admiral Merino. It was the first mention of Merino's name on the radio network that day. Carvajal said Merino would try to make it by helicopter from Valparaíso to

Peñalolén, adding he would also notify Leigh. In an expansive mood Pinochet then said: "You, too," to Patricio. The radio network fell silent.

Inside the gutted palace, amid the acrid fumes of fire and tear gas, the terrifying sounds of gunfire all around them, a handful of people, most too numbed to be frightened, others too fanatical to feel, and one too desperate to reason, huddled together in a darkened corridor along the eastern end of the palace, each lost in the loneliness of his own thoughts.

Salvador Allende still had one card left to play, and now he would play it.

III. "To My Comrade in Arms"

"Give up, everybody—this is a massacre."

The words resounded through the darkened corridor like a thunderclap. It was the voice of Salvador Allende.

"I heard those words clearly," Patricio Guijón said. "He was at the other end of the corridor."

Guijón and the other doctors had spent most of that day in a small room in the basement. They were there during the air attack, "barricaded" behind a stack of papers and the mimeograph machine. Carlos Jorquera sat out the bombing with them there.

"It is curious," Guijón would recall, "but the rocket bombardment actually calmed us. Those missiles make a lot of noise, as if it were a strong temblor, but at no time did they bring things tumbling down. My impression was that no one died a victim of the rockets.

"Our state of mind," he continued, "was not fear; there comes a moment in which you no longer feel panic."

It was around 1:15 P.M. ("the truth is that I had lost any notion of time") when someone summoned the doctors to join the others in that second-floor corridor.

There were twenty-five to thirty persons in the corridor, and Guijón took up position about one-third of the way from the southern end of the group, seated in a single row along the west wall. He did not see Allende, then in the spacious Salón Independencia, behind closed doors.

"I suppose we were there half an hour or forty-five minutes," he said. "There was no conversation. Each of us was lost in our own thoughts. I didn't even see the fire, although some closer to the other end did." His reveries ended with Allende's words.

"La Payita goes first, I'll go last," Allende added.

Although bullets were not impacting in the area of that second-floor corridor, the sounds of gunfire outside were, the young doctor said, "deafening." So it was that, as the group began to make their way cautiously toward the circular staircase leading down to Morandé 80, someone said they ought to show a white flag as they emerged.

"I took off my doctor's apron," Guijón said, "and passed it along. For some reason, I also took off my gas mask and put it on the floor. Then I began crawling along the floor behind the others."

It was at that instant that fate dealt Patricio Guijón the third and final blow, the one that would obliterate the life he had known and substitute for it the melancholy one of reluctant witness to a history he despised.

"I was about to round the corner," Guijón said, "when I remembered my gas mask—even the lettering on it: U.S. Army. This was my first war, and I didn't have a souvenir for my boys. So I decided to go back for it."

Guijón was groping for it when some instinct made him look up.

The door to the Salón Independencia, the scene of so many grand state receptions, was now open, and light streamed through a huge open window of the high-ceilinged room. It sidelighted the figure of Salvador Allende, seated on a sofa, to the right of the window as Guijón faced in. In his hands was a weapon that Guijón—in his unfamiliarity with violence and its artifacts would repeatedly refer to as a "shotgun"—gripped between his legs, the barrel pointed at his face.

For an imperishable instant their eyes met, but no sign of emotion, no sign of recognition, crossed the president's face.

"I did not hear the shot—I SAW it," Patricio Guijón said. "Shot or shots, how could I tell with all that racket outside? When it happened, I ran to him and instinctively reached for his arm to take his pulse."

There was no pulse to take.

"Most of the top of his head was gone," Guijón said. "Skin was folded over his eyes, most of his brains were on his lap and the floor. Brain fragments were also on the ceiling. But there was no blood. It was hard to recognize his face."

There was a small chair at right angles to the sofa. Guijón pulled it up close to the sofa.

"Then I looked around the room and realized that the military would be coming in any moment. I was afraid they might see the gun —it was still propped between his legs—and start shooting before they realized he was dead.

"So I got up and took the gun out of his hands. It was easy. If there is such a thing as a death grip, the president didn't have one on that gun. I then put the gun on the sofa and sat down again to wait."

Outside, General Palacios was beginning the final assault on the palace, rounding the corner from Moneda into Morandé Street. It was then that he saw a white apron, waving from the end of a broomstick at the Morandé 80 entrance.

Astonished, the general and his men quickly surrounded the prisoners. One of them was a woman, weeping hysterically. It was La Payita. All were made to lie face down on the sidewalk, except her. For her, Palacios immediately ordered an ambulance to take her to the Military Hospital. A few minutes later the ambulance pulled up. Unbeknownst to Palacios, at the wheel was an Allende loyalist, waiting for just such an opportunity. He drove off with La Payita, but not to the Military Hospital. Instead, he took her to the Colombian Embassy.

Inside La Moneda no more than seven or eight of the most fanatic GAPS fought on. Palacios led a platoon into the palace and up the stairs. Two soldiers with him fell as the GAPS fired from behind the doors in the tightening circle of resistance. As Palacios himself re-emerged into the long Gallery of Presidents—where Allende earlier had smashed the busts of past presidents—a young GAP of no more than eighteen years of age fired a burst at the general at close range, but missed. A lieutenant at the general's side winged the boy in the arm and then in the head. That bullet ricocheted off the lad's steel helmet and wounded Palacios in the hand. As the general continued advancing, he almost stumbled over the corpse of a GAP with eleven bullets in his body.

With the few remaining GAPs ducking in and out of doorways, firing and cursing as they did, Palacios realized that priceless relics were threatened by the flames and called out order after order: save this, roll up that rug, pull down those drapes. (One item he managed to save: the sword of the liberator, Bernardo O'Higgins.) Everywhere he found discarded arms, and the brief bursts of gunfire were punctuated by the sounds of explosive touched off by the spreading flames.

Meanwhile, at the other side of the palace, Lieutenant Ramírez, with about fifty of the seventy men still fit for action in his company, had completed their pincers movement from the west side and had reached the door of the Teatinos Street side when the walkie-talkie that had served him so well during the battle conked out.

Unable to consult his commander, Ramírez hesitated a moment, then decided to plunge ahead into the palace. The front half of the palace facing the Plaza Constitución was in flames, especially the second floor, and there was only scattered shooting.

"The door was open," Ramírez said. "I would guess that a number had made their escape by that door. We first occupied the south wing, where the Foreign Ministry is—the first, second, and third floors. There was no resistance.

"Suddenly, in one room, I discovered these bigwigs: Briones, Tohá, Almeyda, and Palma, and two officials who identified themselves as Investigaciónes detectives, but I was sure they were GAPs. We opened the door and found them all seated, smoking cigarettes. The two Investigaciónes guys had pistols. Tohá looked serious, but was very dignified. Palma seemed indifferent to what was going on, but I noticed he was nervous. Almeyda and Briones looked just plain deflated.

"I told them that if they resisted, we would shoot them. Otherwise, they were under arrest. I had them all lie on the floor, face down. After we searched them, we let them get up, and then I left two or three guards with them. By then the captain was there.

"We searched other rooms, but found no one. Then we made contact with troops from the Military Academy [Palacios's men] who had gone in on the Morandé side. I went from the second or third floor to the presidential rooms, and that's when I saw Allende."

"Maybe two, maybe three minutes passed," Guijón said, "before the soldiers came. There were three soldiers. A few seconds later, Palacios came in."

Palacios first saw the figure of the dead man—seated on a red sofa, his head lightly resting on a shoulder, hands swollen and black with powder. Next to him, a steel helmet and a gas mask. On the floor, spent shells. Everywhere in the room, a room dominated by a huge painting of the ceremony of the declaration of independence, furniture toppled, a whiskey bottle on the floor.

"Who are you?" the general snapped at the trancelike man seated next to the body.

"Patricio Guijón. I am a doctor, one of the presidential doctors," he replied.

"What are you doing here?"

Guijón explained about the gas mask. And he told Palacios about moving the gun.

"And you did not touch anything else?"

"Nothing else."

Palacios told him to put the gun back exactly as he had found it. Guijón complied. Palacios questioned him further, clearly suspecting that this quiet man might have murdered Allende.

"But he believed me when I told him I did not. And I did not," Guijón said.

Again, a sense of history seized Palacios. He sent word to have firemen, ballistics experts, report on the double. Nothing was to be touched.

"He stayed in the room the entire time," Guijón said. "Maybe an hour and a half, even longer. He never left."

Ramírez, with two or three cadets from the NCO school, came into the room. He described the scene subsequently:

"There were a few others—Lieutenant Catalán, from our school, Captain Rojas and Lieutenant Salgado from the Infantry School, and a few soldiers."

"The room was dark, and there was a stink in the place. The room was a mess, odds and ends lying all around the place, shells on the floor. General Palacios had moved a folding screen in front of the body of Allende. We peeked around it."

"His head was tilted to one side, his right hand was drooping. I recognized the moustache. Even though I looked for only a few seconds—it wasn't an inspection—I have a clear image in my mind. I remember his jacket. I saw a square-shaped whiskey bottle on the floor; I don't know what brand it was. There was smoke in the room. Then I went down to the street for instructions on what to do with our prisoners."

Having taken the first precautions to safeguard the scene (the Salón Independencia was the only room in the entire north end of the palace that would remain intact), Palacios reported what had happened to Carvajal, who immediately got through to Pinochet and Leigh.

Not even the imperturbable Admiral Carvajal could mask the explosiveness of the message he was about to transmit.

"There is a communication, information [he paused] from the personnel of the Infantry School, which are now inside La Moneda. Because of the possibility of interference, I am going to transmit in English.

"They say dat [he pronounced the word in that fashion] Allende committed sue-side [again, his pronunciation] and is dead now. [Back to Spanish.] Tell me if you understand."

Pinochet: "Understood."

Leigh: "Understood perfectly. Over."

There followed a long silence.

The battle had ended, as unexpectedly as it had begun. The months ahead would increasingly cloud the question whether Allende was the vanquished or the victor.

He remained seated on the sofa, clutching the weapon. On it was a gold-plated inscription: "To my friend and comrade-in-arms, Fidel Castro."

IV. The Battle Ended, the War Begins

Inevitably, it was Carvajal, the pipe-smoker, the man of meditation, who broke the silence.

"Uh, with respect to the airplane for the family," he said, an island of practicality in the midst of the tempest, "there would be no urgency, then, that the family leave immediately?"

His words trailed off into static. Back through the crackling came the hoarse voice of Pinochet:

"Put him in a box and load him on an old plane together with his family! Let them bury him somewhere else—in Cuba! We're going to have a mess with the burial. This character, even to die, made problems!"

Carvajal again, still the voice of calm reason.

"Right. Uh, the information is going to be held in confidence, then. . . ."

Pinochet: "Right. Patricio, the plane, put him in a box, embalm him, and send him to be buried in Cuba. Let them bury him there."

Pinochet's voice was, by now, calm. Nor was there any longer any doubt that with Allende dead, he was now indisputably in control of the country's destinies. Yet, after a pause, Caravajal did an unexpected thing: he appealed, in effect, to Leigh.

"Gustavo," Carvajal said, "I await your approval, your understanding."

Leigh chose to duck.

"Patricio, it's all clear, all understood," he said. "I withdraw the helicopter [standing by to take the living Allende to the plane that would have taken him to exile] and await further news. Tell me if the meeting is still on for 6:00 P.M. at Peñalolén? Over."

Carvajal: "O.K. Augusto, from Patricio."

Pinochet: "I hear you."

"Merino reports that he can't make it by 5:30 and asks that the meeting be held at 6:00."

"O.K. O.K. It is a good idea to consider that we have two possibilities: one that we bury him here secretly, the other that we send him off to be buried in Cuba or some other place."

Carvajal also sidestepped a direct answer.

"I believe," Carvajal said, "that this measure could be, could be kept, the situation, quiet, inasmuch as it is going, after the meeting, in the meeting at six. . . ."

In that rare (for Carvajal) jumble of words, one kernel of an idea registered with Pinochet.

"Agreed. Agreed. We keep it quiet."

Carvajal: "Good. As far as I'm concerned, that's all I've got."

"Me, too," Pinochet said.

But the subject of Salvador Allende's death would not, of course, go away so easily. Once the first shock had passed, the commanders realized they would have to handle the matter with the utmost care and discretion.

But first there would be two other matters to dispose of. Leigh proposed, "for reasons of security", moving the junta's first meeting to Military Academy. Why he would regard the Academy, however well guarded its parklike grounds, more secure than Peñalolén is a mystery. The Academy is surrounded by a residential area. Peñalolén is situated in rustic isolation, at the foot of the Andes. Nonetheless, Pinochet accepted.

The second was a grisly idea born of the heat of battle, which died stillborn in the rarefied atmosphere of reason: "For each member of the armed forces who suffer, who are victims of attack, at any time, wherever, Marxist prisoners will be shot, those who are prisoners. Over."

"Put together a communique containing those ideas" came back the reply. "Over."

"Perfectly clear, thanks."

(That order was never given. What was announced was that anyone attacking military men or installations would be shot on the spot so long as martial law remained in force.)

It was Leigh who surfaced with the first practical suggestions on what to do about Allende's death. The subject was so tender, so delicate, that Leigh resorted to the unprecedented device of referring to himself as he spoke, for the first and only time that day, in the third person.

"The commander in chief says," Leigh declared, "that it is indispensable that, as quickly as possible, the chief surgeons of the Army Health Service, of the navy and the air force, and the chief of the Medical Service of Carabineros, as well as the coroner of Santiago, certify the cause of death of Señor Allende in order to avoid that later on the politicians may charge the armed forces with having provoked the death. This as soon as possible, and you should pass the word to the various institutions [in Chilean military parlance "institutions" usually refers to branches of the service]. Let me know if you have understood. Go ahead. Over."

It was Carvajal, not Pinochet, who responded to Leigh's realization that the four of them—Pinochet, Merino, Mendoza, and himself—would soon find they were on trial before a jury of world opinion.

"Agreed. The doctors will be the heads of the medical corps of the three institutions, plus the coroner of the Military Hospital. Right?"

"No," Leigh shot back. "Correction. Correction. The chiefs of the medical service of each institution, plus the Carabineros, and a fifth doctor, who would be the coroner of Santiago, so that he would sign the death certificate together with the military doctors. . . ."

"Got it," Carvajal answered. "Clear." Leigh repeated that time was of the essence. Carvajal assured him the orders would be issued straightaway. Now Leigh was back with still another proposal. (Apparently Pinochet was away from his command post during this entire exchange.)

"We've got to get out a communique, I don't know whether you have done one there, on the cause of death. The way it happened at the end. Do you have anything ready, or not?"

"Right. We are going to take something prepared to the meeting of the junta of the commanders in chief." (It was the first time anyone had mentioned the word "junta" since the proclamation of that morning, a time that already seemed for all of them an eternity between resolve and reality.)

Leigh was not about to miss this opportunity to register his thoughts before the crucial communique coalesced. This time he used the editorial "we" to underscore his thoughts.

"We deem it necessary," he said, "to be very careful to spell out the facts well, because there are two successive aspects, and if they are not well explained, they could easily appear contradictory: one, that he [Allende] softened his stand and agreed to surrender, to give up; and, later, that it has been found he committed suicide. Also, there would be the incidence, the report of the doctors. But we do consider that this entire matter has to be very carefully laid out, in such a way that it doesn't end up vague or unclear and that it reflects the reality exactly to avoid later charges against us making it out that we intervened in this final decision."

"Agreed, understood," Carvajal said. "We will have all of those points in mind; we are going to make, to prepare a draft of the corresponding communique."

Leigh: "Fine, that statement should contain a general picture of the facts: for example, the action of the extremists that delayed the final denouement because of the fire from the neighboring buildings, and, in fact, prevented the surrender or delayed it; the presence of a great number of foreigners, which has been proven; and, right after that, some background on the extremist pockets that still remain; and the general state of tranquility in the country as total. Thus, in general, we believe these ideas should give a general notion of the situation in the communique. Go ahead, over."

Carvajal once again gave his assurances. The death of Salvador Allende would not again be mentioned on the secret radio network, a network itself not far from outliving its usefulness.

At least eight GAPs, the fiercest of the fanatics, died in the final combat. Although no defenders remained in the burning palace, troops in both the Plaza Constitución on the north flank of the palace and the Plaza of Liberty and Plaza Bulnes on the south flank continued to take heavy fire from remnants on the sniper forces still in action. In all, it was estimated that around eight hundred snipers were in action in the downtown area that day.

On the sidewalk along the Morandé side of the palace intelligence officers interrogated the prisoners lying prone on the pavement. One appeared particularly pasty-faced.

"Aren't you the one who had so much to say about armed revolution?" the officer asked Carlos Jorquera, the presidential press secretary noted for his fiery oratory. "Why," the officer added mockingly, "don't you let go with a speech now?"

Late in the afternoon Patricio Guijón spied his fellow doctors as he was being escorted out of the palace to the Defense Ministry. "I took advantage of the good rapport I had established with General Palacios, and, appealing to his humanitarian instincts, I said: 'General, those men are doctors just like me. There is no reason for holding them.' Palacios gave orders that they be allowed to stand up. I understand some of them later helped treat the wounded. Most were later allowed to go free."

Palacios was not so "understanding" about Investigaciónes detectives who formed part of the president's personal guard. To their pleas that they were only following orders, just as he himself would do, Palacios fired back: "And why didn't you surrender when you realized all was lost?" He ordered them bundled off to the Tacna Regiment with the other prisoners.

Nor were all the doctors allowed to go. Drs. Oscar Soto and Arturo Jirón, both personal physicians of the president, were detained. So, too, was Eduardo (Coco) Paredes, who had long before switched from a life of healing to a life of violence. Paredes would later be reported dead. The army said that he, together with his ex-aide, the detective Oscar Aravena, was killed in a skirmish with Carabineros after somehow escaping from the palace; leftists said he was executed shortly after his capture.

If Paredes did escape—as did La Payita in the ambulance that had been standing by for just such a "rescue" opportunity—he was not alone. Seventeen-year-old Renato González made it also.

"On leaving through the door into Morandé Street," the boy said, "I threw myself on the ground and pretended to be having an attack. One of the president's doctors, who was also leaving as a prisoner, told the Carabineros that I was suffering from hepatitis. They believed him, and I went to the Military Hospital as a detainee.

"Another doctor from the Popular Unity government helped me

escape. He had cut my hair like a soldier's in the infirmary itself. He got hold of a dressing gown for me and took me out to an ambulance where there was another comrade. We went out, the driver in front and I behind, like a nurse. Thus we were able to pass through the military posts, six in all. I took refuge in the house of a friend, and on Thursday, once the curfew ended, I came to the Mexican Embassy."

Another to reach the embassy that day had used another ruse to escape the palace. Jorge Uribe, deputy director of the OIR, was one of the last persons out of the palace.

"I went out to the street through the Morandé door," he said, "hung three cameras around my neck, carried another in my hand, and passed without their seeing me for more than half a block. Two Carabineros discovered me and asked me who I was, where I had come from, and what I was doing. I replied that I was a photographer from *El Mercurio* and in the confusion they believed me. After throwing a few insults at me, they told me to get out of the zone immediately or they were going to fire at me. I did so and passed without anything happening. As soon as I could, I requested and obtained asylum in the Mexican Embassy."

He was joined there that Saturday by his wife and two sons, and by his ex-boss, René Largo Farías, the man who had sounded the first alarm and who had walked away from the palace unscathed just before the rocket raid. Although he was on the original "wanted" list, Farías managed to elude capture until turning up at the Mexican Embassy on Thursday.

The last massive redoubts of resistance were about to be obliterated, about half an hour too late for what might have been a chance to take Allende alive. The helicopters Pinochet had requested almost two hours earlier finally appeared over downtown Santiago. Jorge Braña saw them as they closed in on the State Bank Building across the street, their 50-caliber machine guns blazing.

"The walls shook, glass shattered, and the building itself seemed to move as they fired," Braña said. "They actually rocked back and forth as they fired."

Another civilian in the Defense Ministry next door said it was "the most violent action of the day." Jim Halsema, back on one of the top floors of the embassy building, watched out a back window as helicopters strafed other rooftop sniper nests. He also saw flames spout from the Socialist Party headquarters on the Alameda, three or four blocks distant.

At about the same time, Carabineros were moving against another bastion of the Popular Unity—Communist Party headquarters, just two blocks up Teatinos Street. After surrounding the two-story red building, Carabineros lobbed tear gas shell after tear gas shell into it, and finally battered down the main doors and charged in. A total of twenty-nine prisoners were marched out. In the three basements of the building Carabineros found a completely equipped base camp for the permanent detachment of armed guards, as well as whiskey, pisco (a favorite Chilean drink, made from fermented grapes) and a huge supply of arms. The final assault was complicated by cross fire from a suicidal sniper in the window of an MIR office across Teatinos Street. The youthful sniper was finally picked off, and his body tumbled from the window to a parapet of the building just one story above the street. In his hand was his weapon, a virtual popgun: a .22-caliber pistol.

The helicopter sweeps broke the back of serious resistance in the downtown area. Lieutenant Ramírez was now able to take his high-ranking prisoners—Almeyda, Briones, and Anibal Palma—to the Defense Ministry as ordered.

"We went out the south door and across the gardens, across the catwalk over the subway construction, then into the Galvez entrance to the ministry," Ramírez said.

"We walked normally. I didn't make them put their hands up, but I did separate them so they couldn't talk to each other. At the ministry I turned them over to a friend of mine, Lt. Rafael Oyarngurren, of the ministry guard. 'These gentlemen are now in your hands,' I told him."

"That," Briones said, "is when I learned that Salvador was dead. I asked General Nuño the very first thing. He said, 'The president is dead, but not by a bullet of ours.' He said the president had committed suicide. I believed him. The president was a different man that day. I believe he had already decided to sacrifice himself, to immolate himself."

Only a few eyewitnesses and the top military commanders knew the truth at that point. At least one man sensed it, or thought he did. "Around 2:00 P.M. Dan Arzak [of the American Embassy political section] turned to me," Halsema said, "and told me: 'Allende is dead. I feel it in my bones.' "

One who did not know it, or sense it, was Erick Schnake, at Radio Corporación, across the street from the palace. When the station came back on the air briefly, about 3:00 P.M., it was with the playing of the "Marseillaise." Schnake then relayed the message the "anguished" Salvador Allende had asked him to relay three hours earlier: "The president has not surrendered, and calls on the masses to prepare a countercoup." A rifle shot again silenced the station, for the last time, but the message fired the will to resist of the few who had heard it. Much blood would yet be spilled.

From his command post outside a chicken short-order restaurant ("Pollo en Brasas") near the Teatro Continental, Canessa had picked one of his best officers, Captain Caravich, to join with Palacios's troops in the final assault on the palace. Now he concentrated on mopping up a few pockets of resistance in his sector: the newspaper *Clarín*, for so long the leading propaganda weapon in the arsenal, now a fortress of armed struggle (it took Canessa's men half an hour of intense fighting to subdue the nest of snipers in the newspaper); radio stations loyal to Allende (Corporación, the last to broadcast, was the toughest); Canessa also had to repulse an attack on the Officers Club in downtown Santiago. (His men remained in action in the downtown area until eleven that night, and would be thrown back into battle again at dawn the next day, and see action again and again in the days ahead.)

In the anticlimax of Chile's six-hour war, the bloodiest actions yet to be fought were in other sections of the city, though none would match in ferocity the imaginative prose of the Cuban news agency, Prensa Latina, and other lurid accounts appearing in the Communist press.

From midmorning on sharpshooters in the State Technical University (UTE) and Teachers College, both extreme leftist strongholds, peppered the 11th precinct of Carabineros with rifle and machine gun fire. Carabinero Pedro Cariaga Mateluna was killed, a number of his fellow Carabineros wounded. By midafternoon the two pockets of resistance had been neutralized. At the UTE more than six hundred prisoners were taken and a huge cache of arms captured. Carabineros of the Second Section of the First Squadron of the Carabinero NCO school, under the command of Lt. Sergio Jiménez Albornoz, kept a fretful watch on the now ghostly schools from a bus parked at the corner of Jotabeche and Alameda. (Later that night, fighting would again break out there and continue on into the next day.) The men were fretful because over the shortwave radio on the bus they learned of action elsewhere claiming the lives of comrades.

Aboard the bus, Fabriciano González Urzua—"el Negro Fabriciano" to his buddies—led the squawking. What are we doing here, he grumbled, where all is peace and quiet, when we are needed elsewhere? It was natural for González to take the lead: he was number one in his basic training cycle at Los Andes in 1967, and ever since entering the NCO school at Macul, a year and a half earlier, he had won the respect of his instructors and companions.

As reports of the casualties continued to come in, Lieutenant Jiménez decided to act. He got on the radio and said that since all was quiet in this sector, his platoon was available for duty elsewhere. There was a pause. Then, back came the answer Jiménez and his men —above all, "el Negro Fabriciano"—had been waiting for: move out to San Miguel and join the troops in action there attempting to take the big Indumet metalworks. Earlier that day around a hundred Socialist Party "shock troops" had rendezvoused at a predesignated corner on factory-lined Vicuña Mackenna Street. Armed with rifles, carbines, bazookas and a 30-caliber machine gun, they occupied Indumet, a factory with few peers as a bastion of paramilitary strength in Allende's factory defense ring. At Indumet the outsiders joined a well-armed and trained group already inside. After repelling the first Carabinero assault, the Indumet force split into two groups, and under heavy covering fire from the factory complex, the second group occupied the neighboring SUMAR nylon factory, another pivotal point in the Vicuña Mackenna industrial firepower cluster. Still another Carabinero, Manuel Cifuentes Cifuentes, had fallen mortally wounded in the intense action there. Lieutenant Jiménez's group was ordered to assault a large shop in the Indumet complex, with covering fire from an armored car detachment. Fabriciano and Ramón Gutiérrez Romero led the attack. They had no sooner reached the door than Gutiérrez was hit in the face with a bullet. He fell to the ground near the open door, beyond the reach of his companions, who had quickly taken cover. Hearing the cries of his wounded buddy, González began to crawl toward Gutiérrez and was about to reach out to pull him to safety when a machine gun burst raked his own body.

González's heroism galvanized his comrades into a frenzy of action, bursting into the shed with guns blazing. The two wounded men were rushed to the Military Hospital. Gutiérrez lived, but Fabriciano González would pay with his life for his act of valor. He died at dawn on the fourteenth.

With Indumet subdued, the action switched to SUMAR, where the defenders very nearly scored their only air victory of the day. An army helicopter, nicknamed "Puma" by its five-man crew, was assigned to strafe the factory and was over the zone when the big chopper took a volley of fire from the ground. One barely missed the copilot's head, another pierced the blades of the main rotor, and another hit the pilot in the right foot, nicking also the flight engineer.

"Emergency, emergency!" the copilot cried over the radio. "Pilot wounded." The helicopter was ordered to make an emergency landing at the Los Cerrillos Air Force Base, just a few miles to the west. On the ground, the crew counted eighteen holes in the fuselage.

By nightfall, SUMAR, too, was in the hands of the new government. Three other factories also had to be taken by force that day— Cristalerias Chile, Pizarreño, and Viña Santa Carolina—but a number of others where resistance had been expected were occupied without a fight. The huge publishing house Allende had seized early in his government—then called Zig-Zag, changed by him to Quitmandú, later to Gabriela Mistral—was taken without opposition. But another stronghold of the war of words, the MIRista magazine *Punto Final,* had to be taken by force of arms, as was *Clarín.* Along the way, troops picked up 150 Cubans identified as "extremists," as well as a large number of other foreign revolutionaries who had flocked to Chile. They were promptly deported. Several thousands more would follow in the months ahead.

For others, the aftermath of Chile's long night of chaos and the war it fostered was neither asylum nor exile, but prison. Among them were many tumbling from the heights of power as Allende's closest collaborators to the ignominy and indignity of convict status.

It was General Leigh who communicated the news to Isabel Letelier.

"I was on the telephone constantly that day," she said, "trying to reach Carvajal or Pinochet. Finally, that afternoon, I got through to General Leigh.

" 'Don't worry,' he told me. " 'Your husband's situation is going to be clarified soon. He is very well, and there is nothing for you to worry about.' "

"I kept calling others," she said, "using all the numbers Orlando had noted in his telephone log since taking over as Defense Minister, trying because I wanted so badly to speak to him."

It was the following day before she would talk to him, and four months would pass before she would finally get to see him. Together with thirty other high-ranking members of Allende's official family, Letelier was imprisoned on frigid Dawson Island, 1,500 miles south of Santiago, in the Straits of Magellan. He was finally released in mid-1974, thanks in large measure to the quiet intervention of Secretary of State Henry Kissinger.

Two years later, on Sept. 21, 1976, a bomb blew apart a car he was driving in downtown Washington. Letelier and a coworker at the Institute for Policy Studies, a left-wing think tank, were killed in the blast. The murder was eventually linked to Chile's secret police agency, the Dirección de Inteligencia Nacional (DINA), which was later dissolved. Letelier was, by 1976, an agent on the payroll of Cuba's intelligence service, DGI—a connection revealed by documents found in his briefcase.

At the palace, Lieutenant Ramírez watched as the diehards who had fought with Allende to the very end were loaded aboard a lead-colored navy bus and taken to prison.

"The stories about them being executed on Morandé are just plain bunk," Ramírez said. "I saw them, the ones who had been lying on the sidewalk outside, put on the bus and taken away, and they were very much alive."

Most of the big names of the Allende regime, including those on the "most wanted" list, were taken to the Defense Ministry, where, for a time, they milled around in relative confusion before being taken to the first stop in their prison odyssey, a room in the basement of the ministry.

Carvajal radioed Pinochet that there were more there, indeed, than the ministry could handle, and he was waiting for General Brady to decide where to put them. Among those already there, Carvajal said, were José and Jaime Tohá, Anibal Palma, Clodimoro Almeyda, Daniel Vergara, Fernando Flores, Osvaldo Puccio, "a guy named Hurtado from the Interior Ministry," and around fifty members of the GAP. Colonel Sepúlveda, still in the ministry, recalled seeing around two hundred prisoners seated on the floor of the main entrance hall late that afternoon.

Carvajal also told Pinochet that in the aftermath of the fall of La Moneda the troops had found a "great arsenal with all kinds of arms and explosives and gas masks, et cetera." (Lieutenant Ramírez said he was "astonished" at the quantity of arms "lying all over the place in La Moneda—carbines, pistols, revolvers, ammunition, and, in one room, so much armament, including rocket-launchers and machine guns, that there was practically no room left to get in.")

The prisoner question was one of the final ones aired on the secret radio network. The last concerned Cuba.

"Listen, Patricio," Pinochet said, "I think I'll head for the place of that meeting at five-thirty. They tell me also there's a problem in front of the Cuban Embassy. People are gathering there. It would be a good idea . . . I am going to talk to Brady to send someone there. Do you know anything about it?"

It was, of course, a matter the commanders had dealt with hours before. They could, however, be forgiven a lapse of memory after such an emotion-charged day.

"No, no, I don't know anything," Carvajal came back, "but Carabineros have been given instructions to take measures to prevent mass gatherings. I'll make it a special point to have them look into that crowd situation at the Cuban Embassy."

There was, indeed, a "problem" at the embassy. Reports would later conflict. The Cubans charged that they were fired upon, and that their ambassador, Mario García Incháustegui, was even nicked in the hand. There is no question that there was an exchange of gunfire. Eduardo Arriagada, head of the Federation of Engineers, who lived just a few blocks from the embassy, said the shooting continued through the night of the eleventh and most of the day of the twelfth. It ended, in fact, only a short time before Colonel Ewing, together with Tobias Barros, the Foreign Ministry's protocol chief, formally notified the Cubans late Wednesday that diplomatic relations between the two countries had been severed and they were to leave the country. Even before the diplomats left the next day, the 150 Cuban extremists were deported on the twelfth on an Aeroflot jet, which also carried Allende's daughter, Beatriz, and her husband, Luís Fernández Oña.

The report of the disturbance at the Cuban Embassy transmitted, the radio network, the dry voice of an improvised revolution, went off the air.

Volunteers from the Fifth Company of firemen were the first to reach the burning palace, braving scattered sniper fire to fight the flames. Soon other civilians would also enter the palace. Although Palacios believed (correctly) that Investigaciones was shot through with Allende sympathizers, he realized he had nowhere else to turn for a quick, expert examination of the scene, and so he put in a call to the technical section of the Homicide Bureau. A group headed by Inspector Pedro Espinoza reported. With him: Detective Julio Navarro, ballistics experts Jorge Almanzábal and Carlos Davison, technician Alejandro Ossandón, fingerprint expert Hector Henríquez, and homicide photographer Enrique Contreras.

Espinoza's report concluded with these words: "Probable cause of death: brain/skull traumatism [caused] by a bullet wound of a suicidal type."

At 6:10 P.M. their work was done, a little less than two hours after they had begun. Five minutes later the body of the second president in Chilean history to commit suicide was taken out the Morandé side door of the palace, wrapped in a Bolivian poncho, laid out on a stretcher.

Salvador Allende had said over and over that if anyone tried to remove him from La Moneda by force, they would have to take him out in a wooden box.

He was not far from wrong.

V. Night Falls On the City

The back of resistance broken with unexpected speed, the military commanders lifted the curfew briefly that afternoon to enable Santiaguinos trapped by the fighting to make their way home.

"A corporal came back to our office and said it was O.K. to leave," Frank Tonini of the U.S. Embassy said. "He said it would be a good idea to go individually and not in a convoy as we had suggested. I asked him whether there were any guarantees of our safety. 'Of course not,' he said dryly.

"As it happened, we made it home without being shot at, but I can tell you that we did make a run for it from the door of the embassy to the garage next door when we first ventured out. We were stopped and frisked several times along the way. Apart from that, what I remember most was the number of Chilean flags flying from the windows of houses and apartments we saw along the way."

At *El Mercurio,* a few blocks to the northeast, there were similar hasty getaways. Mario Carneyro, editor of *La Segunda,* the afternoon tabloid of the *Mercurio* group, and one of the few newsmen in on the secret of the revolution, saw his hopes of publishing the biggest scoop of his career dashed: no paper would be allowed to appear until Thursday, and the two selected then were *El Mercurio* and Carneyro's arch-competitor, *La Tercera de la Hora.* Dejectedly, Carneyro called the Defense Ministry and asked for, and got, a jeep escort home for the staffers he had mobilized to report Chile's greatest story of the twentieth century. Downstairs in the *Mercurio* building Jorge Figueroa joined a group leaving the building without protection: they tiptoed outside with their hands over their heads. Figueroa, too, was stopped by patrols and searched several times along the way, and barely made it home before the 6:00 P.M. curfew went back into effect. (It would remain so until noon Thursday, and, under martial law, anyone moving on the streets did so at the peril of being shot with no questions asked.) For Figueroa, the next few days would remain tense ones: a known MIRista activist lived just a few doors down the street from him. (Nothing would happen then, but months later, in a raid, troops uncovered in that house a fully equipped field hospital, one of several the Allende underground had set up, siphoning huge quantities of medical supplies away from critically short hospitals in order to do so.) The war was not over, either, for Eduardo Arriagada, boss of the College of Engineers, when he covered three to four kilometers to his home from the downtown office where he had witnessed the revolution from a ringside seat. Arriagada lived just a few short blocks from the Cuban Embassy, and the shooting there continued through the night and most of the following day.

Few that day had to traverse a more dangerous route "home" than Jorge Braña, the Esso executive who flew over from Buenos Aires on routine business and found himself a hostage of the revolution. Hearing on the radio that the curfew had been lifted briefly, Braña and the others in the Esso offices began to move out cautiously. The others went out the back door, away from the circle of fire ringing La Moneda. Braña had to go out the front door, into the eerie emptiness of the Alameda, the once-bustling boulevard where the wounds of war made even more ghastly the muddy maw of the subway construction. The shooting had stopped; the aftershocks of revolution had not yet set in. The skies, clear in the morning, were ashen gray now, and the spring-soft breezes of midday were giving way to the grumpy cold of a fading day. Even Braña's unconscious choice of dress added a somber tinge of its own: he was wearing a dark gray suit. Slowly, nervously, Braña made his way through the big, copper-trimmed, double glass doors out of the building and onto the south side of Alameda, past the adjacent Defense Ministry, then into the open spaces of Plaza Bulnes across from the burning palace.

"I walked slowly, very slowly, and carried my Argentine passport in my hand," he said. "Not that it would have saved me from getting shot, but I thought, if they do shoot me, at least they'll know who they shot."

At the northwest corner of the plaza, where only an hour earlier vicious and frightening battles had been fought, Braña stepped onto the wooden footbridge over the subway construction-gutted Alameda. A few soldiers moved about in the area. No one seemed to pay any attention to the solitary pedestrian with the wine-red booklet in his outstretched right hand. Nearing the south facade of La Moneda, Braña jaywalked across Teatinos Street, crossing to the west side.

"There was a lieutenant checking people," Braña said, "and so I crossed over. But he didn't check me, and so I went on." He walked in the shadow of the flames consuming the west wing of the palace, then on into the west flank of sprawling Plaza Constitucíon, past the Contraloriá, and Finance Ministry, and Economy Ministry, and, finally, to the Hotel Carrera.

"There was one small door open on the Teatinos side," Braña said. "I ducked in. You can imagine my relief."

Why did he risk it?

"I didn't have any clothes with me at the office, and very little food, and I said to myself, if I don't make it now, who knows when I will?"

At the Hotel Carrera-Sheraton, Manager Mike Gallegos was such a providential provider—and life-saving taskmaster—that one admiring correspondent would write: "Gallegos, upon whose thin breast every one of last week's guests would like to hang a medal, evacuated his charges to the cavernous second basement. It took on the atmosphere of a London tube stop during the blitz, but with a notable international flavor." One of the reasons Gallegos was able to provide so well for his 648 guests and employees was because for months he had been prudently stockpiling foodstuffs, using the hotel's blocked and increasingly worthless funds of escudos to buy scarce goods at the only rate they were available: the black-market rate. Entrepreneur that he was, Gallegos did not allow the fact he was running a hotel in the middle of a battleground overwhelm his business sense.

"I decided," Gallegos said, "to set a flat rate of 3,000 escudos per day, all meals included, for the duration of the war. The first night I even threw in a free glass of wine."

Gallegos soon had reason to repent even such a limited liquor ration.

"A lot of people kept pestering me for more; arguments started; and it was getting pretty rough. So I said no more liquor, and there was no more, for two days. Most of all, I was worried about the staff. We had a lot of Communists among the personnel, and I was afraid that some of the guests might start celebrating—you know, something like, 'They killed Allende, hurray, hurray,'—and then we really would have had a mess on our hands. So I said no booze, not at any price. A few of the guests had their own stocks, of course, but as near as I could figure, it was all gone by the end of the first day."

Gallegos's guests were served in groups of ten or so at a time, standing up at a counter. The personable hotelier soon discovered that he had more mouths to feed than he had reckoned on. A few persons with safe-conduct passes wandered in the first night, and so did a small "delegation" from the Carabinero underground station in the Plaza Constitución, just beyond the front entrance of the hotel.

"They asked to borrow some sugar,"Gallegos said. "I asked them why they needed sugar, and they said for their coffee. I asked them what they had to eat, and they said nothing, that they had been marooned down there since 4:00 A.M. with nothing to eat. So I told them to give me an hour and come back then. During that hour, I put together enough food for sixty-nine of them, and also asked them to take some food and blankets to the U.S. Embassy staffers staying on there. Those Carabineros caught hell the next day or day after, by the way, when their commanders found out they had secured food from us. Me, I was glad to be able to help them."

Braña was among those who stumbled into a private liquor stock.

"When I first got to the hotel," he said, "Gallegos told me not to go up to my room—which was right next to his, by the way. He said mine had been completely destroyed, as was his. Anyway, around midnight, he allowed us to go up to our rooms, those of us who wanted to. There were no lights, and the elevators weren't working, so it was a long climb up to my room [Braña was on the eleventh floor]. Luckily, a Chilean friend of mine had a bottle of whiskey, so I had a drink with him.

"My room was a mess, but it wasn't destroyed. I looked around, using a cigarette lighter. The windows were broken, and there were big holes in the ceiling. Plaster had fallen on the bed, and I cleaned that off with a wet towel. Then I took off my clothes, put on my pajamas, and stretched out—only not on the bed, but on the floor, under the window.

"The shooting was still going on. My impression was that every time a sniper would fire once or twice, the military would shoot a hundred times. I don't know how long it was, but I finally decided it was just too cold to stay on the floor, and so I said to hell with the risk, I'm going to bed, and I crawled in and went sound to sleep. They tell me the shooting went on right through the night, but I didn't hear it. What I do remember, before dozing off, was seeing the flames rising from La Moneda. Smoke continued to come out of it for several days, in fact. By the way, the stories about the firemen celebrating around Allende's body are bunk; they didn't even get there until at least five that afternoon."

Braña was up early as usual the next morning, at five or six.

"Since there was nothing to do," he said, "I positioned the blinds in such a position that the sun came in and I could sunbathe. Later on, I asked for a clean room, and they gave me the keys to another. But when I got there, I discovered the beds had been slept in, and so I went back to my own. There I found four bullet cartridges. Speaking of bullets, I had seen lots of spent shells in the street on my way over the afternoon of the eleventh, but didn't bother to pick any up. The next day, or maybe it was the day after, I discovered people were picking them up and selling them."

An adventure in roughing it also awaited Col. Eduardo (Caco) Sepúlveda when he finally managed to head home—at dusk, the night of the twelfth. An army major found a driver for him and said, "From here to the Plaza Italia, it may be a little rough. After that you're O.K." Sepúlveda said they made the dash through that sniper-infested gauntlet at speeds of 100 to 120 kilometers (65 to 80 miles) per hour, but made it unharmed.

At the spanking new Hotel Tupahue, a few blocks northeast of the Carrera and just beyond the fringe of the heaviest fighting, the revolution caught a large delegation of usually poised Russians off balance. When the shooting started Tuesday morning, many of the 102 members of the Russian Berioska Ballet Company rushed to their rooms and began waving small flags from the windows in the mistaken belief that it was a celebration of some sort. An officer stormed into the hotel and told the manager he had better warn his guests to stay away from the windows or risk getting their heads shot off. For the next two days those who neared the hotel's windows did so very cautiously. (The warning was anything but frivolous; *Time* magazine correspondent Charles Eisendrath, in the Carrera, reported that as late as Thursday, he was typing in his room when a man asked if he could peek out Eisendrath's window to see whether his car, parked in the Plaza Constitución below, had been destroyed. No sooner did the man part the curtains than a bullet banged into the room. Eisendrath said before he could crawl over and pull the man away from the window another bullet had thwacked into the room.)

It would be several days before the ballet company at the Tupahue could continue on their journey to Buenos Aires. When they did, they were among 1,100 Russians leaving the country, a number far in excess of the 150 assigned to the bloated Soviet Embassy. Also among the Russians leaving the country were twelve Soviet army officers and eight Russian engineers and technicians arrested September 11 at El Belloto, near Valparaíso. The twenty had arrived there in 1972 when the Russians installed a factory for the manufacture of prefabricated housing, a cover for after-hours training of a cadre of "specially-selected worker revolutionaries in the use of arms, street fighting, and urban guerrilla tactics."

The Russians were relative latecomers to such training in Chile. Long before, it had been reported that the Cubans had organized at their embassy in Santiago a "Latin American Liberation Movement," headed by Juan Carretero Ibañez, number three man in the embassy. Carretero had a ten-man staff for coordinating "liberation" activities. Like Fernández de Oña, he also belonged to Cuba's G-2, and served his apprenticeship during 1963–64 in Bolivia as the reputed liaison between Che Guevara and Havana headquarters.

The guerrilla training center was the Kremlin's boldest step in the direction of playing the "Big Brother" role Allende had given the

Russians during his December 1972 visit to Moscow. But it was by no means the only one. Although the Russians regarded the Allende regime with suspicion from the outset, they realized they had no option but to prop it up, hoping he would survive, and meantime extracting as much advantage for themselves as they could in the process. Their first dramatic overture was to offer Allende $300 million in military equipment in 1971, a move aimed at infiltrating the armed forces, and one the armed forces themselves quashed. Later the Soviets assigned forty-six technicians to the nationalized copper industry, but used them mainly for gathering information on American mining equipment, techniques, organization, and costs and productivity. Similarly, their aid to Chile's fishing industry was also designed primarily to gather intelligence and oceanographic data of use to the Soviet navy in its increasing maritime presence in the South Pacific. Of the $620 million in Socialist bloc credits to Allende, the Russians put up $260.5 million, most of which was never utilized.

For those who made it home, and for those still on the job, like Halsema at the U.S. Embassy, or stranded in hotel rooms, like Braña or the ballet dancers, nightfall marked little more than the end of a momentous day. For others, darkness was a curtain closing on a life they would now leave behind. For some, it was the beginning of a long fall from the power they had so badly bungled. For others, it was an ascent from virtual obscurity to power they had never sought.

Such a man was César Mendoza, a man serving out the last days of his Carabinero career as a forgotten general in a petty post. Now, suddenly, violently, all that had changed.

Late that afternoon an aide reported to Mendoza and told him he was to be at the Military Academy between 5:00 and 5:30 that afternoon for the first meeting of the new junta of the government of which Mendoza was about to become a part.

"We took all kinds of precautions," Mendoza said. "I had a minitank in front, then three cars, and another minitank behind. I rode in one of the cars, but not my usual car, a different colored one. We made the run out to the academy at top speed."

Another man was already en route. At 4:30 that afternoon, Adm. José Merino took off in a helicopter from Valparaíso bound for the fateful meeting. Seated next to him was his close companion and trusted confidant, Marine boss Adm. Sergio Huidobro.

"Along the way," Huidobro said, "I couldn't help remembering that it was just forty-eight hours before that I had been racing to Santiago with the message Merino had scribbled, the one that really touched off the revolution. Now it was all over."

Only a few weeks before, Gustavo Leigh's most fervent wish for the future was to serve out the rest of 1973 and then settle into relaxed retirement. Now, as he covered the few miles separating his headquarters from the academy, he realized that retirement would remain a mirage for years to come.

"I thought it was going to be a strategy session," Leigh said. "Instead, when I got there, I discovered TV Channel 7 [the government station] was already set up, a display of the captured arms, and a great number of newsmen. In fact, the meeting was so that the junta could be sworn in, something that caught both Merino and myself by surprise. Surprise or no, everything was well organized, and around seven we did take the oath."

The man who had arranged it all was, of course, the man in whose hands the country's destinies would now repose: Augusto Pinochet. In common with the other three who would back him up in the junta, Pinochet never wavered once he came to the conclusion that Chile was doomed unless the military ousted Allende. But even when he reached that resolve, he still did not covet political power for himself, as his behavior in the early days of the regime would demonstrate. (In those first days, there were promises of an early return to civilian rule; later Pinochet said caretaker power would, in the meantime, be rotated among the four commanders.) The ultimate—to quarantine the country against renewed political fratricide for a prolonged period of time, while retaining sole control himself—emerged later.

Other business had to be transacted before the new junta could be sworn in. Mendoza and Merino, now destined to share in the responsibility of governing the nation, had never even met before, and it was at the academy that they were introduced for the first time. Then there was a round of backslapping.

"We congratulated each other on the outcome," Mendoza said, "and then we go busy. We were all happy, of course."

One of the first items of business was deciding whether, and how, to break to the country the news of Allende's death. It was decided to do it in a terse communique, which, as Leigh had suggested hours earlier, carefully pointed out that Allende had dispatched emissaries to arrange a cease-fire and surrender. That mission, the communique added, was aborted by intense sniper fire, which prevented the return of the emissaries to the palace. The next decision was kept quiet until afterward: the decision to bury him in Chile rather than shipping the body abroad.

The news of Allende's death ricocheted around Chile rapidly that night. Most, especially those who knew Allende, found it believable that he would have taken his own life.

"I was not surprised, knowing his mentality," remarked Enrique Urrutia Manzano, Chief Justice of Chile's Supreme Court, and an avowed Allende antagonist. Urrutia, a tall and courtly man with the air of assurance that comes from power and position as the scion of one of the country's oldest families, paced the floor as he spoke. He paused to blow his nose, then went on. "Allende must have realized how enormous his responsibility was for what he had done to this country. That does not justify suicide, but it does explain why I was not surprised when I heard the news."

Pelayo Figueroa, the Senate secretary who had watched Allende at close range for so many years and was the man who officially notified Allende he had been elected president of Chile, said the news did not surprise him, either. "I would have been surprised," Figueroa said, "if he had surrendered. That I couldn't imagine—he was too vain. A person so egocentric as he would never accept the humiliation of surrender or of resigning. So when I heard of the plan to bomb La Moneda, I thought then and there that he would never accept surrender, and that he would still imagine the people would rise up to defend him. But there must have been a great turmoil in his mind between going on living—and by doing so submitting to the criticism even of those who had buttered him up in the past—or dying, and by doing so, measuring up to the image he had created of himself."

One who plainly expected Allende to fight on to the death, should the time come, was Fidel Castro. On July 29 Castro dispatched Carlos Rafael Rodríguez, his number two man as deputy prime minister, and Manuel Piñeiro, chief of the Cuban secret service, on an unannounced mission to Santiago. In a letter he sent with them Castro said the "pretext" of their visit would be to discuss plans for the upcoming meeting of the so-called nonaligned countries, but "the real purpose is to find out, from you, the situation, and offer you, as always, our willingness to cooperate in the face of the difficulties and dangers blocking and threatening the process of making Chile Socialist." In that letter Castro wrote: "Your decision to defend the process with firmness and honor even at the price of your own life, which we all know you capable of fulfilling, will draw to your side all those forces capable of combatting and all the worthy men and women of Chile."

Many in the Christian Democrat leadership—particularly those of the Frei faction who, at the end, encouraged the coup—imagined that power would pass quickly to their hands.

A few—very few—knew of Allende's death even before the radio and television broadcasts. Among them were the high command of the Christian Democratic Party. An army officer called to tell them that Allende had committed suicide. Sen. Osvaldo Olguín Zapata, vice president of the party, suggested that an autopsy be performed by the director of the Medical Institute, Dr. Vargas, in the presence of two Christian Democrat congressmen. The officer promised to call back and let him know where and when the autopsy would be performed. The call never came.

At 10:00 P.M., before television cameras and radio microphones that brought the ceremony to a nationwide audience, the four members of the junta took their oaths of office. A man with an ironic last name—Gen. Enrique Montero Marx, soon to become Deputy Minister of the Interior—served as Minister of Faith and took Pinochet's oath as president of the junta. Pinochet then swore in the other three.

Following the swearing-in, each of the four spoke briefly. Pinochet said the junta was studying the naming of ministers, governors, and mayors. (The fifteen members of the Cabinet were announced the next day. All but two, the Ministers of Justice and Education, were military men, although two of the military men were then retired.) Pinochet said the ouster of Allende was not a military coup, but rather a patriotic movement "to rescue the country from the acute chaos into which it was being plunged by the government of Salvador Allende."

He said the junta would maintain diplomatic relations with all nations except Cuba. He said that while Congress would be in recess, the junta would respect the autonomy of both the courts and the Contraloría.

Leigh, following Pinochet, said the decision to act came "after putting up for three years with the Marxist cancer that brought us economic, moral, and social disarray which could no longer be tolerated. In the sacred interests of the fatherland, we have found ourselves obliged to assume the sad and painful task we had undertaken."

Merino said that under Allende the concept of a three-cornered state was collapsing and, in its place, the executive alone ruled. "Perhaps," he said, "it is sad that a democratic tradition had been broken. But when a state loses its meaning, there come forward those who, by obligation, assume the responsibility of maintaining its validity. That we do today. We are certain that all of Chile understands the sacrifice that this represents for us."

It remained for Mendoza, the junior man among the four, but who, because of his training (as a lawyer) and experience (in a quasi-civilian organization closest to the citizenry) would speak in the most conciliatory, and wistful, vein: ". . . it is not," he said, "a case of crushing ideological currents or tendencies, nor of personal revenge, but, rather, one of restoring public order and returning the country to the path of compliance with the Constitution and laws of the Republic. That, then, is the spirit of the junta, to return to the path of true legality. We expect from every citizen, without exception, your cooperation for the best success and best achievement of that goal."

"When Pinochet spoke," said Silvia Díaz, one of the women to keep the long vigil of protest at the Congress, "we [the wives of the truck drivers in the capital] all cheered and embraced and danced—except for the Allende people. They were furious. Until that moment we were afraid this might be another tancazo [the abortive uprising of June 29]. But with the swearing-in ceremony and all that, we knew this was for real. The military aide ordered a real banquet for us in the presidential salon of the Senate. And what a feast it was—ham, avocado, lettuce. Fabulous, because we hadn't seen ham for such a long time. We ate with a silver service and uniformed waiters. In fact, the only thing missing to make it a true state banquet was wine. That night the aide kept special watch to make sure the *Upelientos* [a slang word for members of Allende's Unidad Popular, with the connotation of 'repugnant'] didn't kill us."

VI. Those Who Cannot Go Home

A colonel from army intelligence finished questioning Briones, Vergara, Puccio, and Flores. Next, they were submitted to a cursory medical examination. They were then taken by bus to the Military Academy. Briones said they were treated courteously througout. But the radio "hams" who saw them as they arrived at the Academy recalled it somewhat differently.

"They were brought up to the cadet dormitory wing where we were working. One young cadet asked an officer if we should make them march. The officer said he should, and sure enough, he made them march through the corridor."

For Patricio Guijón, there would be no marching, but there would not, either, be release from the terrible tensions of the day. He remained for several more hours in the the basement of the Defense Ministry. Intelligence officers questioned him repeatedly.

"It was inevitable, I suppose," Guijón said, "that the suspicion should be very strong that I had killed Allende. The questioning went on even afterward, in Dawson. But there came a time when I believe that they believed I was telling the truth."

Finally, around midnight, he, too, was taken to the Academy. He remained there until, suddenly and without warning, at noon on Saturday he and the other prisoners were ordered to gather up their belongings. They were loaded into a bus, and then an airplane from Los Cerrillos, destination unknown.

"Late that afternoon," Guijón said, "Punta Arenas, a barge, and then, in darkness, a march across an island. It was Dawson, a Marine base. The commandant, Jorge Fellay Fuenzalida, told us that we were prisoners of war and would live under military law."

For Guijón, it would end as unexpectedly as it had begun, fourteen weeks later, on December 21, when he would be returned to Santiago to tell his story on nationwide television.

A few others would go free at that time. José Tohá would follow a short time later, a man broken in health and spirit, ending his own life in a military hospital in Santiago. All would be evacuated to prisons up north as the harsh winter of 1974 set in, and a few of them —Orlando Letelier, for one—would then go free. Others awaited trials and the certainty of long prison terms or exile.

Patricio Guijón went free after his television appearance, in time to rejoin his family for Christmas.

"Silvia and I, from the bombing of La Moneda, me inside and her at home with the kids, had a kind of mental telepathy, and both of us never doubted that somehow I would live through the 'war.'

Frankly, the idea that I would die there didn't even flash through my mind. Perhaps that was the complete lack of experience of the two of us with war. Later, in Dawson, neither of us ever doubted that one day we again would be together."

Together they were, and free he was, but as the melancholy days and months ahead wore on, Patricio Guijón realized that his freedom was walled in by the momentousness of an accidental instant.

VII. Burial By the Sea

Enter, briefly, from history's shadows, Jaime Grove Kimber, godson of Salvador Allende, grandson of the president's sister, Inés. His story:

"It was around 10:30 in the evening, and we were all eating, when a navy captain came and told us what had happened, that Salvador had committed suicide. I was not surprised. I knew he would not surrender; it just wasn't his personality. He was a very strong person, and he would fight to the end.

"The captain said that since we were the closest family, they wanted us to take charge of the burial. He asked us where we wanted to bury him—in Santiago or Viña del Mar. He said they [the military] preferred Viña. We had buried my grandmother, Inés, at the tomb of my grandfather in Viña only three months before; in fact, my uncle [Allende] had attended. So my father said Viña, and the captain accepted immediately. Before he left, he gave us safe conduct passes, for my father and for myself—we had decided it would be better for both of us to go.

"The next morning [Wednesday, the twelfth], around 7:00 A.M. we started out for the house of my uncle, Patricio, on O'Brien Street in Vitacura, near the Vitacura Church. The streets were deserted [the martial law curfew was in force around the clock during the first two days]. We were stopped by a patrol. They made us get out of the car and searched us. They asked for our documents, and my father showed them the safe-conducts. They searched the car. The safe-conducts were not stamped, and so they closed up the car and put us on a bus, me on the first seat, my father on the last, and two guards beside us. My father explained what we were doing, but it was to no avail, they wouldn't let him say more. We had no idea where they were taking us, only that we were heading out on Kennedy Avenue.

"Suddenly, a city bus came from the other direction and a Carabinero lieutenant and two noncoms stopped us, talked to the soldiers, and put us on another bus. They took us to the Military Academy. It was around 8:00 or 8:15 by then. We were there around an hour. They didn't tell us anything. My father went and talked to Col. Nilo Floody [director of the Academy]. My father also had Carvajal's telephone numbers and called him. They gave us a new safe-conduct, stamped this time, and a military escort to our own car.

"We then went to Patricio Grove's house. There it was decided he would go get Laura [Allende's sister], and we would get Tencha [his widow]—I think Patricio told him where she was. And so we went to Felipe Herrera's house in Pedro de Valdivia Norte [just a few blocks west of Patricio Grove's]. It was around ten when we got there. We went in, to the living room. There were two other persons there. She [Tencha] came out, looking sort of sad. She had just found out and was sobbing. I said hello to her. She didn't say anything.

"We told her we had orders to go to the Military Hospital. We left around 10:15. We had to go very slow, perhaps 20 kilometers [15 miles] per hour. It took us fifteen minutes [from Herrera's house on El Cerro Street to the hospital, only half a dozen blocks south on Providencia, is normally a two or three minute hop]. We were stopped several times and asked who we were. They [the soldiers] didn't recognize her.

"The three of us got out at the hospital. She was wearing a dress with lots of colors, a pink dress. At the hospital door she asked to go in, and identified herself. The guards didn't want to let us in, they said they had no orders, that they didn't know anything.

"She was sobbing and pleading with them, for perhaps half an hour, saying she only wanted to see her husband. She asked to see the director of the hospital.

"After awhile he came with a chaplain, and they advised us that the remains had been taken to Los Cerrillos, and we should go there. By then it was around 11:15.

"Along the way we were stopped several times again. There was shooting all over the place [their route took them past two of the factory strongholds of paramilitary forces]. We weren't shot at, but we were scared to death. It was around noon or 12:15 by the time we got there. Patricio Grove, Laura, and the air attaché, Commander Sánchez Grove, were already there, plus a few guards, and some high air force officers.

"The two women were sobbing. It was very sad. The day was sunny, it was a springlike day, but it was a sad scene. We went to the plane, a DC-3 parked maybe 50 meters away. Before we got in, all five of us were searched, the men by parachutists, the two women by air force women in uniform. We went in, first, my father, then me, then Tencha and Laura, then Patricio, then the aide. The first thing we saw were jump seats along both sides, ten or fifteen of them, round, metallic. In the middle was the casket, a light gray, covered with a blue-and-beige blanket and tied with cables. It was a very unpleasant instant. We were all silent.

"Tencha went forward with the aide and sat in the flight engineer's seat because she had a problem with her back. My father and I sat on one side, Laura on the other.

"Then the pilots came in. They were young and greeted us, but we did not answer. We took off around 12:55.

"We were all lost in our own thoughts during the entire trip, all silent, looking out the windows. I looked at the motor of the plane, and it sounds like a joke but the plane—it was fifteen years old—the door, instead of being hermetically closed, it was a good ten centimeters [four inches] open, and the wind was coming in, and I looked at the motor through that crack.

"There were two high officers—admirals—and two Carabinero generals at the cemetery, but no one else. There was no indication they were going to bury Salvador Allende. Oh, there were around ten guards, too. The officers came up to us, and Laura and Tencha explained they were very sad and didn't want to talk. 'No problem,' the officers said.

"The hearse went to the vault, and we walked behind—six, ten persons, perhaps three meters behind. In the meantime, Diana Comber, who was married to my father's younger brother, Jorge Grove, had joined us. She lived in Viña, and my uncle Jorge was then in the United States. My father, Patricio, the aide, and I took the body from the back door.

"At the moment we were taking it, the top slipped off a little, about a couple of centimeters [about 4/5 of an inch] and I could see white bandages covering everything. We put the top back as best we could and carried it to the vault. There were about five gravediggers and others who work in the cemetery there. We tied the casket and lowered it into the first niche from the top, at the right—the tomb has six niches, and he was put in the first one from the top.

"No one spoke. Everyone was silent. The women were sobbing."

"At the instant we were putting the casket in the niche, Tencha said some words: 'Compañeros, here our compañero president leaves us. Let us hope that the people don't forget him. Look how he is buried, without so much as a floral wreath, and in complete anonymity.' She then threw a wild red rose she was holding in her hand on top of the casket."

"Then they closed the niche with a marble cover. We walked back to our cars, the same ones we had come in. We asked if we could go to the presidential beach house in Viña, and he [the aide] said O.K. She wanted to get some of their effects, his and hers. He said there would be no problem.

"It was around three when we got there. The household staff had no idea we would be coming. We took some of his clothes—pants, sweaters, the grandchildren's toys, some of her clothes—and put them all in two or three boxes, which we then put in the navy car.

"They took us from there back to the Quintero Air Base. When we arrived at Quintero, someone remembered that we hadn't eaten, and Sánchez invited us to have something to eat. We had sandwiches, but ate them on the plane.

"Nobody in Viña knew we were there. The plane left at 3:30—same pilots, and we all sat in the same places. We arrived in Santiago around 4:30.

"My father, a navy officer and I took Tencha to Herrera's house, and Patricio and Laura went to her house. The officer asked us if we could drop him off afterward at the Defense Ministry. The four of us went to Herrera's house. We all got out and said farewell to her. Then my father and I got back in the front seat and the officer in the back.

"That ride was the scariest of all. When we got to Alameda, we were the only car on it and snipers were shooting from the rooftops. We didn't go all the way—there was too much shooting—but left the officer around 200 meters from the ministry. He got out and walked, and we turned around.

"We were stopped by three or four patrols on the way and one Carabinero searched the car as well as us.

"It was around 7:00 P.M. when we got home. We were upset and nervous from what we had seen and been through and felt that day.

"We stayed home all that night and the next day too.

"I will remember, as I do now, detail by detail, what I saw that day for the rest of my life."

Two days later, his aunt Diana Comber was taken back to the cemetery to identify the body. She went with a high naval chief.

"They opened the niche," Jaime concluded, "and then the urn, for maybe two seconds, long enough for her to see.

"Then they took him out and put him in the lowest niche, perhaps three and a half meters down."

Salvador Allende had returned to the seacoast land of his birth.

Appendix

Even in the very telling of his own story, one detects lassitude, resignation in Patricio Guijón, but one ought to detect more, much more: the image and likeness of a man who has stripped off the mask of pretense, a man who presents himself to the world and to himself as he is, and *what* he is—neither proud nor weaseling, neither petulant nor full of apologies, a man who has made mistakes and will make many more, but who is, by his very nature, unshakably, unbudgingly true to himself. Which makes him a remarkably decent man. A few bits and pieces of his own story, as written in a letter to the author, in his own unrehearsed and unself-conscious words:

"Our house is modest; we rent it. It is a DFL-2 [a special, semipopular floor plan in Chile] with a tiny garden where Silvia tried for several years to grow grass and a few plants but gave up because they are incompatible with soccer, bicycles, three boys, and a six-year-old Doberman.

"I couldn't tell you the size of our bedroom, but it is definitely on the small side. The beds, by the way, are extremely simple, nothing more than wooden rectangles, really. In 1961 that was original indeed.

"We have been renting our house since 1964 when I returned from Arica, where I had fulfilled my two-year commitment to work in the provinces [standard for medical students in Chile in return for free education] after completing my residency in surgery.

"I was born in Santiago June 28, 1932, the third of a family of five children. Two older sisters, two younger brothers. My father, a lawyer, well off financially and professionally, my mother, a housewife, daughter of German parents. My father, Chilean, a hundred percent. He also studied in the German School because it was near his house. There he met my mother.

"All of my brothers and sisters studied in that same school. All of us went on to college. The girls got married before graduating, but of the boys, two of us became doctors and the youngest a lawyer. Two years before finishing high school I decided on medicine. Frankly, I couldn't tell you why; it just happened that one day I decided on it, and never doubted my decision. The same is true of my decision to specialize as a surgeon.

I learned German both in school and at home—we did much better with my mother, permission to go to the movies, for example, when we spoke German. I also learned English in school, French too. And during the six months I spent in Brazil on a scholarship I learned to get along in Portuguese, or, more accurately, 'Portuspanish" [Portuguese pronounced in Spanish—the pronunciation of that language is positively devilish].

"My sentimental life wasn't very unusual. Everything absolutely within the norms of the petit bourgeoisie.

"I knew Silvia twice. The first time was when I was a med student and she a nursing student in the same hospital. I liked her from the first moment I saw her, but at that time she was unapproachable. She has always been very pretty, and inevitably, the older students chased after her, and one or two doctors as well, so a mouse like myself had no chance at all.

"The second time was after I had graduated and was in my residency. She came to work at the same hospital; by then she was an RN. This time I didn't let my chance get away. Whatever else, at least I was a doctor myself. We met in August and were married in March 1961. The first baby was born in November 1961.

"We were both thirty when we married, so we were much more mature than if we had begun four or five years earlier. As a result, neither of us had any doubt whatever when it came time to consider marriage.

"I once read in an interview one of the sanest things I have ever read anywhere, and which fits me to a tee. The person being interviewed was asked the typical question: 'Are you happy in your marriage?' His answer: 'I got married to be married, not to be happy.'"

"I think Silvia and I have worked things out as well as could be expected. We love each other, and we respect each other, and, moreover, we admire one another, and I think that is the foundation of a solid marriage. We have never had any money. Neither of us has ever inherited anything. We have never earned much money, and it hasn't bothered us either that we have to economize. This has been the source of lots of arguments with my family. They say I have no sense of money.

"I have no complaints about my career, but, as a doctor, one does not get rich in Chile, or, for that matter, anywhere else unless you devote yourself exclusively to making money. In that case a doctor, at least, would have to choose another specialty. anyway, the fact is we have never had to go hungry, and we have been able to live decently.

"Toward the end of med school I traveled to Europe with a group of classmates, the famous 'study trip,' which in fact is just plain sightseeing. It was one of the most notable experiences of my life, and I still remember it with emotion. I have always hoped I would one day repeat it, this time with Silvia, but, as you know, I haven't had that luck.

"In 1969 I spent six months in Brazil, studying surgery of the liver. It was tremendously beneficial. It was in São Paulo, but several times I went to Rio. I was alone, because the grant was very small. I missed Silvia and the children terribly (we already had the three then), and because I missed them so much, I did not extend my stay. Silvia came to meet me there. We met in Rio. I had managed to scrape up a few dollars, and Silvia had scraped up a few. We spent the ten most marvelous days of our lives in a hotel (the Regente) on Avenida Atlantida, right on the beach.

"During the time I was in Arica I registered to vote in that city, as did Silvia. We were there for the 1964 election, the one Frei won. I voted for Allende. Later, in 1970, we went back to Arica to vote, since we were still registered there and hadn't bothered to change. . . . Needless to say, I voted for Allende.

"I have never belonged to any party, nor organization, nor movement, for or against anyone. I am a leftist because misery makes me sick, and from what I have seen misery doesn't seem to matter much to the Right.

"I understand nothing of Marxism, or economics, or, for that matter, of politics. The last thing that would ever occur to me would be to join a political party.

"I am an atheist, but I have nothing against religion. I do not belong to the Rotary Club, or to the Lions. My only membership was in a soccer club a number of years ago. Silvia shares fully my position and is as anti-gregariousness as I am.

"But I can assure you that this community of ideas had nothing to do with our decision to get married. At that time politics had nothing to do with human relations. I give you an example. My best friend, a man I have known since we studied medicine together, is the antithesis of me: he is tall and fat, a Catholic, conservative, with aristocratic ancestors, raised in Spain, and is anti-German. Furthermore, he has money. . . ."

". . . And so ends this autobiography of sorts. Please overlook the mistakes, the errors, the use of certain slang expressions, but I have just written without premeditation so that it would come out spontaneously. I have probably overlooked lots of details, but I didn't start out with the idea of writing a complete narrative, because I would have to write a book for that. And honestly, I don't think of myself as a writer. Shoemaker, look after your shoes. . . ."

Glossary

Names

(*denotes those who were among the persons with Allende at the presidential palace the day of the revolution)

Allende Gossens, Salvador—President of Chile, 1970–73.

Allende, Mrs. Hortensia Bussi de—Allende's wife.

***Almeyda Medina, Clodomiro**—Allende's last Foreign Minister.

Altamirano Orrego, Carlos—Secretary-General of the Socialist Party.

Arellano, General Sergio—commanded troops in downtown Santiago.

Baeza, General Ernesto—Number-three-ranking army general, but not an insider in anti-Allende plotting. He was, briefly on the afternoon of the revolution, a telephone intermediary between Allende, in the besieged palace, and Baeza's fellow military commanders with him at the Defense Ministry.

***Barrios, Jaime**—Communist head of the Central Bank and former adviser to Ernesto (Che) Guevara when Guevara was the czar of Cuba's economy.

Benavides, General Raúl César—Commander of the army's training schools in metropolitan Santiago; responsible for neutralizing Allende's guerrilla-infested industrial cordones (ring of factories).

Bonilla Bradanovic, General Oscar—Number-four-ranking army general, picked by Pinochet to succeed him in case Pinochet should be taken or killed during the revolution.

Brady Roche, General Herman—Commander of the army's Santiago garrison; in overall command of troops deployed in Santiago during the revolution.

*****Briones, Carlos**—Allende's last Interior Minister and one of those who shared Allende's last dinner.

Canessa Roberts, Colonel (later General) Julio—Key commander in intense fighting in the area of the presidential palace.

Carvajal, Admiral Patricio—Chief of Staff, Joint Chiefs of Staff, and the key link between Pinochet, Leigh, and troop commanders in combat.

"César"—Pseudonym for one of the civilians who designed and operated the secret radio network linking the top commanders during the revolution.

*****Contreras Bell de Ropert, Miria** (nicknamed "La Payita")—Allende's private secretary and confidante.

*****Garcés Ramón, Joan**—Shadowy Spaniard on the payroll of UNESCO in Santiago, but who actually served as an adviser and confidant to Allende, He also was invited to the "last supper" strategy session on the eve of the revolution.

*****Grez, Commander Jorge**—Allende's naval aide-de-camp.

Grove Kimber, Jaime—Allende's nephew; one of those who buried the fallen president.

*****Guijón Klein, Dr. Patricio**—One of several presidential physicians, and the man who saw Allende die.

Halsema, James—Public Affairs Officer at U.S. Embassy in Santiago.

*****Joignant, Alfredo**—Head of Investigaciones, a nationwide plainclothes police force.

*****Jorquera, Carlos**—Presidential press secretary.

Leigh Guzmán, General Gustavo—Head of the air force and a member of the first post-Allende military junta.

Letelier, Orlando—Allende's last Defense Minister and another guest at the "last supper" strategy dinner. Letelier's murder on a downtown street in Washington, D.C. in September 1976 brought already tense and strained relations between the U.S. and Chile to the near-breaking point. That murder was laid at the doorstep of Chile's secret police organization, DINA (later disbanded).

Lutz, Colonel Augusto—Head of army intelligence and one of a handful involved in Pinochet's prerevolution plotting to oust Allende.

"Mario"—Pseudonym for another of the civilians who put together the secret radio network linking military commanders directing the revolution.

Mendoza Durán, General César—Fourth-ranking general in Carabineros but the man picked to seize command on D-Day; subsequently director-general of Carabineros and a member of the military junta.

Merino, Admiral José Toribio—Number-two-ranking navy admiral, but the man who spearheaded the revolution and emerged on the eleventh as navy commander; subsequently a member of the military junta.

Montero Cornejo, Admiral Raúl—Navy commander in chief drydocked by the revolution because of his indecisiveness.

*Olivares, Augusto—Director of the government television network; thought by many to be the man closest to Allende, who treated him as a son. Olivares committed suicide on the eleventh when all appeared lost.

Palacios, Javier—Army's training chief, given command of troops in downtown area.

Pinochet Ugarté, General Augusto—Army commander in chief, and the man who directed the revolution; presently President of Chile.

Polloni Pérez, Colonel Julio—Chief of army telecommunications and a conspiratorial insider; worked with "Mario," "César," and other civilians in creating the secret radio command network.

Prats González, General Carlos—Army commander in chief from time Allende assumed office in 1970 until his resignation (under intense pressure from fellow officers) a few weeks before the revolution. Prats's loyalty to Allende was the chief bar to earlier military action to oust Allende. He was murdered in a terrorist bombing in Buenos Aires in 1974.

*Puccio, Osvaldo—Allende's secretary. Among those who remained with him during the rocket attack on the palace.

Puga, Alvaro—Acting general manager of Radio Agricultura, peppery radio station in Santiago which fought Allende throughout his rule and which emerged as the principal "voice of the revolution" on the eleventh. Puga was a principal civilian plotter during Allende's final months.

Sáez, Ayala, Cpl. Iván—Army noncom who went from his girl-friend's house to the heat of battle in downtown Santiago.

*Tohá, Jaime—Allende's last Agriculture Minister.

*Tohá, José—Jaime's brother, and a former Defense Minister. Together with Briones, he tried to persuade Allende to surrender. Tohá died a few months after the revolution in a military hospital, apparently of natural causes.

*Vergara, Daniel—A phenomenon of the Allende regime: he served during the entire administration in the same high post, under-secretary of the Interior (Allende reshuffled his Cabinet and other top posts repeatedly, frequently to thwart congressional impeachments of his appointees.)

Places

La Moneda—The eighteenth-century building in downtown Santiago which, since 1841, had served as Chile's presidential palace. It was there that Allende made his last stand on September 11, 1973.

Tomás Moro—The palatial (and unprecedented) presidential estate Allende occupied after assuming the presidency. (The two presidents who preceded Allende had remained in their own modest residences.) Tomás Moro was the scene of intense fighting on the eleventh.

El Cañaveral—Another palatial, but more sprawling and rural, estate Allende used as a combination of weekend retreat and training camp for his private guerrilla army, the so-called GAPs.

Estadio Chile—Sports arena where Carlos Altamirano's inflammatory speech Sunday, September 9, gave military leaders the pretext they needed for staging the revolution. The arena was later used for housing prisoners rounded up in the first days of the revolution.

Peñalolén—Signal Corps garrison on the outskirts of Santiago, which Pinochet made his command post on the day of the revolution.

Terms

Academia de Guerra—Army War College (rather than War Academy), because its functions parallel those of the U.S. Command and General Staff College at Ft. Leavenworth, Kansas.

Academia de Guerra Naval—Although it translates literally as "Naval War Academy," I have translated it as Naval War College because its functions correspond to those of the U.S. Naval War College at Newport, Rhode Island.

Bando—Communique. A number were broadcast in the days following the revolution.

Carabineros—The paramilitary and nationwide police force.

COFA—Centro de Operaciones de las Fuerzas Armadas (Armed Forces Operations Center) located in the Defense Ministry.

Contraloría—A unique Chilean governmental institution that combines many of the functions of the U.S. General Accounting Office (the translation I have used) and the Solicitor General. In the U.S., the GAO is attached to the Congress, while the Solicitor General is a dependency of the presidency; by contrast, Chile's "contraloría" is independent of both branches. The Contraloría building is located directly across the street from La Moneda, the presidential palace.

Cordones Industriales—A ring of factories surrounding Santiago that were converted into guerrilla fortresses Allende hoped would serve as his Maginot Line, warding off any attempted military strike from outside the city, encircling any uprising within the city. Numerous battles were fought at several of the "factory fortresses," but they at no time constituted the counterforce Allende had hoped they would when the fighting actually broke out on September 11.

Escuela de Aviacion—Air Academy.

Escuela Militar—Literal translation: Military School. I have translated it as Military Academy because it resembles the U.S. Military Academy at West Point in the Chilean scheme of things.

GAP—(Grupo de Amigos Personales)—A private guerrilla force created by Allende shortly after he assumed the presidency, supposedly because he feared for his own safety and did not trust the regular security forces. The GAPs fought hardest for and with him the eleventh.

MIR—Movimiento Izquierdista Revolucionario (Movement of the Revolutionary Left); Maoist-leaning organization committed to revolutionary violence. Legal during the Allende years, illegal since.

Tanquetas—Rubber-wheeled minitanks capable of speeds up to 75 mph.

Key to Map of Metropolitan Santiago

1. La Moneda
   (presidential palace)
2. Air Force Academy
3. Military Academy
4. Non-Commisioned Officers'
   School
5. Tacna Regiment
6. San Bernardo Infantry
   Regiment
7. Army War College
8. To Peldehue Garrison
   (24 miles distant)
9. State Technical University
10. Buín Regiment
11. Home of Patricio Guijón
12. 2nd Armored Regiment
13. Signal Corps Regiment
14. Tomás Moro
    (Allende's in-town estate and
    fortress)
15. El Cañaveral
    (Allende's rural estate and guer-
    rilla garrison)
16. National Stadium
17. Carabineros School
18. Air Force Hospital
19. Transmitter towers for Radio
    Agricultura, Radio Balmaceda,
    Radio Portales, and Radio Ma-
    gallanes
20. Cuban Embassy
21. Home of Gen. Prats
22. Scene of the "tongue incident";
    After a woman passenger in a
    car proceeding along the Costan-
    era stuck out her tongue at Gen.
    Prats as his official car pulled
    alongside, Prats pulled his ser-
    vice revolver and threatened to
    shoot her. That incident, in June
    of 1973, weakened the authority
    and credibility of the then-chief
    of the Army, leading to his even-
    tual downfall two months later
    —the downfall which cleared
    the way for the revolution that
    toppled Allende.
23. 2199 Julieta Avenue—Secret
    transmitter site
24. García Reyes 562—"Filadelfia,"
    intended secret seat of govern-
    ment under siege in case revolu-
    tion came.
25. El Bosque Air Force Base
26. Guardia Vieja Street—Allende's
    home until he assumed the presi-
    dency in 1970
27. Chile Arena (Estadio Chile)

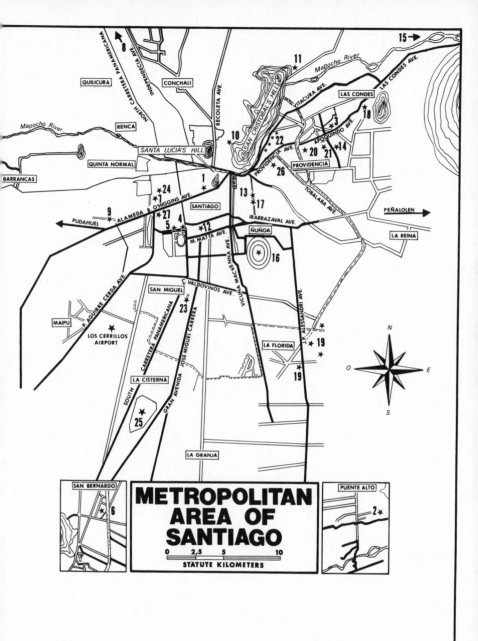

METROPOLITAN AREA OF SANTIAGO

0   2,5   5   10
STATUTE KILOMETERS

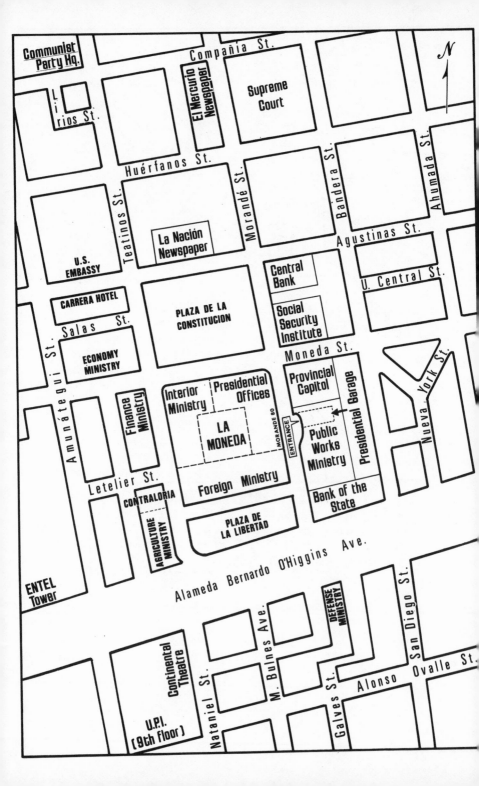

Selected Bibliography

A. *Interviews*
B. *Books*
C. *Reports/Studies*
D. *Newspaper/Magazine Articles*
F. *Reference Works*

A. Interviews

Much of the material in this book is based on personal interviews. The following is a partial list of those interviewed by the author of the book. In most cases the date as well as place of interview is specified.

"Aide-de-camp," in Santiago, Oct. 23, 1974. The former Allende aide requested anonymity, but consented to have the interview tape-recorded.

Alarcón, Ricardo, in Santiago, April 4, 1974

Arriagada Moreno, Eduardo, in Santiago, April 15, 1974

Baeza, Gen. Ernesto, in Santiago, October 16, 1974

Barros, Tobias, in Santiago, April 11, 1974

Bernath, Dr. Zoltán, in Santiago, April 24, 1974

Brady Roche, Gen. Herman, in Santiago

Braña, Jorge, in Santiago

Briones, Carlos, in Santiago, May 13 and October 10, 1974

Caamaño, Juan (Juanito), in Santiago, May 1, 1975
Canessa Roberts, Col. Julio, in Santiago, April 30 and May 1, 1974
Carmona Peralta, Sen. Juan de Dios, in Santiago, April 7, 1974
Carneyro, Mario, in Santiago, March 25, 1974
"César," key civilian in planning and operation of the secret radio
    network that linked military commanders on September 11, 1973;
    fearing later reprisals, he also asked for anonymity. Interview in
    Santiago, October 17, 1974
"CIA agent," in Washington, June 2, 1975. A retired officer, he
    requested anonymity
Cumsille Zapata, Rafael, in Santiago, October 11, 1974

Díaz, Mrs. Silvia Galarze de, in Santiago, May 9, 1974
Donoso, Teresa, in Santiago, May 7, 1974
Durán Cáceres, Hector, in Miami, over several months in 1975

Ferrari S., Roberto di, in Santiago, May 1, 1974
Figueroa, Jorge, in Santiago, April 1, 1973
Figueroa Toro, Pelayo, in Santiago, May 8, 1974

Gallegos Dubost, Miguel (Mike), in Santiago, March 14, 1974
Garrido González, Vicente Adrian, in Miami, April 9, 1975
Grez, Commander Jorge, in Santiago, October 24, 1974
Grove Kimber, Jaime, in Santiago, October 23, 1974
Guijón Klein, Dr. Patricio, a series of interviews in Santiago, begin-
    ning April 4, 1974, and continuing over the next five weeks, carried
    on subsequently by mail, and resuming personally over a three-
    week period in October, 1974
Guijón, Mrs. Silvia, several conversations in April and May, 1974
Guzmán Errázuriz, Jaime, in Santiago, October 13, 1974

Halsema, James J., in Santiago, March 29 and May 2, 1974
Hernández, Francisco (Gabito) in Santiago, April 3, 1974
Hinojosa, Mrs. Esther, in Santiago, April 3, 1974
Huerta Célis, Gen. Vicente, in Santiago, October 9, 1974
Huidobro, Rear Adm. Sergio, in Santiago, October 24, 1974
Humeres, Hector, in Santiago
Leigh Guzmán, Gen. Gustavo, in Santiago, October 14, 1974
Leiva Lillo, Sgt. Alfredo, in Santiago, May 12, 1974
Letelier, Mrs. Isabel, in Santiago, May 8 and 12, 1974

"Mario," key civilian in organizing and operating the secret radio network which linked military commanders on the day of the revolution; fearing later reprisals, he asked for anonymity. Based on a series of interviews with him in Santiago, beginning on May 4, 1974 and extending over the next ten days, and again on October 17, 1974

Mason, Roberto, in Santiago, April 17, 1974
Massa Armijo, Jorge, in Santiago, October 10, 1974
Medina, Mrs. María, in Santiago, May 11, 1974
Mendoza Durán, Gen. César, in Santiago, October 14, 1974
Merino Castro, Adm. José Toribio, in Santiago, October 18, 1974

Navasal, José M., in Santiago, May 7, 1974

Ossa, Mrs. Nena, in Miami, July 1975

Pinochet Ugarte, Gen. Augusto, in Santiago, October 22, 1974
Pizzarro Mora, Cpl. 2nd Class, Pedro, in Santiago, October 14, 1974
Polloni Pérez, Col. Julio, in Santiago, October 23, 1974
Puga, Alvaro, in Santiago, a series of interviews in October 1974

Ramírez Jald, Lt. Hernan, in Santiago, May 13, 1974
Ravera, Hugo, in Santiago, October 21, 1974

Sáez Ayala, Cpl. Iván, in Santiago, May 9, 1974
Sepúlveda, Col. Eduardo, in Miami, beginning in December 1974 and continuing into early 1975
Sepúlveda, Mrs. Marisa, in Miami, late 1974, early 1975.
"Steward," Navy steward in the presidential household at Tomás Moro, interviewed in Santiago October 24, 1974. Although the interview was tape-recorded, he requested anonymity

Tonini, Frank, in Santiago, March 29, 1974
Terreros Fernández, Vicente, Mrs. Torreros, and their daughter, María, in Santiago, numerous conversations in Santiago, in March, April, and May, 1974
Toro, Pedro A., in Santiago, May 7, 1974

Urrutia, Col. Carlos, in Santiago, April 24, 1974
Urrutia Manzano, Chief Justice Enrique, in Santiago, May 9, 1974

Valenzuela Valderrama, Hector, in Santiago, April 25, 1974
Vilarín, León, in Santiago, October 15, 1974

B. Books

Agor, Weston H., *The Chilean Senate: Internal Distribution of Influence.* Austin, Texas: University of Texas Press, 1971.

Allende Gossens, Salvador, *Allende: So Pensamiento Político.* Buenos Aires: Granica Editor, 1973.

Arriagada Herrera, Genaro, *De La Vía Chilena A La Vía Insurreccional.* Santiago: Editorial del Pacífico, 1974.

Baltra Cortés, Alberto, *Gestión Económica de la Unidad Popular.* Santiago: Editorial Orbe.

Bethel, Paul D., *The Losers.* Westport, Conn.: Arlington House, 1970.

Boizard, Ricardo, *El Ultimo Día de Allende.* Santiago: Editorial del Pacífico, S.A., 1973.

——*Proceso A Una Traición.* Santiago, Ediciones Encina, 1974.

Breve Historia de la Unidad Popular. Santiago: Editorial Lord Cochrane, S.A., 1974. A chronology of key dates and events during the Allende years, 1970–73, taken from the pages of *El Mercurio* and compiled by that newspaper.

Chamudes, Marcos, *Chile: Una Advertencia Americana.* Santiago: Ediciones P.E.C.

Correa Morandé, Maria, *La Guerra de las Mujeres.* Santiago: Editorial Universidad Técnica del Estado, 1974.

Debray, Régis, *The Chilean Revolution: Conversations with Allende.* New York: Vintage Books, Random House, 1971.

Donoso Loero, Teresa, *La Epopeya de las Ollas Vacias.* Santiago: Editora Nacional Gabriela Mistral, LTDA, 1974.

Echeverría B., Andrés and Luis Frei B., Eds., *La Lucha por la Juridicidad en Chile.* Santiago: Editorial del Pacífico, 1974.

Filippi, Emilio, and Hernán Millas, *Anatomia de un Fracaso, La Experiencia Socialista Chilena.* Santiago: Empresa Editora Zig-Zag, S.A., 1973.

Gouré, Leon and Morris Rothenberg, *Soviet Penetration of Latin America.* University of Miami, Center for Advanced International Studies, 1975.

Horne, Alistair, *Small Earthquake in Chile.* New York: Viking, 1972.

Labrousse, Alain, *El Experimento Chileno—Reformismo o Revolución?* Barcelona-México: Ediciones Grijalbo, S.A., 1973.

LaFourcade, Enrique, *Salvador Allende.* Barcelona-México: Ediciones Grijalbo, 1973.

Libro Blanco del Cambio de Gobierno en Chile. Santiago: College of Engineers, 1973.

Libro Blanco del Cambio de Gobierno en Chile. Santiago: Editorial Lord Cochrane, S.A., 1973.

Magnet, Alejandro, *Operación Primavera.* Santiago: Editorial del Pacífico, 1973.

Marchetti, Victor and John D. Marks, *The CIA and the Cult of Intelligence.* New York: Dell, 1974.

McHale, Tomás P., ed., *Chile: A Critical Survey.* Santiago: Institute of General Studies, 1972.

Millar, Walterio, *Historia de Chile,* 29th edition. Santiago: Editorial Zig-Zag, 1973.

Moss, Robert, *Chile's Marxist Experiment.* New York-Toronto: John Wiley, 1973.

Pinochet Ugarte, General Augusto, *La Acción del Ejercito en la Liberación de Chile, Historia Inedita.* A 50-page booklet printed on newsprint quality stock believed to have been written by Pinochet. Devoid of any identifying marks or dates, it appeared in Santiago at about the first anniversary of the revolution, or September 1974. It was not released to bookstores and copies were extremely hard to come by. The booklet describes Pinochet's own role in the revolution—no other military commander is named in it—and that of the army.

————*El Día Decisivo: 11 de Septiembre do 1973.* Santiago: Editorial Andrés Bello, 1980.

Pinto, Silvia, *Los Días del Arrco Iris.* Santiago: Editorial del Pacífico, S.A., 1972.

Powers, Thomas, *The Man Who Kept Secrets: Richard Helms and the CIA.* New York: Alfred A. Knopf, 1979.

Puga, Alvaro, *Diario de Vida de Usted.* Santiago: Ediciones Encina, LTDA, 1973. The book appeared under his pen name, "Alexis."

Rama, Carlos M., *Chile: Mil Días Entre La Revolución y el Fascismo.* Barcelona: Editorial Planeta, S.A., 1974.

Ravines, Eudocio, *El Rescate de Chile.* Santiago: Empresa Editora e Impresora Edimpres, LTDA, 1974.

Silva, Lavtaro, *Allende: El Fin de Una Aventura.* Santiago: Ediciones Patria Nueva, 1974.

Theberge, James D., *The Soviet Presence in Latin America.* New York: Crane, Russak & Co., 1974.

218   *Allende: Death of a Marxist Dream*

Thomas, Hugh, *The Spanish Civil War,* revised edition. Harmonds-worth, Middlesex, England: Penguin Books, 1965.

Uribe, Armando, *The Black Book of American Intervention in Chile.* Boston: Beacon Press, 1975. First published in French by Editions du Seuil in 1974 under title *Le Livre Noir de l'Intervention Améri-caine au Chili.*

Varas, Florencia, and José Manuel Vargara, *Operación Chile.* San-tiago-Buenos Aires-México-Barcelona: Editorial Pomaire, 1973.

———*Conversaciones con Viaux.* Santiago: Impresiones Eire, 1972.

C. Reports/Studies

Elección de Parlamentarios 1973, Boletín de Información General No. 67, Oficina de Informaciones, Senado de Chile, June 30, 1973.

Elección Ordinaria de Presidente de la Republica, Viernes 4 de Sep-tiembre de 1970, Dirección del Registro Electoral.

Report on the Status of Human Rights in Chile, Commission on Human Rights of the Organization of American States, Washing-ton, D.C., Nov. 21, 1974.

Observations of the Government of Chile on that Report, OAS Docu-ment AG/500/75, Feb. 25, 1975.

Multinational Corporations and United States Foreign Policy, based on hearings in March and April, 1973, before the Subcommittee on Multinational Corporations, U.S. Senate. Published in two vol-umes, U.S. Government Printing Office, Washington, D.C., 1973.

Situation, Principal Problems and Prospects of the Chilean Economy. Study by the Ad-Hoc review group of the Inter-American Eco-nomic and Social Council (CEPCIES) of the Organization of American States, Washington, D.C., March 6, 1975.

The Theory and Practice of Communism, Part 5: (Marxism Imposed on Chile—Allende Regime), based on hearings Nov. 15, 1973, and March 7 and 13, 1974, before the Committee on Internal Security, U.S. House of Representatives. U.S. GPO, Washington, D.C., 1974.

Recent Developments in Chile, Oct. 1971. Report of the Subcommittee on Inter-American Affairs of the Committee on Foreign Affairs U.S. House of Representatives. U.S. GPO, Washington, D.C., Oct. 15, 1971.

United States and Chile During The Allende Years, 1970–1973. Re-port of the Subcommittee on Inter-American Affairs of the Committee on Foreign Affairs, U.S. House of Representatives, based on hearings in 1971, 1972, 1973, and 1974. U.S. GPO, Washington, D.C., 1974.

Alleged Assassination Plots Involving Foreign Leaders. Interim report of the Senate Committee to Study Governmental Operations with respect to Intelligence Activities, U.S. Senate, Report No. 94-465, Nov. 20, 1975. U.S. GOP, Washington, D.C.

D. Newspaper/Magazine Articles

Baltimore Sun
"U.S. Backed Coup, Allende Envoy Says," A Rome-datelined dispatch by Kay Withers, Sept. 19, 1973.

Chicago Tribune
"Cowards Don't Head Revolutions—Allende's Final Words," A Reuters dispatch based on a series of interviews done by Mexican newsman Manuel Mejido, published in the *Tribune* Sept. 20, 1973.

El Mercurio (Santiago)
"Funcionario de La Nu Mexclado En Política Chilena," Sept. 11, 1973.
"Infancia y Juventud de La Junta," in the newspaper's Sunday magazine, "Revista del Domingo," Feb 3, 1974.
"¿Como Llegaron Las Fuerzas Armadas A La Acción del 11 de Septiembre de 1973?", Sept. 11, 1974
"El Papel de Joan Garcés Como Asesor de Allende," Oct. 14, 1972.
"Era Un Deber Patriótico," Sept. 13, 1973.
"Un Millón de Trabajadores En Paro," Sept. 5, 1973.

Encounter Magazine
"Allende and the Myth Marker," David Holden, Jan. 1974

Ercilla Magazine (Santiago)
"General Pinochet, El Hombre del'Día D,' " week of March 13–19, 1974.
"Prats El Hombre, El General, El Vice-Presidente," week of Nov. 29–Dec. 5, 1972.

Inter-American Press Association (Miami)
"The Chilean Presidenta," an article written by IAPA scholarship-

winner John Adam Moreau and distributed to North American and Latin American newspapers by IAPA, Dec, 8, 1971.

La Prensa (Lima, Peru)
"Demócratas Christianos Condenan Golpe en Chile," Sept. 21, 1973.

La Segunda (Santiago)
"Joan Garcés, el Español que Traza la Política Chileña," by Teddy Córdoba, Oct. 10, 1972.
"Tomás Moro, Una Aguja en el Pajar," Sept. 10, 1974.

La Ultimas Noticias (Santiago)
"La Payita Cuenta Su Versión del 11," Oct. 12, 1974 (taken from an interview with her published in the Cuban magazine *Bohemia*)

Miami Herald
"Fidel Hits Defeat in Chile," Sept. 12, 1964.
"Allende Claims Plot On His Life," Sept. 13, 1970.
"Kissinger Angrily Denies He Misled Chilean," an AP story datelined Washington, Feb. 5, 1975.

The New York Times
"Salvador Allende: In Memoriam," by Régis Debray, Sept. 26, 1972.
"Chile's First Lady: An Ardent Feminist," Nov. 4, 1970.
"Mrs. Allende Confirms Husband Killed Himself," a Reuters dispatch datelined Mexico City, Sept. 16, 1973.
"Italy's Reaction Strong," a Rome-datelined dispatch, Sept. 15, 1973.
"U.S. Expected Coup but Decided Not To Act," a Washington-datelined story, Sept. 14, 1975.
"Chile Junta Says It Kept U.S. In Dark," a Washington-datelined story, Sept. 15, 1973.

New York Times Magazine
"A Revolution Without the Execution Wall," Bernard Collier, Jan. 17, 1967.

New Yorker Magazine
"Letter from Santiago," by Joseph Kraft, Jan. 30, 1971.

¿Qué Pasa? Magazine (Santiago)
"Estado Mayor Técnico Para La Junta," March 22, 1974.
"El Who Is Who de Carabineros," Sept. 6, 1973.

San Francisco Examiner
"Chile's Kissinger Blueprints Future," by Percy Foster, Aug. 30, 1972.

Time Magazine
"The Coup: The View From the Carrera," Sept. 24, 1973.
Washington Post
"U.S. Helped Allende in 1964," by Laurence Stern, April 6, 1973.
"Chile Junta Bans Leftist Parties," Sept. 22, 1973.
"Soviets Cut Relations with Chile," a Moscow-datelined dispatch by Robert G. Kaiser, Sept. 22, 1973.
"No Direct U.S. Role Seen In Chile Coup," Jack Anderson's column as it appeared in the *Post,* Sept. 22, 1973.

E. Reference Works

Almanaque Mundial, 1973, (Editorial América, S. A., Virginia Gardens, Fla.)
Annual of the Institute of Strategic Studies, 1973–1974 edition, London
Current Biography (H. W. Wilson, New York, Sept. 1971)
Fuentes, Jordi, & Cortés, Lia, Eds., *Diccionario Político de Chile, 1810–1966,* (Editorial Orbe, Santiago, 1967)
The Latin American Scene of the Seventies, A Basic Fact Book, (Irving B. Reed, Jaime Suchlicki, and Dodd L. Harvey, Eds., Center for Advanced International Studiés, University of Miami, Fla., 1972)
The New York Times Encyclopedic Almanac, 1971 Edition (The New York Times Book and Educational Division, New York, 1971)
Nueva Enciclopedia de Chile, Francisco Javier Diaz Salazar, editor (Ediciones Copihue, Fotomecánica Futura, S.R.L., Ediciones Libra, Buenos Aires, 1974)

INDEX